A Jean Toomer Reader

A
Jean Toomer
Reader

Selected Unpublished Writings

Edited by

FREDERIK L. RUSCH

New York   Oxford
OXFORD UNIVERSITY PRESS
1993

Oxford University Press

Oxford   New York   Toronto
Delhi   Bombay   Calcutta   Madras   Karachi
Kuala Lumpur   Singapore   Hong Kong   Tokyo
Nairobi   Dar es Salaam   Cape Town
Melbourne   Auckland   Madrid

and associated companies in
Berlin   Ibadan

Published by Oxford University Press, Inc.,
200 Madison Avenue, New York, New York 10016

Oxford is a registered trademark of Oxford University Press

Library of Congress Cataloging-in-Publication Data
Toomer, Jean, 1894–1967.
[Selections. 1993]
A Jean Toomer reader : selected unpublished writings / edited by Frederik L. Rusch.
p. cm.   Includes bibliographical references.
ISBN 0–19–507733–4.
ISBN 0–19–508329–6 (pbk.)
1. Afro-Americans—Race identity—Literary collections.
2. United States—Race relations—Literary collections.
I. Rusch, Frederik L. II. Title.
PS3539.O478A6   1993   813'.52—dc20   93–16374

1 3 5 7 9 8 6 4 2

Printed in the United States of America
on acid-free paper

Acknowledgments

Permission to publish the Toomer material herein has been granted by the Yale Collection of American Literature, Beinecke Rare Book and Manuscript Library, Yale University. I would like to thank the staff of the Beinecke Library, especially Patricia Willis, Curator of American Literature, and Karen V. Peltier, Beinecke cataloger of the Toomer Papers, for their help.

Permission to publish the excerpt from the letter to Lola Ridge of December 1922 has been granted by the Lola Ridge Papers, Sophia Smith Collection, Smith College, Northampton, Massachusetts. I also gratefully acknowledge permission from Margery Toomer Latimer to publish this excerpt.

The following works have been extremely useful to me in compiling *A Jean Toomer Reader*: *The Lives of Jean Toomer: A Hunger for Wholeness*, by Cynthia Earl Kerman and Richard Eldridge; *In a Minor Chord: Three Afro-American Writers and Their Search for Identity*, by Darwin T. Turner; *The Wayward and the Seeking: A Collection of Writings by Jean Toomer*, edited by Darwin T. Turner; *Jean Toomer, Artist: A Study of His Literary Life and Work, 1894–1936*, by Nellie Y. McKay; *Jean Toomer's Years with Gurdjieff: Portrait of an Artist, 1923–1936*, by Rudolph P. Byrd; and *The Collected Poems of Jean Toomer*, edited by Robert B. Jones and Margery Toomer Latimer.

Contents

Introduction

JEAN TOOMER, 1894–1967

"Life, human life, we must use, but its use should be accompanied by dimensional transformation." Thus wrote Jean Toomer to *Double Dealer* editor John McClure in 1922. He was writing about his art, but the subtext was his life. The attainment of self-realization and psychic wholeness leading to a new personal and social harmony was Toomer's aim throughout his life, and it was often through his writing that he strove to discover and express this desired transformation. Toomer believed that human beings could change, transcend their ordinary lives and selves, and find true being and unity with others. Furthermore, artistic creation was self-creation, and self-creation demanded transformation.

Transformation and the quest for a meaningful identity underlie a number of the pieces in *Cane,* Toomer's powerful, avant-garde collection of lyrical portraits of black rural and urban life, published in 1923. The restless searching and aching discontent displayed by many of the characters in *Cane* were representative of its author, and so it is not surprising that by 1924 Toomer had abandoned black writing in favor of more didactic and philosophical work. While the critics and publishers were asking him for more black material, Toomer turned to different settings, still preserving in the post-*Cane* writing his desire for transformation and the search for being. And although the early admirers of *Cane* had mostly concentrated on its African-American aspects, presenting striking portrayals of black America, the latter-day reader with hindsight and knowledge of the vast amount of Toomer's post-*Cane*, unpublished writing can discern a more personal level in *Cane*—the quest for transformation.

An example of the pursuit and realization of transformation is "Bona and Paul," a story Toomer wrote in 1918, probably the earliest piece in *Cane*. Paul is a light-skinned African American whose "red-brown face" puzzles white people, who cannot decide whether he is white or black. While other people are agonizing over Paul's racial identity, confused by their inability to categorize him, and frustrated in their very American need for clear racial definition, Paul comes to the realization that he is

> apart from the people around him. Apart from the pain which they had unconsciously caused. Suddenly he knew that people saw, not attractiveness in his dark skin, but difference. Their stares, giving him to himself, filled something long empty within him, and were like green blades sprouting in his consciousness. There was fullness, and strength and peace about it all. He saw himself, cloudy, but real.

Paul, refusing to let people define and categorize him, takes strength from their stares because their confusion about his racial identity has shown him to be unique and individual, with their stares "giving him to himself." Giving him to himself is a beginning, but Paul goes further. As he leaves the nightclub where he has had this epiphany, he says to the black doorman, "I came back to tell you, brother, that white faces are petals of roses. That dark faces are petals of dusk. That I am going out and gather petals." As a gatherer of white and dark petals, Paul will embrace all people regardless of their color. And although Bona, Paul's date, leaves him because she cannot deal with the racial and social complexity he represents, Paul has made definite progress toward self-realization and persoanl identity.

In transforming the negative self-consciousness of being stared at and thought odd and out of place into a positive understanding of himself and an embracing of others, in a harmonious rose garden of human diversity, Paul embodies the desire of his creator. Jean Toomer, like Paul, was made up of mixed racial and ethnic strains. He had seen the white and dark petals of America and knew them to be also in himself. Furthermore, he believed that through the spiritual transformation latent in all individuals, Americans could live together on a transcendent plane.

An important influence on Toomer as he was finding his way as a writer was Waldo Frank, a novelist and essayist well established by 1920, when he and Frank first met. During their short-lived but intense friendship, Toomer and Frank critiqued each other's work and sharpened their ideas about what modern American literature should be. Both writers stressed the unity of the individual with being. "Unity is truth. This is a universe, not a multiverse," Frank declared in *Salvos: An Informal Book About Books and Plays* (1924). "Culture implies a Whole. . . . The great work of art invests the individual with the ecstasy of participation in the

Whole." However, Frank continued, "We are in misery because we have lost the control which comes with the experience of unity and wholeness. We are in misery because we are in chaos. . . . Ere we can be whole again, we must create a new spiritual body." For both Frank and Toomer, the new spiritual body first had to be developed in the individual—and for the writer, in his art—and then in the life of America.

In 1923, the year of *Cane's* publication, Toomer broke with Waldo Frank after falling in love with Margaret Naumburg, Frank's wife. Around this time, along with some of their literary friends in New York City, Toomer and Naumburg were developing a keen interest in the psychological and philosophical ideas of the Eastern mystic Georges I. Gurdjieff. After completing *Cane,* Toomer felt burned out. He sensed a growing spiritual and psychological malaise within himself. Gurdjieff's philosophy, promising to open the door to being and personal unity, further developed some of the ideas Toomer and Frank had discussed during their friendship. By 1923, Toomer felt that he had to "re-from and transform" himself, and he was attracted to Gurdjieff's philosophy in the hope that it would help clear his mind and rid him of the chaos he found there. And so, in 1924 he traveled to France to study with Gurdjieff himself at his Institute for Man's Harmonious Development.

Gurdjieff believed that there were two aspects of human beings: "personality" and "essence." Personality is created by people's social environment and is superficial. But despite its superficiality, personality is strong and in most people, hides their essence, which is their true nature and the core of their being. Gurdjieff proposed to help people find their essence. Toomer hoped that if he could rediscover his essence, he would find within him what would make him whole and unite him with all people. Gurdjieff's emphasis on the importance of a person's true essence as opposed to the superficial personality created by society attracted Toomer, who felt constricted by the burden of America's rigid and simplistic racial and ethnic categories. Consequently, by 1924 he was an ardent believer in Gurdjieff's philosophy, and his writing began to reflect that ardor.

Toomer believed he was a man of "scattered parts," a man "born to be divided." Gurdjieff wrote, in his long allegorical work *Beelzebub's Tales to His Grandson,* that in the individual "all the separate parts should harmonize together." Gurdjieff understood the problem of personal scatteredness and disharmony. He believed that many people are, in the words of his disciple and interpreter P. D. Ouspensky, "divided into different 'I's' all contradicting one another." Only when the different "I's" become unified can we reach being, for "being means state, inner conditions, all together, not separate." Furthermore, Ouspensky continued in *The*

Fourth Way, "Being is power, power to 'do'; and power to 'do' is power *to be different.*" Toomer responded favorably to such ideas. In fact, they corresponded nicely to the process he had described in "Bona and Paul" when Paul reacted positively to his "scattered parts" and united them into a unique identity.

Rudolph P. Byrd, in *Jean Toomer's Years with Gurdjieff,* notes that the unity of the individual's "I's"—the "unchangeable 'I'"—produces the third state of consciousness, after the "sleeping state" and the "waking" state in human development. The fourth and final state is "objective consciousness or, as Toomer termed it, 'cosmic consciousness.'" In Part II of *A Jean Toomer Reader,* Toomer describes an experience of cosmic consciousness during a mystical episode in New York City in 1926, when he believed he was "being transported from exile into Being." Indicating his attainment of the third state, personal unity, he proclaimed, "I was one and whole. I was one being, one consciousness, alive in a life so different from ordinary life that there seemed to be absolutely no relation between the two. . . . High in me I was joined with myself. Deep in me I was connected with my roots and source. Here in being I became my realness, this extraordinary I AM." From these feelings of personal unity Toomer then moved to the fourth state, cosmic consciousness: "I was discovering that my being was in vital contact with the vast Universe. Through being, as had never been possible through body, I was connected with the all-embracing world. Now I realized with certainty and astonishment—*I live and move within the Universe.*" At least for the moment, he had attained in reality what he had striven for from the time of "Bona and Paul," if not earlier, on through his work with Gurdjieff.

It is interesting to ponder why Jean Toomer—more than most people, it seems—was so acutely aware of a psychic chaos and an alienation from other people and why, as he expressed in his autobiographical writing, he felt uprooted, standing alone in the world. Certainly the matrix of personality is complex, and to discover all the sources of Toomer's feelings would be impossible. However, it is clear from a substantial number of his written works that one aspect of his personal confusion was his ambivalence about his racial identity. Growing up in Washington, D.C., he had lived among both middle-class whites and poorer blacks. His maternal grandfather was Pinckney Benton Stewart Pinchback, one-time acting governor of Louisiana, the offspring of a white farmer and a freed mulatto slave. When P. B. S. Pinchback moved from Louisiana to Washington in 1890, he was a rich man, but by the time Toomer was a teenager, the wealth had substantially diminished. Toomer's father, of white, black, and Native American blood, left his wife three months after their marriage, and Toomer never really knew him. For the most part, Jean grew up in the home of his grandfather Pinchback, the dominant member of the family. Physically, Toomer had an olive complexion; according to Toomer's early friend Mae Wright Peck, "If one had not been told that he had Negro blood in him, one never would have known it. He would have had no trouble whatever passing for white." With such a background and complexion, it is not surprising that Toomer felt uncertain and ambivalent about his identity. It is also not surprising that much of his writing expresses not only a search for identity but also, as with his character Paul, a desire to gather both white and dark petals. And it was in the land and people of America that he searched, because one thing Toomer knew with certainty was that he was an American.

However, "it is a complex fate to be an American" as James Baldwin notes, quoting Henry James, in the opening sentence of *Nobody Knows My Name*. Continuing, Baldwin writes, "The very word 'America' remains a new, almost completely undefined and extremely controversial proper noun. No one in the world seems to know exactly what it describes, not even we motley millions who call ourselves Americans." Toomer, as one of those motley millions, would have agreed with Baldwin; in much of his writing he concentrated on defining America as well as himself. *Cane* represented the initial step in this task. Through the pieces in *Cane,* Toomer explored the blackness within him. On visiting the rural South, he found the African-American peasant a revelation of beauty and pain, and he was immediately stirred to write the stories and poems that make up the Southern sections of *Cane*. At that time he felt a strong identity with the black people he was writing about, but the identity did not last. Complete identification with black culture was not possible for him; he regretted that literary critics and editors wanted him to write another *Cane*.

Henry Louis Gates, Jr., in a January 1990 *PMLA* essay, "'Tell Me, Sir, . . . What *Is* "Black" Literature?'," observes, "One must *learn* to be 'black' in this society, precisely because 'blackness' is a socially produced category." Because of Toomer's "black blood" America defined him as black, and yet his socially mixed, predominantly middle-class upbringing had not "taught" him very well how to be black. In the same essay, Gates quotes James Baldwin in *Notes of a Native Son* on the obsession with "race" in his fiction: "I have not written about being a Negro at such length because I expect that to be my only subject, but only because it was the gate I had to unlock before I could hope to write about anything else." Toomer, who in contrast to Baldwin had not grown up in the solidly black society of a Harlem, nevertheless desired to unlock the gate. He did so in *Cane*. What he found fascinated, excited, and inspired him, but it did not sustain him. Black life could not be his only subject.

However, although after *Cane* his fiction moved away from portrayals of African Americans, Toomer continued to be concerned with the meaning of being black in America, as is evident in his long essay "Race Problems and Modern Society," published in 1929, and some of the pieces in the present collection. He believed that our national racial divisions could be overcome with the attainment of personal harmony and the discovery of being. His 1926 mystical episode had shown him the possibility of social harmony just as it had shown him a glimpse of personal harmony. He believed himself to have seen that separate people could come together in one consciousness, which would lead to true brotherhood. His out-of-body experience showed him that people could free themselves from "bondage of the body" and could end "the cravings and prejudices that arise when people believed that they and others *are* their bodies." This freedom would bring "the beginning of being-life."

Furthermore, unity of being would put an end to the rigid and limiting system of classification that Toomer so hated and found so prominent in American society—the classification his character Paul resisted and Toomer fought against much of his life. In his mystical state he saw that

> People were people, stripped of the labels and classifications they foist on each other, stripped too of the ratings they give each other. I saw an earth-being, not an American or a New Yorker or a foreigner. I saw an earth-being, not a white or a colored man. I saw an earth-being, not a street-cleaner or taxi-driver or a salesman.

The stripping away of labels and classifications revealed the individual, the unique person: "Each man's uniqueness showed forth strikingly. Each one was himself and none other—and so should be met, valued, treated," while at the same time, due to the realization of the unity of being and the experience of cosmic consciousness, "the membership of all in one kind was just as evident. All were vital interrelated parts of an unimaginable whole—and so should be rated and appreciated." In actuality, Toomer discovered, "All men, as beings, are kin." E pluribus unum.

The complementary forces of exhaustively mastering the Gurdjieff philosophy and undergoing the mystical experience of 1926 color a great portion of Toomer's oeuvre. Much of the Gurdjieff-influenced work is heavily didactic and lacks the lyricism so characteristic of *Cane*. While it is clear that a bright imagination is still at work, the fiction, drama, and poetry often suffer from the weight of Gurdjieffian preaching. Consequently, after *Cane* Toomer had great difficulty getting his creative writing published, with notable exceptions like his stories "Winter on Earth" and "Mr. Costyve Duditch" (published in 1928), "York Beach" (1929), and the long poem "Blue Meridian" (published in 1936). However, Toomer's scanty published output obscures that he produced a tremendous amount of writing after the publication of *Cane*. The Toomer collection at Yale's Beinecke Library contains over 30,000 items, made up of plays, poems, short stories, novels, literary criticism, philosophical pieces, and letters. Yet readers who look eagerly to Toomer's vast unpublished literary output for work with form and content similar to *Cane*'s are mostly disappointed.

Because of his sparse publishing record after 1923, and the fact that much of what was printed did not deal with African-American subjects, Toomer, the author of *Cane*, faded from the memories of readers and critics. It was not until *Cane* was rediscovered and republished in the 1960s, thanks in part to such scholars as Robert Bone, Darwin T. Turner, and S. P. Fullinwider, that Toomer became part of the canon of African-American literature.

Toomer's exploration of his Gurdjieffian essence and his search and hopes for himself were intimately connected with his feelings about America and being an American. American democracy could break down the simplistic and prejudicial categories that so unfairly stereotyped individuals; American pluralism acknowledged people of every type, and these people could live together in harmony. Such hopes and desires give much of Toomer's writing the flavor of Whitmanesque prophecy, while also containing, like Whitman, whom Toomer much admired, strong criticism of aspects of American society that are destructive to its promise.

The 1929 essay "Race Problems and Modern Society" is an example of such prophecy, containing both the hope and the criticism of a piece like Whitman's "Democratic Vistas." While Toomer condemns the "anti-social urges" that "stimulate acquisitive passion for money power," he is encouraged by the dialectic of history enabling "the movement of forces that have at least in part broken from old forms and that have not yet achieved stability in new forms." Indeed, "we *must* create new forms of thinking and bring about a transformation of attitude." On racial matters, Toomer anticipates the Black Power movement of the 1960s and the "new tribalism" of today: "The new negro is much more negro and much less American than was the old negro of fifty years ago." "The races cannot draw nearer together; nor can they draw much farther apart—and still remain races in America. But they will undoubtedly push away from one another, until they have completely occupied what small room for withdrawal is still left." Furthermore, "it may be that a solution does lie in the direction which calls for an increase to bursting point of the existing conditions. Circumstances have been known to change as a result of the accentuation of their negative factors." But Toomer, believing in the unity of being, holds out for "the positive possibilities contained in the emergence of a large number of the type of people who cannot be classified as separatist and racial. These people are truly synthetic and human. They exist all over America."

Today, when a strong sense of racial-ethnic identification, self-respect, and group solidarity appears to many activists and social thinkers to be the best way of dealing with the racial exclusivity of American society, Toomer, with his proclamation of the oneness of all people and his denial of specific ethnicity within himself, seems to be an anomaly. But now, as we draw closer to the "bursting point" both in America and the world, Toomer should not be dismissed. In both his feelings of aloneness and his hope for harmony he was a product of America: His eschewal of specific racial-ethnic identity came from an honest rebellion against the narrowness of his society, and his utopian hope for a harmonious future reflects the universalism implied in the best of what we call the American Dream. Toomer abhorred the disunity within himself and among the people of the United States. For him categorizing people, emphasizing their differences rather than their similarities, caused only personal pain and social disunity. He would agree with Clarence Major, who said in a *Poets & Writers Magazine* interview of January-February 1991, "We are all essentially, at the deepest level, the same, except for our cultural differences. What happens is that the cultural differences become, somehow, more visible, rather than the equally significant universal elements."

In his 1967 biography of Waldo Frank, Paul J. Carter wrote: "Frank's career is an attempt to make man aware of his bond with the cosmos and at the same time to create a culture in which spiritual values can survive and flourish through art. He has tried to transform America, to shape organic wholeness out of the fragmentation and chaos of contemporary existence." The same can be said of Jean Toomer. In Frank's 1919 introduction to *Our America*, he proclaimed, "We go forth all to seek America. And in the seeking we create her." In *Cane*, Toomer was creating the South and testing his own identity against that creation. This creating and testing continued throughout his career as a writer. In "Blue Meridian" he wrote, "We suffer to create—what we are,/What we have become, American." Like Paul in "Bona and Paul," suffering from the narrow American view of racial identity, Toomer sought to counteract it by gathering both dark and white petals and creating a new American flower. In so doing, Jean Toomer became an American of the future—as he wrote in "Blue Meridian," a "blue man"—with a dream of the promised land.

Note on the Text

For this collection's introductory piece, "To Move from Place to Place" (my title), I have chosen a handwritten entry called "Travel—France," from a notebook Toomer named "Paris," dated September 20, 1929. The sources of the other selections in this collection are given in the Editor's Notes at the beginning of each chapter.

I have used both manuscripts and typescripts of Toomer's hitherto unpublished writing. To indicate where I have cut material from a piece I have placed three asterisks (* * *) and explained the deletion in the textual notes at the end of the book. With Toomer's letters, I have kept the original idiosyncrasies of spelling, punctuation, and so on to retain their flavor and informality. In other pieces, I have corrected occasional misspellings and typographical errors, and very occasionally have altered punctuation for clarity. In the few instances where Toomer has interlined alternatives to original words or phrases, I have chosen those that I judged most effective. When a word is unclear, I have put my guess in brackets with a question mark; when I have added words for clarity, I have put them in brackets. When working with more than one draft of the same piece, or with handwritten notebooks, I have occasionally changed the original order of sections for greater coherence. Sometimes I have drawn together two separate pieces into one. All these changes are explained in the textual notes.

In a 1949 letter to his friend Howard Schubert, Jean Toomer wrote, "It is possible that . . . my writings will be 'discovered' one of these days, and be published, and do all I had hoped they would do. It is also possible and even probable that none of them have really come off, that they are not worth publishing because I was not able to put the real stuff into them." The reader will judge. It is my belief that *A Jean Toomer Reader* will be a discovery.

Chronology

1894 Nathan Pinchback (Jean) Toomer born, December 26.

1895 Father leaves family.

1899 Parents are divorced.

1909 Mother dies.

1914 Graduates from high school; begins agricultural studies at University of Wisconsin.

1915 Leaves University of Wisconsin.

1916 Enters American College of Physical Training in Chicago.

1917 Leaves American College of Physical Training; takes classes at City College of New York and New York University.

1918 Writes "Bona and Paul."

1920 Meets Waldo Frank; changes name to Jean.

1921 Is substitute principal at Sparta Agricultural and Industrial Institute, Georgia; writes many of the Southern sketches of *Cane;* Grandfather Pinchback dies.

1922 Visits Spartanburg, South Carolina, with Waldo Frank; finishes *Cane.*

1923 *Cane,* with foreword by Waldo Frank, published by Boni and Liveright; breaks with Waldo Frank.

1924 Goes to Georges I. Gurdjieff's Institute for the Harmonious Development of Man, at Fontainebleau, France.

1925 Leads Gurdjieff workshops in Harlem, New York; visits Taos, New Mexico.

1926 Has mystical experience in New York City.

1927 Second printing of *Cane* published by Boni and Liveright.

1929 "Race Problems and Modern Society" published in *Problems of Civilization*, edited by Baker Brownell.

1931 Leads Gurdjieffian living experiment in Portage, Wisconsin; marries Margery Latimer; *Essentials: Definitions and Aphorisms* privately published.

1932 Margery and Jean live for a short time in Carmel, California; they move to Chicago; daughter Margery born; Margery Latimer dies in childbirth.

1934 Marries Marjorie Content; Marjorie and Jean live in New York City.

1935 Breaks with Gurdjieff.

1936 Marjorie and Jean move to Doylestown, Pennsylvania; "Blue Meridian" published in *The New Caravan*.

1938 Starts going to Friends Meeting.

1939 Travels in India.

1940 Joins Society of Friends.

1949 Starts Jungian analysis; Gurdjieff dies.

1950 Ends Jungian analysis.

1953 Renews his interest in Gurdjieff work and study.

1967 After about two years in nursing homes, dies March 30; third printing of *Cane* published by University Place Press.

1969 Paperback of *Cane*, with introduction by Arna Bontemps, published by Harper & Row.

1975 Paperback of *Cane*, with introduction by Darwin T. Turner, published by Liveright.

1980 *The Wayward and the Seeking: A Collection of Writings by Jean Toomer*, edited by Darwin T. Turner, published by Howard University Press.

1988 *The Collected Poems of Jean Toomer*, edited by Robert B. Jones and Margery Toomer Latimer, published by the University of North Carolina Press; Norton Critical Edition of *Cane*, edited by Darwin T. Turner, published by W. W. Norton.

1991 *Essentials* reprinted, edited by Rudolph P. Byrd, published by the University of Georgia Press.

A Jean Toomer Reader

I do now and always have attached more importance to manhood than to mere kinship or identity with one variety of the human family. Race, in the popular sense, is narrow; humanity is broad. The one is special, the other is universal. The one is transient, the other permanent.

—Frederick Douglass, Speech at dedication
of the Manassas Industrial School,
Virginia, September 3, 1894

Lo, soul, seest thou not God's purpose from the first?
The earth to be spann'd, connected by network,
The races, neighbors, to marry and be given in marriage,
The oceans to be cross'd, the distant brought near,
The lands to be welded together.

A worship new I sing . . . .

—Walt Whitman, "Passage to India"

This deeper wish was a wish for the perfect place, the perfect place of dwelling on earth.

—Jean Toomer, "York Beach"
The New American Caravan, *1929*

———————

To Move from Place to Place*

I appear as a travelled person and give the impression of having been most everywhere. Few people on first acquaintance take me to be a "home" type of man, liking a settled habitat. On the contrary, they quickly form the opinion that I am cosmopolitan, a citizen of many countries, one who has seen all or most of Europe. Should I say I have been in many oriental countries also, this statement would be accepted far more readily than an assertion that I had never seen beyond the borders of America. They assume, not only that I like to travel and that I have travelled, but that moving about is for me a natural form of life. I can, they think, meet all kinds and classes of people and speak a number of (to them) foreign languages, with facility.

In truth, I have moved about quite a bit; but most of my excursions have taken place in and over America. Not till last summer did I visit Canada. France is the only European country I have been in, to date. Yet, in a sense, people are quite right in feeling that I am not a settled, home, or stationary type. I am locomotive, nomadic—and this for many reasons.

As a child I was conditioned to move from place to place. My family often changed residences. In the first year of my life I was moved from the house of my birth, to another house and then to the house of my grandfather; and, while still living in Washington, we went to different places each summer. We went to several towns in Virginia, one of them, Culpeper Springs. (Just let me note here in parentheses that this choice of southern places for our summer outings indicates my family's attachment to the South.) We went to Harpers Ferry, to Arundel in Chesapeake Bay. We went to Saratoga Springs, thus occasioning visits to Brooklyn, to New York and Albany. Thus, while my life was still rooted in

*["Travel—France," from the notebook entitled "Paris," dated September 20, 1929.—Ed.]

Washington, I had experiences of travel and of a fair number of different localities.

The time came when we definitely left Washington and moved to Brooklyn. This was a complete and, in a sense, acute change of habitation, causing me to make basic and often difficult adjustments to different conditions of life: new playmates, not only new schools but a different kind of schooling, and so on. In Brooklyn we changed place of residence three times.

Shortly afterwards we went to live in New Rochelle. After two years in New Rochelle—back again to Washington. In Washington during a four year period we lived in five houses, each one of which contained a set of conditions unlike the others.

Then came the period of my solitary wanderings back and forth between Washington, Madison, New York, Chicago, Washington, New York.

With this kind of early history it would be difficult now for me not to move from place to place.

I have already indicated the major mal-adjustments I suffered as a youth and young man.* These acted as negative stimulants to movement.

On the positive side, I was perhaps born a potentially locomotive type. My essence had developed beyond the vegetable to the animal stage; and I had, therefore, all the needs and urges which are proper to this stage. Also, I had and I developed the ability to move from place to place. Once one has an ability, this ableness must exercise, must function. It does so. In a sense it compels a man to use it. And, in functioning, it compels the person to manifest in corresponding ways.

I felt the need to see and understand locales, cities, regions, men of all kinds.

I was compelled to search for a constructive way of living.

[September 20, 1929]

---

*[In his extensive and mostly unpublished autobiographical writings, Toomer describes these "mal-adjustments" as his transient family life, his searches for a career, and his feelings of uprootedness and lack of strong personal identity.—Ed.]

I

Cane

Editor's Note

Toomer began writing fiction as early as 1918, completing "Bona and Paul" while living in Chicago. By 1922 he had published a handful of poems and sketches in small literary magazines. Many of these pieces became part of *Cane*, which he finished in December 1922. In 1923 *Cane* was published by Boni and Liveright, with a foreword by the essayist and novelist Waldo Frank.

In August 1920, Toomer had met Frank at a party in New York City given by Lola Ridge, an editor of *Broom*, a small literary magazine. Their friendship grew intense by 1922, with a mutual fascination and respect for each other's ideas about life and literature, and Frank, the successful, established author, encouraging Toomer to write and publish. In the fall of 1922, while Toomer was working on *Cane*, and Frank was writing his novel *Holiday*, set in the South, the two authors traveled to Spartanburg, South Carolina. At this point in their careers, both deeply immersed in their work, Toomer and Frank were intellectually and emotionally close to each other. However, this intense relationship ended in 1923 when Toomer and Margaret Naumburg, Frank's wife, fell in love.

Toomer wrote his letter to Frank of July 19, 1922, in anticipation of their traveling together in the South, the trip that brought them to Spartanburg. The references to Georgia reflect Toomer's sojourn in Sparta, where he was a substitute principal of Sparta Agricultural and Industrial Institute for two months in 1921. "Murder" is part of *City Block*, a novel by Frank, privately printed in 1922. *Double Dealer* was a little magazine from New Orleans, edited by John McClure. Gilbert Seldes was an editor of *Dial*. *The Liberator* was a magazine based in New York City, edited by Floyd Dell, Max Eastman, Michael Gold, and Claude McKay, among others. "Withered Skin of Berries" is a short story; it was posthumously published in *The Wayward and the Seeking,* a collection of Toomer pieces edited by Darwin T. Turner in 1980.

Georgia Douglas Johnson (1886–1966), referred to in the letter to John McClure of July 22, 1922, published four volumes of poetry and had her 1928 play *Plumes* performed in New York City.

In his July 23 and 25, 1922, letters to Frank, Toomer is probably referring to Mae Wright when he says he fell in love at Harpers Ferry. Wright was eleven years younger than Toomer; the relationship was over by year's end.

The letter to *The Liberator,* August 19, 1922, is in response to a note of August 17 from that magazine, accepting "Carma" and "Reapers" for publication. The text of this acceptance reads: "We like your CARMA and REAPERS, particularly the latter, and are taking both for publication. You know, of course, that the Liberator is not in a position to pay for contributions. Could you let us have the poems on that basis? We admire your work and should like to know something about you."

Many Marriages (Toomer to Sherwood Anderson, December 18, 1922) is a novel by Anderson, published in 1923.

Gorham B. Munson, editor of the little magazine *Secession,* was part of a group of literary friends and acquaintances with whom Toomer was enthusiastically involved in the early twenties. This group included, among others, Frank, Ridge, and the poet Hart Crane.

Kenneth Macgowan (letter of March 21, 1923) was a theatrical producer and editor of *Theatre Arts Magazine;* he was also the director of the Provincetown Playhouse in New York City. Toomer's letter is in response to the following note from Macgowan concerning "Kabnis," dated March 20: "Frankly the THEATRE ARTS MAGAZINE can't very well use a play quite so long as yours, but what you write interests me so much that I am going to suggest that you send the mss. along. But if you ever have an [sic] shorter dramatic work, will you remember us?" In fact, "Kabnis," was rejected by Macgowan; however, sections 1 and 5 were published in *Broom* 5, August and September 1923.

In the undated letter to Frank that follows the letter to Macgowan, Toomer refers to *Rahab,* Frank's novel published by Boni and Liveright in 1922.

Horace Liveright was editor and publisher at Boni and Liveright. In his letter to Liveright of March 9, 1923, Toomer is referring to Gorham Munson's *Waldo Frank: A Study,* which the literary magazine *S4N* had sent him to review. Toomer's review, "The Critic of Waldo Frank: Criticism, An Art Form," appeared in *S4N,* Number 30, January 1924.

History has made the March 9 letter to Liveright sadly ironic because the exciting projects that Toomer writes of were not completed. Instead,

Toomer came to realize that he could not continue writing in the vein of *Cane* and must turn elsewhere for inspiration and subject matter. In 1923 this search for new meaning led him to the philosophy of the mystical psychologist Georges I. Gurdjieff, who was popular among some intellectuals at the time. Gurdjieff's influence would profoundly change Toomer's writing style.

Pre-Cane

Letter to Waldo Frank

Mountain View House,
Harpers Ferry, West Va.,
19 July 1922.

Dear Waldo, dear brother

it [sic] will be fine to be with you. I certainly want to, and I am almost certain that I can. Instead of staying here a week or so longer, I'll go back to Washington and save the money against the coming of fall.

I had to get away for a few days. During the last six months I've drawn myself so unstintedly that I had run dry,—abnormal mental excitation with no corresponding physical vigor or emotional flow. A week here has worked wonders. I have been receptive to life and nature, and it would seem that they have healed me. No writing, not even rewriting or polishing. . [sic] no desire to. The responsibility which is so heavy an element in my normal living seems, in fact did melt into the easy inconsequence of the other summer boarders. And three young girls have routed my seriousness and restored my instinct of play. The transition has been so sharp to those looking on that they are somewhat bewildered in ascribing my thoughts (some of which have filtered through to them) to the boy that [was] so evident to them. I picture their faces when they read my book!

Life here has not the vividity [sic] and distinction of that of middle Georgia. Racial attitudes, on both sides, are ever so much more tolerant, even friendly. Oppression and ugly emotions seem nowhere in evidence. And there are no folk-songs. A more stringent grip, I guess, is necessary to force them through. But southern life is surely here. Stringy; [sic]

ruddy whites, worn; [sic] fullblooded blacks. And I think I see a strain of Indian blood. Localisms are somewhat diluted by the influx of summer boarders, week-enders, and transients. It has its history, however, and its landmarks. John Brown's fort (now on the grounds here—this is Storer College, an institution for Negro youth—not more than a hundred feet from where I write this letter. The main building was used as a headquarters during the Civil War) Jefferson's Rock, buildings peppered with musket shot, etc. There are paper mills here. And of course, the Negro church, a shade less dramatic and musical than that of Georgia, but essentially the same. Here the Shenandoah and Potomac meet. Here also meet three states: West Va., Virginia, and Maryland. The opportunity for a vivid symbolism is wonderful. I have made a partial use of it in my last long piece. While not the best place for our trip, it would be an easy matter to go farther and fare worse. It has this distinct advantage: transition between the races is neither [difficult] nor hazardous.

I read Murder in Broom. In form and design, in depth and directness, it not so much makes most stuff seem puerile and inane as it outlaws them from serious art consideration.

Will City Block be ready by the time you come south? If length of time is anything, BROOM seems to have taken a few of my pieces. Double Dealer thought it inadvisable to print what I sent them. Gilbert Seldes returned Becky, Withered Skin of Berries (my last long piece). He now has Karintha, and Fern. Fern you have not seen. Liberator wants some. BROOM, I guess, is my best chance.

I dont [sic] want to be precipitant nor force myself, but I've had the impulse to collect my sketches and poems under the title perhaps of Cane. Such pieces as K. C. A. ["Karintha," "Carma," "Avey"?] and Kabnis (revised) coming under the sub head of Cane Stalks and Chorouses [sic]. Poems under Leaves and Syrup Songs. Vignettes under Leaf Traceries in Washington.

Jean

Letter to John McClure

1341 You Street, N.W.,
Washington, D.C.,
22 July 1922.

Dear John McClure

that [sic] was a fine letter from you. Very fine. It sets one more solid pillar beneath me. I managed to get away to Harpers Ferry for two weeks. Most of my mail was forwarded. Yours, however, I just received a day or so ago.

I am sending a batch of Mss. and hope that a few at least will meet your needs. I have more on hand, of course, but those sent are among the ones which I will include in my book. If things go well it should come out sometime this coming Spring. I think that I shall call it CANE. Having as sub-heads Cane Stalks and Chorouses [sic] (Karintha, Fern, etc. and two longer pieces), Leaves (poems), and Leaf Traciers [sic] in Washington, under which I shall group such things as For M.W., and other sharp, brief vignettes of which I have any number. I do not wish to force myself, and havent [sic]. But I feel that a precipitant is urgently needed just at this time. The concentrated force of a volume will do a great deal more than isolated pieces possibly could. And then, of course, more than anything else, I have the *impulse* to its creation. After all, whatever my mind says, I can only go [sic] things when I have a deep "feel" for them.

I do conceive of literature as an art. It is innate in me. The other sort of stuff I cannot write, as easy as many of my friends think it should be for me. They are a world apart, like the third is to the second dimension. I want to live the greater measure of the strictly human passions. When I use words I wish to create those things which can only come to life in them. I am violated to think of literature as nothing more than a vicarious experience of what one should be strong enough to wring from the social life. A simple rustic lyric has the power to touch me; but I do not confuse it with art. Life, human life, we must use, but its use should be accompanied by dimensional transformation. I do not think it good, though, for an artist to aesthetitize to [sic] much. To do so leads to sterility and absurdity. Of my writer friends (other than those you already know) only one has possibilities in the way you speak of. And she manifests them more in an appreciation of my stuff than in anything she has done. She has an undoubted instinct for good words and lines. I am certain that in her best moments she experiences a very genuine aesthetic emotion. But her faculty of expression is not up to her sensibilities. Nor is she sufficiently conscious. I do not think she ever will be. The inhibitions and taboos and life-limitations she labors under make even her modest achievement remarkable. I speak of Georgia Douglass [sic] Johnson of this city. I hear most of her best things. If at any time she attains your standard, I shall suggest that she send it to you. And I shall be increasingly awake for other efforts.

Thanks for the July number.

I too feel, in a very sincere way, that the Double Dealer cannot afford to hazard its existence for any single contributor. Whatever the momentary disappointment, any genuine artist in the long run will profit by your policy.

Fraternally, Jean Toomer

From Letter to Waldo Frank

1341 You Street, N.W.,
Washington, D.C.,
23 July 1922.

Dear Brother

* * * Yesterday I sent a bunch of Mss direct to the Liberator office. I hope that you will like them and be able to use one or two at least.

I want to see you. Perhaps I shall be able to make it before you get away. Russia must be very stimulating just about now. But somehow I do not envy you your trip. The Experiment here in America has an almost complete hold upon my interests and imagination. Were it not that I am broadly curious and sympathetic I should be in danger of falling into provincialism. The strange turns of life even here in Washington (which is usually rated as an unspeakably dull place), the tragic consequences of spiritual abortion, the complacency, the warmth and color and waywardness—I love them all. I love this southland of my ancestors. In New York I have been nostalgic for the streets and faces of Washington. In Paris or Moscow I think that I would be the same. And my work, I guess, is progressing as good [sic] as it could in any other place. Besides, while at the Ferry I fell in love. . . [sic]

That is a great place, that Ferry. Its hills and rivers were the scenes of two youthful love affairs. This time, as night came on, its dusk blended with a face whose eyes held more love than any I have ever seen. I'll tell you, brother, the South means love. It has always happened so. Its lies and prejudices are dirty. Well, I'll eat the dirt provided that the life be sufficiently sweet.

Come down, if you can, before you go away.

Jean

From Letter to Waldo Frank

134 [sic] *You Street, N.W.,*
Washington, D.C.,
25 July 1922.

Dear Waldo

the [sic] postman didnt [sic] know that I had returned—he sent your letter to the Ferry. It was forwarded to me and I received it this morning. You are right. Harpers Ferry is not the place for you, nor for myself in light of the new significance I place on our trip. It could never have been the starting point of such a thing as Kabnis. The vivid thrust of LIFE simply is not there. Your letters, together with a bit of analysis on my part, have convinced me that the impluse [sic] which sprang from Sparta, Georgia last fall has just about fulfilled and spent itself. My book, whether it matures next month or next year, will place a period. A fresh, and I hope a deeper start will come from our coming venture.

What do you think of Kentucky? The name itself has a special charm and beauty for me. Men I have met and asked about the place. . [sic] porters, race-track men, preachers, students, etc. . [sic] tell me that nowhere in the country can such a riot of life be had as in Lexington and Louisville, and that in many of the outlying districts things have changed but little since the Civil War. The actual Kentuckians whom I have seen seem to carry the vividity [sic] and color, the dash and love and waywardness conjured to the art mind by 'nigger.' I'd love to go there. At worst, it can serve as a convenient door into regions farther south. * * *

I think that you are right about. [sic] Dial. Seldes returned Fern and Karintha this morning. "Those manuscripts are interesting, but it seems to me, unfulfilled." So be it. Four years, perhaps, will serve to age them to their 'standards.' Double Dealer came across with quite a decent letter. "The blend of races has produced remarkable literature in the past. It will do so in the future, and the work which you showed us three weeks ago seems to all of us not only full of rich promise but, to a great extent, of rich fulfillment. It will afford us great pleasure to be able to print something of yours, if you will keep us in mind for other manuscripts." (John McClure). But they do triffle [sic] a lot. And their half-sophistication and mock vivacity do not help matters. Witness July number.

That book of mine is by no means ready. The shere [sic] fact of typing will take me some weeks, I guess. And then, besides, Kabnis has not reached its real fusion. I had hoped that my stay at the Ferry would give me energy for this. I dont [sic] think it did. I didnt [sic] stay there long enough. More than this, I fell, or came very near falling in love. A wonderfully emotional, rich dark skinned, large eyed girl. Complications. . [sic] a clogging rather than a freshet in my passionate life. I have been partially numbed ever since I left her. . . [sic] I shall try to get away again within a week or so.

You are wonderfully dear to me, my brother.

love

Jean

Letter to The Liberator

1341 You Street, N.W.,
Washington, D.C.,
19 Aug 1922.

Dear Friends,

Whenever the desire to know something about myself comes from a sincere source, I am always glad to meet it. For in telling other folks I invariably tell my own self something. My family is from the South. My mother's father, P. B. S. Pinchback, born in Macon, Georgia, left home as a boy and worked on the Mississippi River steamers. At the beginning of the Civil War he organized and was commissioned captain of a Negro company in New Orleans. Later, in the days of Reconstruction, he utilized the Negro's vote and won offices for himself, the highest being that of lieutenant, and then acting governor of Louisiana. When his heyday was over, he left the old hunting grounds and came to Washington. Here, I was born. My own father likewise came from Middle-Georgia. Racially, I seem to have (who knows for sure) seven blood mixtures: French, Dutch, Welsh, Negro, German, Jewish, and Indian. Because of these, my position in America has been a curious one. I have lived equally amid the two race groups. Now white, now colored. From my own point of view I am naturally and inevitably an American. I have striven for a spiritual fusion analogous to the fact of racial intermingling. Without denying a single element in me, with no desire to subdue, one to the other, I have sought to let them function as complements. I have tried to let them live in harmony. Within the last two or three years, however, my growing need for artistic expression has pulled me deeper and deeper into the Negro group. And as my powers of receptivity increased, I found myself loving it in a way that I could never love the other. It has stimulated and fertilized whatever creative talent I may contain within me. A visit to Georgia last fall was the starting point of almost everything of worth that I have done. I heard folk-songs come from the lips of Negro peasants. I saw the rich dusk beauty that I had heard many false accents about, and of which, till then, I was somewhat skeptical. And a deep part of my nature, a part that I had repressed, sprang suddenly to life and responded to them. Now, I can not conceive of myself as aloof and separated. My point of view has not changed; it has deepened, it has widened. Personally, my life has been torturous and dispersed. The comparative wealth which my family once had, has now dwindled away to almost nothing. We, or rather, they, are in the unhappy position of the lowered middle-class. There seem to have been no shop-keepers or shysters among us. I have lived by turn in Washington, New York, Chicago, Sparta, Georgia, and several smaller towns. I have worked, it seems to me at everything: selling papers, delivery boy, soda clerk, salesman, ship-yard worker, librarian-assistant, physical director, school teacher, grocery clerk, and God knows what all. Neither the universities of Wisconsin or New York gave me what I wanted, so I quit them. Just how I finally found my stride in writing, is difficult to lay hold of. It has been pushing through for the past four years. For two years, now, I have been in solitude here in Washington. It may be begging hunger to say that I am staking my living on my work. So be it. The mould is cast, and I cannot turn back even if I would.

If this brief sketch leaves unsaid anything that you are especially interested in, tell me, and I'll give you all I know.

Its [sic] all right about the pay. If the Liberator can keep going, that fact will compensate me.

Glad you liked those two pieces, and are going to use them. What about "Georgia Dusk"? Didnt [sic] I send it in with the large batch? I thought I did. And "Becky" and "Tell Me"? These two I remember sending separately, and later. If you have them, and are considering them—all right. I just want to know.

Best wishes, always.

Jean Toomer

From Letter to Lola Ridge*

1341 You St
Wash. D.C.
[Dec., 1922]

Dear Lola Ridge,

* * * The aesthetic of the machine, the artistic acceptance of what is undeniably dominant in our age, the artist creatively adopting himself to angular, to dynamic, to mass forms, the artist creating from the stuff he has at hand,—these things have life and vitality and vision in them. They release. They punch. They stimulate. I like them. They are clean and fine and healthy. A trifle crude, but only because the process of spiritualization has not gone far enough as yet. It will, though. And I think my own contribution will curiously blend the rhythm of peasanty [sic] with the rhythm of machines. A syncopation, a slow jazz, a sharp intense motion, subtilized, fused to a terse lyricism.

Jean

Letter to Sherwood Anderson

1341 You Street, N.W.,
Washington, D.C.,
18 Dec 1922

Dear Sherwood Anderson,

Just before I went down to Georgia I read Winesburg, Ohio. And while there, living in a cabin whose floorboards permitted the soil to come up between them, listening to the old folk melodies that Negro women sang at sun-down, The Triumph of the Egg came to me. The beauty, and the full sense of life that these books contain are natural elements, like the rain and sunshine, of my own sprouting. My seed was planted in the cane- and cotton-fields, and in the souls of black and white people in the small southern town. My seed was planted in *myself* down there. Roots have grown and strengthened. They have extended out. I spring up in

---

*At the top of this typed letter Toomer handwrote: "A note from Sherwood Anderson says that I'm striking what he had long been wanting to hear. How long will I continue to, I wonder . . ."—Ed.]

Washington. Winesburg, Ohio, and The Triumph of the Egg are elements of my growing. It is hard to think of myself as maturing without them.

Ther [sic] is a golden strength about your art that can come from nothing less than a creative elevation of experience, however bitter or abortive the experience may have been. Your images are clean, glowing, healthy, vibrant: sunlight on forks of trees, on mellow piles of pine boards. Your acute sense of the separateness of life could easily have led to a lean pessimism in a less abundant soul. Your Yea! to life is one of the clear fine tones in our medley of harsh discordant sounds. Life is measured by your own glowing, and you find life, you find its possibilities deeply hopeful and beautiful. It seems to me that art in our day, other than in its purely aesthetic phase, has a sort of religious function. It is a religion, a spiritualization of the immediate. And ever since I first touched you, I have thought of you in this connection. I let a friend of mine, a young fellow with no literary training but who is sensitive and has had a deep experience of life, read Out of Nowhere into Nothing when it first appeared in Dial. After having finished it he came back to me with face glowing, and said, "When any man can write like that, something wonderful is going to happen." I think that there is. I think that you touch most people that way. And when my own stuff wins a response from you, I feel a linking together within me, a deep joy, and an outward flowing.

Yesterday a letter came from John McClure in which he told me of your stopping past the Double Dealer office, of your reading the things of mine he had on hand. McClure was the real thing, at the *right* time. The impetus I received from him, and from the Double Dealer, has been wonderfully helpful to me. Dec Double Dealer has just come. It features Harvest Song. Good!

Naturally, my impulse was to write you when I first received your note. But at that time I was re-typing my stuff, writing three new pieces, and putting Cane (my book) together. I felt too dry to write. Now, the sap has again started flowing. . . [sic]

I am following Many Marriages with deep interest.

Wont [sic] you write and tell me more in detail how my stuff strikes you? And at first opportunity I would certainly like to have a talk with you.

Cane

Letter to Gorham Munson

1341 You Street, N.W.,
Washington, D.C.,
31 Oct 1922

Dear Gorham B Munson,

Your letter came this morning. It stimulates. It contains just what I want: criticism that rubs me against myself; opinions, appreciations, interests, whose inherent fuel sets me going; thoughts that I value to the extent that I must test myself against them; and a general tone which makes me desire that my creations be intelligible to other people. (My position here has been such that I unconsciously discount or ignore the reader.)

Theatre [sic] sprang to life a few weeks back when I was helping to manage the Howard. For a week or so my job kept me from writing it. The minute I was released, I brought it out. The piece was written in a single day. When the last word was down, something within me said FINIS, so I knew that any rewriting or elaboration would have to come at a later day. I was conscious, however, of a questionable brevity, a possibility of misunderstanding, and of Waldo Frank. But I wanted to touch you, so I sent it on.

I cannot *will* out of Waldo. With the exception of Sherwood Anderson some years ago (and to a less extent, Frost and Sandburg) Waldo is the only modern writer who has immediately influenced me. He is so powerful and close, he has so many elements that I need, that I would be afraid of downright imitation if I were not so sure of myself. But I know my own rhythm (it has come out fairly pure in a formative way, in some of my southern sketches. It is when I attempt a more essentialized and complex pattern that Waldo comes in.) and I feel with you that I will "eventually make a successful amalgamation with (my) own special contribution." I must *grow* out of him.

The general design of Theatre [sic] you certainly get. (I have made that clear.) And you see and [sic] John and Dorris until "the theatre flings off into chaos." Perhaps you still follow them as I meant that you should, perhaps I have failed to make my meaning clear. Perhaps I dont [sic] quite get your criticism. I dont [sic] know. I'll tell you what I'm driving at: there is a barrier between John and Dorris (from her point of view) not of race, but of respectability. Stage-folk are not respectable; audiences are. Dorris' pride and passion break through the stage attitude (which is voiced by Mame) and she uses the only art at her command: dancing, to win him. John's mind discounts Dorris, first, because he knows that she cannot satisfy him, second, for the reason that he is aware of the way in which this particular set of show girls look upon him: that he is dictie (respectable) and stuck up, and will have nothing to do with them. Dorris' dancing, however, pulls his passion from him to it. Dorris and John unite in a sort of incorporeal animalistic ecstasy. Dorris feels this union, and naturally expects John to be moved to action by it, to clap, to come up on the stage, to make love to her, at least to make a date with her. Instead, John rebounds from the actuality of Dorris, from the reality of his own passion, into a dream. (The part inclosed in * * * [Toomer's asterisks] is dream.) In this, he gives her an impossible beauty, and achieves an impossible contact. He is startled from his fancy by the bumper chord which is the actual end of Dorris' dancing. It is evident that he will never do more than dream of her. Dorris, on her part, failing to find in John's face the desire she had calculated on, and being incapable of seeing him except in terms of the two alternatives, concludes that what Mame said was right. The humiliation of having failed, drives her into her dressing-room. The implication of the story is that of a dual separation: one, false and altogether arbitrary, the other, inherent in the nature of the two beings. This coincides loosely with a conception I have of the theatre, and of art in general, in its relation to life. (One side of the conception only, of course.)

In terms of this outline, would you say that Dorris experiences the crescendo? She does, of course, physically. But John's curve starts with intellection, swings down to passion in Dorris, and sweeps upward into dream. Except for physical motion, Dorris is largely inarticulate. This motion should be felt as an undercurrent all through the dream. As I reread my work, I see that I have failed in this. I have interposed some stuff that not only disolves [sic] her [im?]pulses, but throws the reader off the track. Dorris dances (I can say no more about her for her mind is simply a lush glow) John dreams. They both come to themselves at the same time. By statement in Dorris' case, by implication in John's, they both know their separateness. Because of his consciousness, and because of the actual range of his experience, John seems to me to be the logical one to emphasize. If you still see it in terms of Dorris, please tell me, for your thoughts will greatly help.

I'm particularly glad you liked "Stage-lights, soft, etc." and the autumn leaves figure, for in these I experienced immediate satisfaction. The sort of thing that accompanies image, that accompanies *expression*.

Your sentence that begins "I would urge crystallizing and crystallizing" strikes me as an usually [sic] fine piece of thinking. Mystery cannot help but accompany a deep, clear-cut image. Conscious mystery, like conscious profundity, is false and cheap. The great elements in literature are inherent in its designs, and cannot be willed or tacked on. In my reflective moments I desire the profound image saturated in its own lyricism. When I write, my imperfections have a way of closing the eyes of my ideal.

I am trying to get to New York. But the people to whom I have written asking for an advance of money have no precedent along this line—it is a slow business. Things have usually come my way, however, and I guess I'll be up that way before so very long. I want to talk to you. Your clarity, your horizons, your interest, will do much for me. And for my own part, I shall not come to you with empty hands.

John McClure wrote for something for Nov Double Dealer. As I have not heard from him, I'm expecting something to come out.

Thanks for SECESSION. And I'll send in the first piece I write which I think measures up to you.

From Letter to Gorham Munson

19 March 1923.
5:30 PM

* * * I see the importance of form. The tree as a symbol comes to mind. A tree in summer. Trunk, branches: structure. Leaves: the fillers-out, one might almost say the padding. The sap is carried in the trunk etc. From it the leaves get their sustenance, and from their arrangement comes their meaning, or at least, leaves upon the ground do not make a tree. Etc. This symbol is wanting, of course, because a tree is stationary,

because it has no progressions, no dynamic movements. A machine has these, but a machine is all form, it has no leaves. Its very abstraction is now the death of it. Perhaps it is the purpose of our age to fecundate it? But its flower, unlike growing things, will bud *within* the human spirit. . . [sic]

So my own stuff from now on will have more to do with conscious structure. Up till now I have not wholly neglected it. I think Theatre [sic] and Box Seat evidence of this. For Box Seat I had a very definite design. . . . The point is, from now on I'm going to shoot the sap into the trunk, where it belongs. And this leads me to a consideration, or a reconsideration of my own materials and of my own probable esthetic. I have a great need to talk to you about these, in fact, I dont [sic] feel like writing until we have gone over them.

Adieu

Letter to Kenneth Macgowan

1341 You Street, N.W.,
Washington, D.C.,
21 March 1923.

Dear Mr Macgowan,

Your interest is stimulating. I surely hope Kabnis will sustain it. I was afraid, in fact I was almost certain that the piece (unless it can be cut) would be too long for THEATRE ARTS, but somehow I at least wanted you to see it in ms. The truth is that I'm feeling, reaching out for my forms and for my esthetic. The material is all here. Some of it has gone naturally into poems, prose poems, sketches, short stories, and dramas. As I see it, the best of my stuff is basically dramatic. Whether or not I am 'of the theatre' remains to be seen. But this I do know: there is no social unit I love as I do the theatre. Something within me springs to life the minute I enter one. And my two best short stories are placed within theatre walls. My experience of theatrical art, however, has been very meager. You know what Washington is. And then, up till now, raw life has for the most part held me and absorbed my energies. In the matter of written plays, my knowledge of what I dont [sic] like exceeds my knowledge of what I do. I respect Galsworthy, for instance, but if he be naturalist or realist, then these two types are not for me. Eugene O'Neil comes nearer. The Russians. Etc. What I really want, I believe, (Kabnis may or

may not be evidence of this) is a close-knit, deep-rolling, dynamic structure whose language tends more towards poetry than towards what is flat
and commonplace. I do not want art to be a mere transcription of life,
technically OK; I want it to be the most vital and thrilling experience that
life has to give. That is, I want my own art to be this. And thus far, in a
tentative, nascent way, it surely is. Well, I could go on like this for ever
and a day. It is a fine thing that Kabnis is to secure your reading. And
when I write some shorter stuff, I'll certainly submit it to you.

Cordially,

Letter to Waldo Frank

[*no date*]
[*1923?*]

Brother,

Even before last fall I am certain that you saw race and color as surfaces. Perhaps your mind still retained a few inhibiting wraiths. But the
fact is, that you were *ready* for the miracle to happen. For myself, I could
sense no dissonance or qualification whatsoever. I dont [sic] look for
these things. I dont [sic] have to. If they're there, I simply *know* it. Nothing could have been more natural and real than our experience in Spartanburg. And the difficulties were extreme. All along, your consciousness
of life was [sic] been too deep and strong a thing to suffer restrictions and
distortions. I felt this (in a vague way, of course) during the hour we had
in Central Park. Our America sharpened the impression. After I had
read Rahab and the Dark Mother, I then seemed to know. Without this
knowing I doubt if I would ever have sent those mss. Or if I had sent
them, they would have been in the nature of a test. My sending them to
you was a natural step in their *expression*. And so it is with CANE. There is
not another man in the world that I would let touch it. Any more than I
would let someone write Karintha or Kabnis for me. You not only understand CANE; you are *in* it, specifically here and there, mystically because
of the spiritual bond there is between us. When you write, you will express me, and in a very true way you will express yourself. This combination I believe to produce the only worthwhile Introduction.

Sherwood Anderson has doubtless had a very deep and beautiful emotion by way of the Negro. Here and there he has succeeded in expressing
this. But he is not satisfied. He wants more. He is hungry for it. I come

along. I express it. It is natural for him to see me in terms of this expression. I see myself that way. But also I see myself expressing *myself*, expressing *life*. I expect artists to recognize the circle of expression. When they dont [sic], I'm not disappointed; I simply know that in this respect they are second-rate. That in this respect they differ but little from the mass which must narrow and caricature if it is to grasp the thing at all. Sherwood's notes are very deep and sincere. Hence I attribute his attitude to a natural limitation. This limitation, extended, is noticable [sic] in the bulk of his work. The range of his sensitivity, curiosity, and intelligence is not very wide. One's admiration suffers, but one's personal liking need not be affected by this.

There is one thing about the Negro in America which most thoughtful persons seem to ignore: the Negro is in solution, in the process of solution. As an entity, the race is loosing [sic] its body, and its soul is approaching a common soul. If one holds his eyes to individuals and sections, race is starkly evident, and racial continuity seems assured. One is even led to believe that the thing we call Negro beauty will always be attributable to a clearly defined physical source. But the fact is, that if anything comes up now, pure Negro, it will be a swan-song. Dont [sic] let us fool ourselves, brother: the Negro of the folk-song has all but passed away: the Negro of the emotional church is fading. A hundred years from now these Negroes, if they exist at all will live in art. And I believe that a vague sense of this fact is the driving force behind the art movements directed towards them today. (Likewise the Indian.) America needs these elements. They are passing. Let us grab and hold them while there still is time. Segregation and laws may retard this solution. But in the end, segregation will either give way, or it will kill. Natural preservations do not come from unnatural laws. The supreme fact of mechanical civilization is that you become a part of it, or get sloughed off (under). Negroes have no culture to resist it with (and if they had, their position would be identical to that of the Indians), hence industrialism the more readily transforms them. A few generations from now, the Negro will still be dark, and a portion of his psychology will spring from this fact, but in all else he will be a conformist to the general outlines of American civilization, or of American chaos. In my own stuff, in those pieces that come nearest to the old Negro, to the spirit saturate [sic] with folk-song: Karintha and Fern, the dominant emotion is a sadness derived from a sense of fading, from a knowledge of my futility to check solution. There is nothing about these pieces of the buoyant expression of a new race. The folk-songs themselves are of the same order. The deepest of them. "I aint got long to stay here." Religiously: "I (am going) to cross over into camp ground." Socially: "my position here is transient. I'm going to die, or be absorbed." When I come up to Seventh Street and Theatre [sic], a wholly new life confronts me. A life, I am afraid, that Sherwood Anderson would not get his beauty from. For it is jazzed, strident, modern. Seventh Street is the song of crude new life. Of a new people. Negro? Only in the *boldness* of its expression. In its healthy freedom. American. For the shows that please Seventh Street make their fortunes on Broadway. And both Theatre [sic] and Box-Seat, of course, spring from a complex civilization, and are directed to it. And Kabnis is *Me*. Holiday? Brother, you are weaving yourself into the truth of the South in a most remarkable way. You need it to complete [y?]our own spiritual experience. Because of your need, a beauty that is in solution will continue to live.

Post-Cane

Letter to Waldo Frank

12 Dec 1922.
Washington DC
[*sic*]

My brother!

CANE is on its way to you!

For two weeks I have worked steadily at it. The book is done. From three angles, CANE'S design is a circle. Aesthetically, from simple forms to complex ones, and back to simple forms. Regionally, from the South up into the North, and back into the South again. Or, From [sic] the North down into the South, and then a return North. From the point of view of the spiritual entity behind the work, the curve really starts with Bona and Paul (awakening), plunges into Kabnis, emerges in Karintha etc. swings upward into Theatre [sic] and Box Seat, and ends (pauses) in Harvest Song.

Whew!

. . . . [Toomer's dots]

You will understand the inscriptions, brother mine: the book to grandma; Kabnis, the spirit and the soil, to you.

I believe that before the work comes out, Little Review, Dial, and Secession will have accepted certain of its pieces. The ones I mention are the certain ones.

Between each of the three sections, a curve.* These, to vaguely indicate the design.

---

*In the original edition of *Cane,* Toomer placed arcs on separate pages before each of the three sections.

26

I'm wide open to you for criticism and suggestion.
Just these few lines now. . . [sic]

love

HOLIDAY?

Letter to Horace Liveright

1341 *You Street, N.W.,*
Washington, D.C.,
27 *Feb 1923.*

Dear Mr Liveright,

Under separate cover I'm sending CANE.
Waldo's Foreword. [sic] is included.
The book is done.
I look at its complacency and wonder where on
earth all my groans and grunts and damns have gone.
It doesnt [sic] seem to contain them.
And when I look for the power and beauty
I thought I'd caught, they too thin out
and and [sic] elude me.
Next time, perhaps. . . [sic]

Cordially,

Letter to Horace Liveright

1341 *You Street, N.W.,*
Washington, D.C.,
9 *March 1923.*

Dear Mr Liveright,

Your enthusiasm for CANE gives me a deep pleasure. And it also gives
me an energy which I shall try to put to good purpose in the shaping of
my next book. I have on hand here the crude material of two pieces that
approximate Kabnis in length and scope. I have another long story forming in my mind. With these three I'm thinking to make my second volume. The milieu is constantly that of Washington. The characters are

dynamic, lyric, complex. I am not quite ready for a novel, but one is forming. As I vaguely glimpse and feel it, it seems tremendous: this whole black and brown world heaving upward against, here and there mixing with the white. The mixture, however, is insufficient to absorb the heaving, hence it but accelerates and fires it. This upward heaving is to be symbolic of the proletariat or world upheaval. And it is likewise to be symbolic of the subconscious penetration of the conscious mind. Doubtless, before it is finished, several smaller dramas will have been written. At any rate, the horizon for the next three years seems packed and crowded.

I have had Munson's Study of Waldo sent to me by S4N for review. When the thing is done, I'll send you a copy. I have read the book through once. I think it an outstanding piece of critical writing.

The editor of the Modern Review, Fiswoode Tarleton, has promised to boost CANE up his way. He has written to know if he can get a copy for review in his July number. What shall I tell him?

I am planning to come to NY sometime this Spring. I look forward, anxiously, to seeing and having a talk with you.

And of course I'm waiting for the proofs of CANE.

Cordially,

II

The Mystical Experience

Editor's Note

In 1926, while standing on an elevated train platform in New York City, Toomer suddenly went into a mystical trance that demonstrated to him the possibility of a "higher consciousness" able to transform him into a "radically different being." The intense mystical feelings that began on the train platform lasted for about two weeks, and although Toomer could not sustain this heightened consciousness indefinitely, the experience demonstrated to him the possibility of a world of harmony in contrast to the world of chaos with which he was all too familiar. It was a moment of crystallization, and Toomer felt reborn.

In fact, he had been preparing himself for this experience from at least the time when he had articulated his unhappiness with his life by going to Gurdjieff's institute in 1924. Although in writing about his experience he expressed amazement that what he had been trying to do consciously suddenly came to him unconsciously, without effort at all, it was probably the years of *conscious* effort that had laid the ground work for his mystical episode. This is not to say that Toomer's experience was not spontaneous. On the contrary, Toomer's narrative discribes some classic characteristics of traditional mystical states, like the above-the-body phenomenon, for instance, that William James documents in *Varieties of Religious Experience*.

At any rate, not only did Toomer's episode of 1926 give him a feeling of personal wholeness, it also reinforced his antipathy to separateness and rigid classification, and demonstrated the possibility that all human beings could be united in a "Brilliant Brotherhood." Looking back on his ecstatic two weeks, he felt they had shown him that it "is possible for the whole of mankind to become one in consciousness," and that this could then be "the real basis of our potential ability to realize the brotherhood of man."

"The Experience" is taken from the first 102 pages of Part II of the unpublished autobiography "From Exile into Being," which Toomer worked on from 1937 to 1946. The typescript was Toomer's fifth and final draft, and needed very little editing. Mostly I have taken out sections that I feel detract from the narrative by being too abstract and repetitious.

The Experience

I. THE UNEXPECTED

On an April evening in 1926, having taken a friend home, I was on my way back to my rooms. The first stage of the return trip had brought me onto the platform of the 66th Street "L" station; and there I stood, waiting, I would have said, for a downtown train. Surely I had no sense of waiting for anything else. Spring was in the air. After the confinement of winter it was good to be out of doors; so I just rested there, leaning against a railing as one does on shipboard.

A train came up; I let it pass. Another went by. I had decided, it seemed, to remain where I was until prompted to move. Here on the platform I had an enjoyable feeling of being at large in the world, at peace with myself. There was no rush or reason for returning to my place at any set time. The night, as we say, was mine; and so was this all too rare mood of quiet aliveness and freedom; better experience it while I could. This was the extent of my awareness of my state and motives.

The time was around ten o'clock. Quite a few people were abroad, walking the streets, standing on street corners, as if they too felt the call to be out and at large. Over on Broadway, the glittering front of a movie house accentuated the artificial brightness of the main avenue. The cross-town streets, in contrast, seemed like dark alleys that turned men into shadows. Above the roofs of houses the night sky arched immensely. From my point of elevation, the stars seemed as close as the people down below; New York's inhabitants seemed as remote as the stars.

I doubtless reflected on the condition of man, as I stood there. Thoughts of the possibility of higher states of consciousness may have presented themselves, but without evoking in me the slightest intimation that I was about to undergo any such transformation. I was given no hint, no warning. My mind might as well have been an utter blank. Then, just suddenly, it began.

I was startled by an uncommon inward event. It was as though I had been touched from within in an extraordinary quiet way that stilled my functioning and momentarily suspended me between what had been and what was to come. My very life had been stopped, so it seemed, and yet I was about to live again, live anew, and strangely. Somehow I understood I was going to be moved, regardless of my wish or will, into a nameless experience.

My attention was held to a mysterious working in my depths that instantly impressed me as an authentic action utterly different from any I had hitherto known. It bore no likeness whatsoever to anything I had ever experienced, nor to anything I had ever read or heard of others experiencing. As this unfamiliar inner-action increased I became increasingly incredulous, expectant. My sensations could not have been more strange had my body quietly left the ground and soared into the air. I had just that feeling—the impossible is happening. It can't be!

But it was!

I was changing. Throughout my entire presence I was changing. It seemed I was being taken apart, unmeshed and remeshed. I seemed to become malleable and flowing. My very substance was in motion.

I did not exclaim, This Is It! I had no way of knowing that here was the beginning of my rise into the level of life and the experience I had worked and hoped for. This is *it* was said in me with undeniable authority by the action itself. What *it* might be I could not imagine.

But this I knew. I had not started it, nor could I stop it or influence it in any way. What had begun would unfold. What had started would be carried on and irresistibly accomplished. I would go where I was moved. For I was helpless, now that help had come.

My body and my life were in the power of a Power. Some kind of revolution was occurring in the named and unnamed parts of all of me, occurring with sheer ease and complete harmony. It was perfectly quiet. It was quietly perfect. But how strange!

My very being was at the disposal of the Power that had come. That Power was drawing me. Regardless of me, it was moving and making. I recognized—A master is at the controls. My master has come and I have met him. And in that moment my will became his will; and I felt—Thy will be done. Thy wonderful will!

I became as a child, captivated by a wonder-work. At a stroke my mind was emptied of thoughts. As a child I gazed raptly. Myself was melted down to a single simplicity. Constrictions and fears, desires, plans, all vanished. I had no thought of myself, no wish for anything other than this amazing present happening. *Now* was important. Now was all. Past and future were no more. Place, people, passed out of sight and reckoning. The world itself temporarily disappeared. I was taken out of all that, and felt a rapture so serene, so interior, that no sign of it would have been visible to another person even had he been watching.

The entire rigid frame of the habits of the body-mind was quite dissolved, and I was made ready for I knew not what.

Now there was a growing, as of an inward seed. What remained of myself was as a pod being outgrown by a great seed. A life within my life was in motion. A being within my being was rising and gathering. All within was wondrously fertile and portentous.

The moving was not of me. I felt this distinctly now. The chief moving was not of me but of something other than me. The moving seemed, now, not in me at all, but outside, behind me, occurring in *another* being.

Another being was in motion. Another being, in action, by action, was rising as Consciousness.

I beheld that other being as a stranger entering my life. To that other being I probably was a stranger entering its life. Stranger was meeting stranger on the border of a mysterious world. And what would be the issue?

There was creating, but not by me. Quite evidently, I was not creating. I could not so create. I was being created anew by the Power that had created me.

Yet it became increasingly clear that I was not the center of this working in any way. Not the source, not the main objective. Not subject, not object. I was as if decentered, off to the side as a spectator. That other being was the center, the source and chief recipient of its own actions. Sprung from a seed, it was creating itself, using living substance, using me and my life, and life drawn from a higher order, beyond me.

I was losing my life. It was being taken away for a more noble creation. Life was in that other, in that wondrous visitor. There was Being, Consciousness, an Existence so large and deeply powered that it would surely absorb me as a mere particle.

Now the moving was in light. The light was moving. The moving light was in changing design. My inner world was softly illumined. If, more deeply in, there was a great source of light, I did not yet behold it. I surmise I was still closed to the Inner Light itself, to the Eternal Beam beheld by Dante. There was no blinding flash, no overpowering splendor. I witnessed, rather, the events that proceeded within the sphere of this soft lighting.

I was given insight. I seemed gifted with psychological clairvoyance. My eyes simply opened inwardly; and, though it seemed miraculous at first, I came to know that it is as normal and as necessary for one's eyes to open to the inner world as for them to open to the outer. Blindness is the unnatural condition. Blindness to the world outside and to the world within, is abnormal. Outsight *and* insight are faculties that every human being needs, and should have, for the right process of his whole life and orientation. I saw inner events as clearly as one sees outward forms in the luminosity of dawn or twilight, with this significant difference: one's outward sight is usually of objects only, whereas this inward vision was a seeing of processes—and forms that ordinarily are invisible.

I beheld, inwardly, I saw the main forms of my total human being. I witnessed the workings of the Power. I beheld creating. I beheld myself awakening!

I continued to feel—The impossible is happening. It cannot be. I could not credit it that such marvel exists in man. I could not believe that this was a true disclosure of inner reality. Time had to pass, I had to become more used to this order of experience before I could accept the real as real. And now another feeling became prominent.

The wonder was at hand, yet I felt it to be inaccessible. Though it was within my human totality I felt I could not touch it or contact it in any way. It was "off there," like a star a child beholds but cannot take into his hands.

The moving seemed to have a center whose location, as accurately as I can designate it, was in the torso and to the rear, as though behind me. In my sense of it, it was not in my body at all, or in any part of myself with which I was familiar. This must be repeated. The center of the entire experience seemed outside of this-me. I had the impression that I was witnessing, not subjective but objective phenomena. These extraordinary events seemed to be taking place as much outside of me to the rear as the events of the external world seem outside to the front. No external object has ever appeared more clearly not-me than this internal subject. No other man has seemed as different from me as this inner being.

These impressions, I think, were true to the facts. Later phases of the experience showed beyond doubt that that being was another being, not my ordinary self, and that consciousness was a different consciousness, not my ordinary awareness expanded. The Power, the center of creative action, was outside of this-me, though residing somewhere in my total being.

The motion started, insofar as I was aware of the beginning, as a simple motion. It seemed literally to grow, to become increasingly complex. It became, as it were, a field of motions, waves of moving. The spreading pattern was beautiful beyond description. The motions unfolded, gathered, spread, interweaving, sometimes spiraling. So far as I know, the only visible workings of the external world which bear some resemblance to these of the inner world are to be seen in the art of the color-organ. And, yes! the Northern Lights. Here, however, there was no color, simply light in threads and bands, against a darker background.

So the living light gathered and spread in waves that continually built up, built up. So, in time, the living waves came to envelop my whole self, extending downward as far as the base of the spine, perhaps farther, upward as high as the crown of the head, higher, and frontward as well as rearward.

They seemed to acquire thickness, solidity. They seemed to form a veritable body, a body that enveloped this-me and the physical body, a voluminous body, a vehicle capable of great stretching, a new form with new faculties.

How shall I say it? I did not know the truth of it, so what shall I say? Shall I say that this was in fact a *body*? Shall I say it was a second body, a body in addition to the physical, composed of subtler matters, having its own forces and appropriate functions? I felt it as a body. Indeed I saw it as a body. But neither to myself nor to anyone do I insist it was that.

What I know is this. By the mysterious operations I have tried to describe, there was a transformation and an arising of a new form. This was no extension of my personal self, no expansion of my ordinary awareness. I awoke to a dimensionally higher consciousness. Another being, a radically different being, became present and manifesting. And, for a time, this-me remained this-me, that-being developed as that-being, each distinct from the other.

So was I visited by Grace. For the Power is Grace when it manifests to us. (To be in the Power is to be in Grace. To be out of the Power is to be in dis-grace. Dis-grace and exile are one and the same condition.)

So Grace, as a bright hand with prescient fingers, worked in my total human being.

So the Power touched this life, touched it perfectly, radically changed it without halt or flaw, effortlessly wrought an intricate and sweeping revolution, ordered everything, opened the creature to the creator within, and brought me, together with that manifesting being, through the initial stages of the unimaginable.

O wonderful that Power!

II. TRANSPORT

For a time, exactly how long I cannot say, there were two of us, this-me and that-being, contiguous, yet perceptibly distinct, as though each were an independent entity.

In this-me I continued to locate. For yet awhile, I remained identified with this-me, so that I felt, as I always had, "This is me." Thus I looked in and beheld the coming-into-life of that-being, that self-behind-me, and felt it to be not-me. Now, of all times, it did not occur to me that that-being was my real being. Had someone wise in these matters told me the truth I would not have believed him, so contrary would the truth have been to my sensations.

Nothing that I had ever heard or read helped me to recognize this reality. This seemed utterly new and unique, as if no man had ever experienced it and passed on his findings to others, as though it had never been present even as an idea in the mind of anyone. Nor did my past experiences of my "inner being" provide the slightest basis for recognition of this extraordinary entity. In this writing I call it "that-being," and this term is true to the actual experience; but at the time I could not name it.

I did see it. I also saw this-me. A light seemed to be thrown on both of us, so that presently I realized where I was locating. As clearly as a man sees in what part of a lighted room he stands, so did I see that I was in this-me, and that this-me was the front or outer part of this astonishing combination.

There I was, stationed on the surface, out of the center. There, I suddenly realized, I had been, all my life, but without realizing it. Always I had been out in front, knowing but not knowing it. Occasionally, my inward powers had come out to me. Never had I had a deeply inward centering. I had moved around as on the rim of a wheel, all the while assuming that that was my natural place, that so, in the nature of things, I must move. Never had I been poised in the hub. But why not? Apparently I had been *held* where I was.

These perceptions flashed and passed. These realizations came and receded. But they were indelibly impressed on my memory. They formed the basis of later understandings of self-imprisonment, uprootedness, exile.

One does not make inquiries when such events are taking place; one simply marvels. Yet questions must have been wrung from me. *What is this? What is it doing? Where is it taking me?* And the thought may have occurred that, whatever the eventuality, there simply could not long continue being *two* of us, *both* in consciousness.

Meanwhile that-being was growing in size, solidity, power. It was rising as a tide of life. Presently, we may assume, its force of attraction became stronger than that of the personal self, became irresistibly strong—and then the transit began. I was withdrawn from this-me, from the body-mind, extricated from life-long involvement in the personal self, and set in motion towards that-being.

I was moved across from this world of the self to that World of Being; and as I moved I lost some of my life, never missing it, and the rest, liberated, followed where I went.

There was no choice. I was touched and taken. I was claimed. The Power had me in its power. I had to go.

Without the slightest feeling of dislocation I was radically changing location, leaving every known thing—and there was no clinging, nor any need for surrender; I had been surrendered, and was moving into the unknown.

I was being transported. *I* was. Not my body. It stood there motionless on the "L" station. Not my being. It was there in its world, waiting to receive me. Precisely *I* was being transported from exile into Being.

Transport is the exact term; so is transcendence. I was rising above my habitual level. I was coming over all that formerly had kept me from my real life and being. Liberation is the exact term. I was being freed from my ego-prison. I was going to a strange incredible place where I belonged, even though I did not yet recognize that I belonged there.

And then, in less time than it takes to tell, I was at my destination. I was there. I fulfilled the first stage of the ancient testimony—"Thou art That."

O the wonder of it!

I was taken into that-being, and instantly that-being became this-being, my being, and that-me ceased to exist, and I was one and whole. I was one being, one consciousness, alive in a life so different from ordinary life that there seemed to be absolutely no relation between the two.

Had I been asked—Are you alive?—I would have looked [with] my astonishment and said—I don't know, I don't know where I am or what this is, or even if I am any more.

Yet I *was,* was as never before.

Here in this-being I located. Here I centered. High in me I was joined with myself. Deep in me I was connected with my roots and source. Here in being I became my realness, this extraordinary I AM.

I AM! And AM is greater than I!

Something in me knew it to be real, as I had never before experienced reality. For the rest, I knew nothing at all, except that everything was starkly unfamiliar.

And so for a while there was an involuntary contest between a new certainty and intense incredulity.

It *was*—but *how could it be?*

I was being shown that resurrection can happen; that the resurrected do really live; but the question persisted—Am I living?

I was being shown what my real being is, but I could not accept it as me, so utterly different was it from my ordinary person. Though in myself, I did not yet recognize myself.

One thing, however, I knew without doubt. My ordinary self had vanished. It was gone, and therefore I could not go back to it even if I wished. I was on a voyage, and what I had left ceased to exist when I left it. Return to the familiar was impossible. I had no choice but to accept this incredible being as myself. I had no choice but to be in this being and become accustomed to its life and world. There was this sharp feeling of irrevocable necessity.

My knowing that my ordianry self had vanished was later confirmed. The personal self no longer existed in my thoughts, or in my feelings, or as part of my totality, except as a memory which had no reality. All that pertained to it completely dissolved for the duration of the experience.

Why did that self vanish? I do not know. I simply state the facts of the occurrence. That self began changing and dissolving when my real being became present and manifesting. It ceased to exist as an entity when I was withdrawn from it. And yet, when I eventually fell from Grace, there, bless me, was the personal self waiting to receive me!

In my new state of being there seemed to be but two carryovers from my former condition. One of them was I. I had been transported—but I was I. It was the same I that had inhabited the body-mind throughout the thirty-one years of the body-mind's life. Now it was the I of the revealed being—thus showing itself to be a unit of the human totality, detachable from other parts and therefore capable of changing location.

I was I, in being as in body. There was an *identity*—a tenuous but persistent identity that survived the radical changes. (Is "I," then, the seat of one's sense of oneself? Does it enable each one somewhat to recognize himself, no matter what transformations occur? Is it the core of our sense of continuity? This is certain. "I," its location, and change of location, are the most strategic factors of a man's life.)

The other carryover, strange as it may seem, was my everyday awareness. Though the personal self vanished, my ability to be aware of and move about in the world of daily affairs remained with me, as was shown when the test came. This was no trance I had entered, but a higher state of consciousness in which many of my ordinary faculties were retained.

When a man wakes from the sleeping state, he leaves the sleeping state behind. Certainly he is not in the sleeping *state* and in the waking *state* both at the same time. In this experience I awoke again, that is, awoke from the waking state, yet did not lose It. I left its limitations.

What had happened was this. Once I entered Being-Consciousness, at that instant my ordinary consciousness became an integral part of this greater consciousness. There was a merger into one seamless whole. * * *

I was absorbed in the inner events. The outer world seemed nonexistent. The time came, however, when I gazed outward, and then it was shown that I retained the ability to relate myself to the usual surroundings as one does in the ordinary waking state. There the world was. I saw the "L" station, my body resting at the railing, and, down below, the people on the streets, the traffic, the glittering front of the movie over on Broadway. I saw these things through the glow of my new state; I, as a being in Being, looked at them; but they were the same things with the same shapes. Trains were trains. Streets were streets. Human bodies were human bodies. How extraordinary, indeed how impossible it would have been had it been otherwise!

When I looked up above the roofs of houses and beheld the night-sky, there was nothing apocalyptic in it. High in the heavens were the same sparkles called stars, pin-points of light piercing the black dome of the world. I saw the same night-universe I had seen all the nights of my life. But how purely those stars shone, and what quality in the darkness! No night had ever seemed so sheerly beautiful, so fresh, so complete, so *original.*

Everything seemed original, as if the world out there had just been created, as if I were beholding the newly finished work of the First Creator.

That there was and is a Creator was the most evident fact and mystery of my experience. The existence of the Reality we refer to as God was more real to me than my own existence. But now I used no label for that Reality, or for myself. I was discovering the Life behind labels.

III. BIRTH ABOVE THE BODY

From my depths came a thanksgiving, a rejoicing, a hymn to the Nameless. I was penetrated with aliveness in every particle. I was and felt newborn, utterly exposed to a reality whose quality was electric. I felt everything I had ever wanted to feel, and none of it was as I had thought it would be.

How strange to have awakened and to be!

And when I looked at my body—how strange! It seemed removed from me, placed "out there," and below me, as though there were space between myself and it. It seemed to have become small, a mere appendage. Though I knew I was still attached to it, or it to me, I felt no relation to it whatsoever. It could have walked off and gone about its business, vanished, and I would not have missed it.

I had been born above the body. To me the body was an object. This was no attempt to objectify it, or to detach. This was complete, accomplished nonattachment—a new relationship, a psychological reality, existing not in attitude only but in full experience.

Gone was the feeling—I am a body, I am my body. Identification with the body was so utterly dispelled that it seemed impossible I had ever been in such a condition. Present was the knowledge—I have a body. I have it, but it is not "mine." * * *

If people could only bring themselves to realize that they are beings, primarily; not bodies, not personal selves, but *beings*. I had a sense of the profound inner and outer changes that would inevitably occur if men awoke to this truth. An end of bondage to the body. An end of the cravings and prejudices that arise when people believe that they and others *are* their bodies. An end of imprisonment in the little self. An end of the strife and false goals sought when men believe they are their false selves. The beginning of being-life. The beginning, everywhere on earth, of a world created by human beings for human beings. I also had a sense that in no other way would these changes come about. It seemed to me that the revolution which mankind awaits depends upon this one realization above all others.

We know that the vitals of the body are not in the hands and feet, but in the head and torso. The hands and feet may be cut off; the body will live. I now knew that the vital centers of my life were not in my body but in my being, in my spiritual torso. It was starkly clear to me that I was in no way critically dependent upon that small, insubstantial physical frame. I knew as surely as I could know without it actually happening, that should the slender threads that held me to the body be cut, I would continue being, existing, living. Should the body die, my earthly life would of course terminate for this time. But, just as the body was only a part of my being-totality, so my earthly life was only a segment of my total universal existence.

Universal existence? I could not doubt it. What I was experiencing made me sure of it. As a being, I had a life enduring. The body is bound to this space, to this time. Just as certainly, the being is not so bound. The being has its own great space and long time. The being precedes the birth of the perishable body and succeeds its destruction. In a total human being there is that which is imperishable—and therefore perfectible. We can develop and perfect our beings because, as I realized, our beings remain in existence long enough for this long-range purpose to be accomplished.

This came to me not as a pleasant belief in an easy and guaranteed immortality, but as a reality, stark and relentless as it was hopeful. Our beings *have* to endure, regardless of our wish. They *have* to accomplish what they were created to accomplish, however long it takes, whatever the labor, whatever the suffering, no matter what the unenlightened will of man may do to the contrary.

IV. FIRST SIGHT

Inward moving continued. Growing, expanding, proceeded. This-being, now that I had entered it, continued creating itself. I continued developing. I became voluminous, towering. It was as if some miraculous yeast were in me, so that I was rising, rising. It was as though a cubit actually were being added to my stature—and not by my taking thought.

Below me spread a strange earth. Above me arched a strange universe. Down in front of me stood a strange man.

As I seemed above my body, so I seemed above New York, only more so. I saw the dark earth, and it seemed remote, far down and removed from the center of the Universe, a small globe on the outskirts. I was close enough to see the nightlife of the city, but the traffic of cars and people seemed "way down there." These are the exact words I used.

As I was nonattached to my body (and because I was nonattached to it), so was I nonattached to the ordinary world and its objects. As my body did not seem to belong to me, so I did not seem to belong in the world that met my eyes. Not only was I not of that world, I could not feel myself even to be within its boundaries. I was as if outside, in the Universe, beholding a planet that only recently had come into my view. Though I knew I had seen it before, it felt as though this were my first sight of the earth, its people, their buildings, their city.

I realized—The Earth is the Earth. Of all the bodies of the Universe, Earth is just this particular planet. Here it is, in all its unfamiliar reality. Not my pictures of it—the planet itself. Not some small part of it, but the whole globe. This was a consciousness of the Earth not such as is gained by travel and study but as directly perceived from a cosmic vantage point. Perhaps a man in a plane flying high enough to have some sense of the whole planet yet low enough to discern its features might have a similar awareness. This awareness, once it had come, remained with me thereafter. It came to be my natural awareness whenever I had occasion to take cognizance of the Earth. I continued to be what we may call Earth-conscious.

I saw people on Earth, a strange body bearing my name among them.

People, I realized, are earth-beings. Of all the places of the great cosmos they arise just there. They live just there. I gazed at people intently, as one does at things of interest that one is seeing for the first time. I took in what I could witness of their life. As I continued to look a new feeling came over me. Something was missing from that life.

Earth-people walked the streets, drove motor-cars, went in and out of buildings, but they were not awake, not aware of themselves, did not realize they lived, did not realize they were beings with bodies, did not *realize*. They were closer to unconsciousness than to real consciousness—and that was the way I had been before awakening. I was viewing somnambulists. * * *

I felt a sort of horror, and pity, and indignation. *Something must have been done to people.* It was unnatural that human beings pass their lives as somnambulists. It was diabolical that men be unequipped with the consciousness needed to enable them to live as men.

But how could it be? How was it possible that human beings were sleepwalkers? Why do not all human beings awake? Why did not the Power touch all people as it had touched me, and lift the human race into a consciousness adequate for the life of man?

Why—but there it was. People were sinking under the accumulating weight of their own complicated unconsciousness, blindly fighting each other as they went down.

V. EXPANSE

I was discovering that my being was in vital contact with the vast Universe. Through being, as had never been possible through body, I was becoming connected with the all-embracing world. Now I realized with certainty and astonishment—*I live and move within the Universe.*

Universal life, the limitless spread of creation, became ever so much more real to me than the particularized life of men and bodies. The whole world became ever so much more real than the partial reality of the tiny planet called Earth. The Universe became real to me.

Now I was aware—*The Universe exists.*

The Universe *is*. It is not a conception of man's brain, not a projection of his dreams. It is a stupendous reality. In its own grand right it is living.

From this moment, whatever the particular focus of my attention, something in me was constantly aware of the living Universe, and that I was in it. And it was at this time that I began to have the knowledge and the feelings that became overpowering later on. We are in the Universe, and we cannot escape from it. Not by death, not by any means whatsoever. It is not for us to decide whether we shall or shall not be. It is not for us to say whether we shall live or not. We are being and living in the Universe, and cannot cease.

Ever more vividly I recognized that the Earth is but a small province of the great world. Those who dwell on it as if it were the one and only place of life, are provincial. Travel the Earth around, and if that is all, you remain provincial. Increase your mental cognizance of it; this will not make you a citizen of the world. Direct your thoughts to distant stars; but you will be viewing them from the standpoint of a man on Earth. One must rise above the Earth to become universal. One must experience the Universe, not in thought alone but with his whole being, in order to become aware of himself as a being of the Universe; and to do this, one has to rise above himself, to be born above the body, above the personal self.

I seemed to understand that there are two directions of moving, one horizontal, the other perpendicular—and a third, the spiral, which includes the other two.

Bodily motion is horizontal. It moves outward on a surface that seems flat but actually curves, so that the motion ends where it started. Personal self motion is similarly horizontal. Being-motion is perpendicular and spiralling. It moves outward and inward and at the same time upward, attaining level after level of ascent.

A man may keep his body in constant motion and send it to the ends of the Earth; he remains a body, on its level, in consciousness body-bound, earth-bound. He may extend his personal self; he remains a personal self, ego-bound. (Power over others does not help a man to transcend himself; it prevents; it increases the self-imprisonment of both parties.) Only by being-moving is a man set free to evolve and develop.

The Universe attracted me. Drawn into it, I had a sense that I was ascending. The Universe became increasingly close; the Earth ever more remote. I was of the Universe—and it was as if I had never been of the Earth. I was a being, having no known place of origin, able to exist everywhere.

The remote Earth also attracted me. My attention, in part, was definitely earthward bent. And so, in a way impossible to describe, I had a sense that I was descending to that planet even as I was ascending to the larger world. As I "came down," I had a panoramic view of this globe, these earth-beings, these objects and forms.

Suddenly I felt—I have just landed here. I have just alighted on this "L" platform. Here I am!

I looked around, newly, as if this had not happened before. My impressions were incredibly vivid. They so far surpassed all former ones that it seemed I was now having my origianl meeting, with the earthly sphere.

This is the Earth. These are earth-beings. This is one of their cities. What a strange place! What strange beings!

I observed the various types of bodies, the houses, the motor-cars, the streets, the electric lights. I took in everything that met my eyes, and seemed not to understand any of it. What I felt now was intense curiosity. It was an entirely visual experience, a rapt observing unaccompanied by interpretations. It was, perhaps, pure contemplation directed to an outward scene.

Presently, perceptions became linked with thoughts, impressions were translated into understandings. People were earth-bound, but were they in touch with the Earth? It did not appear so. They seemed unrelated to their globe. Bound, yet separated. Though they moved over its surface, there was no inter-penetration, no exchange of living forces. They might as well have been on the surface of a large shell made entirely of metal.

Body-bound, were they in touch with their bodies? Was the body a living thing to them? To me, as I watched bodies walking the streets, as I saw how rigidly they moved, how few their expressions, how set and confined their ways, it seemed that I was seeing not organisms but machines. Between the people and their machines there was no vital connection. Here it was again—bound, yet separated.

The Earth was in the Universe. So were people. Did they realize it? Not those I was observing. They were wrapped up in themselves, as if their heads were down and their arms wrapped tight around their bodies. In effect, they were existing outside the Universe. They were outsiders. Their lack of realization that they were in the cosmos shut them out. Through unconsciousness they were outcasts from the great life of the world—as they were from the life of their own beings.

Unrelated to the Earth, unrelated to their own bodies. Unrelated to their beings, unrelated to the Universe. Exiles in every possible way. And they accepted that appalling condition as a matter of course, as though it were natural, and were content, or blindly discontent, to mole along.

Newly come to Being, newly come to the Universe, and to the Earth, I was a newcomer in every sense, inexperienced in my new birth, without sure bearings.

As I voyaged further into this new life, I left behind for a while every even remotely familiar thing. It was as though my body had dropped dead, so that I was completely released from it. I no longer had even that strange small link. I soared up and away, out of reach of the Earth and its beings.

I penetrated a vast unknown, a formless world of formless life, wherein I seemed to be the only definite entity. To my perceptions there was no other being of my kind or any kind, no finite living thing. It was as a great field of living force that flowed without obstruction. It was as an ocean of life without waves, without creatures, without markers, sky or horizon—limitless.

I felt—*I have died, and I am the only soul alive.* I have passed away, yet exist. Lifted up, moving, I know not how or where. On I must go, carried by the surge of my incredible resurrection.

It seemed I was in the illimitable reservoir of life before it is poured into moulds. I was as a lone traveller in a living desert where there was no night or day but a constant diffused radiance. How I had come to this trackless expanse I did not know; but I had a sense that I had somehow gained admittance to a sphere that beings dare not penetrate. A voice in me said—You better go back.

I felt myself to be the first being ever to enter this awesome realm. Struck with awe, with a kind of terror, I wanted to close my eyes, hide.

No one knew I had started on this voyage, nor expected my return. No one awaited my arrival anywhere. I had checked out of the inhabited world, departed on a journey watched over neither by man nor God. I was on my own; and on and on I went through a mighty sweep of luminous vitality. I felt destined to press on, forever without companionship, without communication, without guide or map, through the unmarked ways of this awesome Universe of Life.

VI. DOWN TO EARTH

How long had my body been standing on that platform? All I know is that when I again became aware of the earthly sphere, people were still abroad on the streets of their city, but fewer of them. It may have been near the time called midnight by earth-beings.

How did the thought come that I might as well move body away from the railing, onto a train, and into the apartment on 23rd Street? The idea did present itself, but only as an amusing and rather fantastic notion. Walls of brick, chairs, bed, bathroom—that, my home? Mine, that small accumulation of earthly belongings? Those rooms and their contents were as unrelated to me as a rodent's burrow to a flying bird. Certainly not for myself, nor for my body either, could I see any reason for going there.

Body did not need a hole to crawl into. Then why move that inconsequential object? Let it remain where it was indefinitely. Or, if it wanted to change place, let it go anywhere. Yet, just those rooms were its place. If it didn't return it would be missed. People would become concerned and start a search for the "missing" body. So why not go there? Wherever it was, whatever it did, however body fared, I would conitnue being, growing, adventuring in the Universe. I knew this so surely that I could not take body and its circumstances seriously, one way or the other. Outdoors or indoors, what difference? Here or there.

Could I move it? This question somewhat startled me. Here was an entirely new angle of the situation. It seemed to me that body would not move of its own accord. If it were to be done I'd have to do it. Could I? I became quite curious, and tried. For the first time since entering Being I tested my ability to control my earthly appendage. It worked! In some mysterious way my body obeyed me, its arms and legs moving as bid. It seemed as light as a feather. But how were my commands communicated to it? Why did it follow my orders? Incredible! I proceeded to manipulate it, like a boy with a newly acquired toy.

The next thing was to move body away from the railing. Get going, my friend. It did! It made ready to board the next train. Strange fascinating body! I watched it walk. I was aware of it moving somewhat below and in front of me.

A thought struck me. Inasmuch as I was newly come to this planet, it was lucky that I was in league with a body that had been born and reared here. It spoke the language and knew how to get about. A number of other bodies were its friends. It had money in its pockets, more in the bank. Not bad at all. We'd get along quite well.

A train drew up. Body and I got on. Though not a bit tired from standing in one place so long, it sat down on a seat that ran lengthwise. Across the aisle was a similar seat occupied here and there by other bodies. Facing them, I was getting my first close-up view of earth-beings. I looked intently at them. They glanced casually at me, or, to be exact, at my body. They could no more see *me* than I could *them*.

I thought to myself—You never really know what state of consciousness another is in. You but assume that others are in the same state as yourself—unless something has happened to make you realize that different states are possible. Otherwise, it simply does not occur to you that there may be difference. Even should the idea come to mind, how would you find out? By what sign or signs could you ascertain whether a human being were in the waking or in the Being-Conscious state? The man beside you on a train, one passing on the street, someone at the next table in a restaurant, might be in Cosmic Consciousness itself, and you'd not suspect it.

It was fun looking at people from my new vantage point. It was thrilling just to exercise my new faculties: to gather impressions, to think, to feel, to wonder, *as a being.*

Suddenly I stopped having fun. What I saw bit into me. The grimy bodies of these beings, the haggard faces, the pained sullen eyes, the weariness, the hopelessness. How terribly they had fared. And these were beings. They were beings of the Universe. Somewhere in them was the wonderful Power—and they had lost out. But why, how? What destructive force, within them or without, was strong enough to neutralize or counteract the operations of the inward power? Precisely what pushed them down, making them lose all sense of who they were, shrinking their souls, cramping and twisting their bodies? Feelings of outrage and sorrow gathered in me again.

Above the heads of my fellow passengers was a line of ads running the length of the car: cough remedies, dental nostrums, headache cures, skin beautifiers, hair tonics, aids to digestion, reliefs for constipation. I winced at the thought that these were not so much advertisements of merchandise as of the various ailments afflicting the poor people seated beneath them.

One man, happening to glance my way, seemed curious. He kept looking as though trying to size me up. Evidently he was scrutinizing my body only, assuming that he was thereby taking my measure. No doubt of it, he was equating my body with myself. What a queer sensation it gave me to be taken for my body when I was so starkly aware that I was a being.

Suppose you were carrying an umbrella and saw someone looking at it, taking it to be your body. Or suppose a man looked at your chest but believed he was seeing your face. Not only would you have queer sensations; you would know that should that person have dealings with you he would behave at variance with your reality and with his own better intelligence. Whether he meant to or not, he would mistreat you, and himself.

I now knew that should the man across the aisle have occasion to deal with me he would behave at variance with my and his reality. I further saw that this was just what people were continually doing to each other, insofar as they were unaware of themselves as beings and took the body to be the man. Here on this train were samples of the results. The bodies of men and women, as well as their beings, suffered mistreatment resulting from the fact that people were body-aware, being-blind.

When the train stopped at 23rd Street, body and I got off. Down we went to the street level on which I had seen the bodies of earth-beings walking across the surface of the Earth, horizontally.

Though body still seemed strange and off there, I found that we were becoming more connected. How easily, how happily it moved. As I was above and behind it, I not only was aware of its every movement but experienced a sense of leverage over it. It seemed, in fact, that I had complete control of it. At the same time and as never before I recognized it as a self-moving organism. Quite evidently it had its own springs of action, its own mysterious life.

As body walked the half block to number 439, the whole Universe was open to me, and I to the Universe, and I felt an immense freedom. I had this sense—Body walks on the Earth, I move through the Universe. I am in Life limitless and unobstructed.

We came to the house. Body got out the key, opened the door, and we entered. It was as though I were seeing the interior of an earth-being's dwelling for the first time; the dimly lit hallway, the closed doors along it, the stairs to the second floor. I had this awareness—This house, the people in it, all houses, all people, the Earth and everything on it, are in the Universe.

Body went upstairs, used another key, and we were in the apartment. Keys, locks, doors, walls—said I to myself with a chuckle—Earth-beings keep things locked up.

Body walked in and stood still. The room seemed strangely quiet, vacant, uninhabited. A hush was upon everything as though something mysterious were about to happen.

I looked around, amazed. I had seen this room before, yet I hadn't. I, in another condition, had seen it. I, in this condition, never had.

How small it seemed. Hardly large enough for a pygmy. I was as a full grown man returning to a place he had known as a child. Could it be possible that I, in any condition, had lived here and regarded it as "home"? Was it I, who not many hours before, had left this room to go uptown with a friend?

Small the room was, but the great Universe came in. Walls might exclude the outside world fashioned by men; they did not exclude the Universe, but were penetrable curtains in it—little limits within the limitless. Though body was here in its shelter, I was as much in the vast spread of creation, and as exposed, as when body had been out in the open on the "L" platform.

So this was the inside of a house, one's own private quarters, where, presumably, one could live to himself without others seeing you and interfering. No, the eyes of men could not see you. The eyes of Life? I had a sense that just as I was aware of being in a vast Life, so Life was aware of me being in it. I was connected with Consciousness. It was a two-way relationship, with a constant stream of communications passing between the small and great poles. I saw and was seen. I moved and was moved upon, registered and was recorded. More surely than I knew I was within the Universe, the Universe knew that I and all beings and all things were within it, interconnected.

Of a sudden I felt affection and pity for this room and its things: the couch and chairs, the work table with its typewriter, the dark orange curtains at the windows. It was the place that had belonged to my dead self. It was the special place where that self had lived what it believed to be its private life, where it had gone about its self-given work and, indeed, tried to improve itself, tried to make contact with what it dreamed to be reality. Yes, here it had dreamed and, if I remembered aright, here, in its terms, it had loved. And now that self was as dead as its illusions. A segment of my life was represented by this place, several years of unconsciousness.

Body and I moved about, looking at things, discovering them as it were. The toilet, which body promptly made use of; the shaving articles, which it would use the next day; the pots and pans and food in the kitchenette. We clicked the typewriter, picked up and replaced the phone. In the bedroom there was the bed that body had slept upon many a night. And all was new and strange. Yes, I, in another condition, had seen these things; but I, in this condition, was seeing them now for the first time. I was not unlike an archaeologist making "finds" on the site of an ancient city.

When body sat down in a chair, I recognized with some surprise that neither it nor I was the least tired or sleepy. It seemed that I had come upon an inexhaustible spring of quiet energy. I felt I could remain awake, without need of rest of any kind, as long as I remained in existence.

Then what introduced the idea that it would be just as well to get a bit of sleep, and why did I take the notion seriously? All I know is that at the thought of going to sleep I was suddenly touched with a self-concern like that which grips the personal self.

Suppose that while I slept my being were to leave me, my consciousness to disappear, and when I awoke in the morning I'd find myself an ordinary person again? Could I become ordinary again? It did not seem possible. Yet it might happen. Suppose it did. I'd kick myself for not having stayed awake to enjoy this consciousness longer. Imagine forfeiting this wonderful experience for the sake of a few hours' sleep which I did not need!

But was my new condition so volatile that it would vanish if and because I slept? Then no matter what I did, it would disappear before long.

It wasn't mine. It wasn't mine to hold or relinquish. Given me by Grace when I least expected it, it would continue for its time, and would be taken away when Grace saw fit.

So be it. I decided to sleep.

As I reached this decision there arose a glowing sense of what the experience had already revealed. It was not in me to ask for more. My high consciousness might pass; memory of what I had discovered through it would remain. My being might vanish, but the realizations that had come through it would continue in my life, whatever came to pass. Gratitude welled up. With my whole self I was grateful to the Nameless for what had been granted me this night of my life, this day of my being. And now, for the first time, I had a feeling of what my findings might mean to other beings of the Earth. Perhaps some day I would try to communicate them.

Body went into the bedroom, hung its coat in the closet. I was aware—this coat, this closet, are in the Universe. Body removed its shoes and pushed them under a chair—in the Universe.

As body got into bed I had the sense—all bodies, all houses, all cities, the lands and waters, this planet and the myriad stars, are in the Universe.

As I settled down and knew that sleep would soon be upon me, I felt an irrepressible expectancy and hope. At the center of my heart was the question—To what will I awake?

I dropped off into an unusually tranquil sleep.

VII. FIRST MORNING

Dawn came—another day on Earth.

Bright sunlight entered the room in which my body lay. I awakened and was wide awake. How perfectly extraordinary. The experience had not vanished while I slept. It continued!

I looked around the room that was somehow familiar yet not quite probable. What was this place, this little cubicle? How had I come to be in it of all the places in the Universe?

I listened. The noises of trucks lumbering along the street outside came as from a valley to one high on a hill. Though the street sounds gave me an idea that the city was going about its affairs as usual, I had a strong impression that all of it was a make-believe.

Men, with the range of experience possible to men, narrowing themselves down to truck-driving? They couldn't be doing it seriously. Human beings, rich in their own resources, hurrying to shops, factories, offices as if that were the sole purpose of their life and they were destined never to do anything else? Beings of the Universe focused on doing business as if earthly commerce was their full life's work?

Since body was in bed, let it lie. For my purposes it need not get up. I was already up, in Being.

There came to me a sense of what I had experienced the night before, and as vivid a sense of what might unfold this day. Never had the promise of coming outer events so quickened me with anticipation as this prospect of coming inner events. Not as a child on Christmas morning had I been so thrilled by what was in store.

Body, of its own accord, presently got up. As it moved about the rooms I was in a glow as radiant as sunlight. Joy possessed me. Not a mere absence of pain or sorrow, but joy itself, a singing gladness. I could have sung the Lord's song, for I felt close to His land.

All morning I was in this sheer being. I came to be aware of life as a sacred process moving towards the kingdom. I also had an intimation that though the kingdom, as the goal of the entire evolutionary trend, is distant, as an expression of God's life it is at hand, everywhere, always. One need not go far to find it; one need not labor for it as men labor to build their cities and empires; one has simply to open his heart.

Meanwhile there were other events, comparatively minor but more readily described. On this morning, as on others, my body followed its routine for beginning a day. And I, interested in its behavior, somewhat surprised to see that its habits were seemingly unaffected by what had happened to me, observed it. There was a noticeable difference in my relation to it. Though still nonattached, I seemed closer to it. There was a new nearness. Body was more real to me, and in a sense, more "mine." Also it seemed not so small, more "life-sized."

The force that had taken me out of and far away from body, now seemed to be returning me to it. Curious about these changes, I did not really question them. Only later did the meaning become clear. During the first night I had reached the maximum disassociation; already on this first morning a set of new connections was being established. I was re-taking my body. It was becoming, in a new way, an integral part of me. It was becoming, to me and in fact, an instrument of my being—a means of contact, not a confinement, an ability, not a liability.

As my body appeared more life-size, so did these rooms. My rooms? No, not that. Not now, not ever while I remained in Being, did I come to regard these quarters as mine. They were body's shelter. Their furnishings were the belongings of my impossible dead self.

Nearer to my body, I was also in closer contact with the things of its world. Continuing to see earth-objects as earth-objects, they no longer seemed so far down there, but were more on the same level. I was sort of surprised to find them here and was pleased with the thought that my presence surprised them.

Suddenly I experienced the things of these rooms with wonderful immediacy, as though I were in direct communication with them, appreciating them.

The tingle of water was upon my body as it stood under the shower. Suddenly I felt—Water! The wonder of water! I looked at it with new eyes—touched it with new hands. I experienced water with a feeling of regard akin to tenderness.

The cloth of the towel that body used to dry itself was almost a living thing. I recognized it as an entity with a character of its own. So with the metal of faucets, the wood of chairs, the flannel of trousers, the leather of shoes. . .

Breakfast was the first food eaten since I had entered Being-Consciousness. A small quantity sufficed; the quality stood out. An orange, milk, rolls, coffee, each disclosed its unique vital personality.

This keen contact with the Earth's materials came and went. But during the following days the experience was renewed often enough so that I came to understand the extraordinary communication there can be between beings and things. What meaning in the simplest relationships!

When a man opens and awakes he becomes real to himself. When he becomes real to himself the world becomes real to him. The outer world of Nature is discovered to be as marvelous as the inner world of Being; the real physical as wonderful as the real spiritual. Each is revealed as an order of reality.

But those closed to themselves are closed to the world. Those not yet born to their own beings are not awake to the things of the world. The unquickened in spirit are unquickened to spirit *and* to things. They do not make contact. They do not appreciate. Are they "materialists"? Then they are very poor ones.

Breakfast finished, body did something quite contrary to habit. It washed the dishes right away. Usually they were stacked, because in my former condition the morning hours had been the best time for what I referred to as "my work," and I wanted to get to work first thing. So I used to go to the typewriter; dishwashing was not allowed to interfere. My feelings of whether the morning had been spent profitably or futilely had depended upon how the writing progressed.

Now, it was quite all right with me that body was at the kitchen sink instead of at the Corona. Now I had a new work that had begun the night before and was proceeding. Now I had a wonderful occupation that progressed of itself, neither helped nor hindered by body's particular job.

Now I functioned as I had never dreamed possible. As body washed the dishes, I was growing in being and in consciousness. What more important work? As body dried the dishes, I was discovering, meeting, circulating. What more important doing? As body put the dishes in the cupboard I was moving nearer to the Presence that interweaves the Universe. Of all occupations this is chief.

I was *being.* Therefore I was *doing.* Being and doing are not different things, but one and the same. It is impossible really to be without doing. It is impossible really to do without being. There is one thing: being-doing. If you have the one you have the other. If you lack the one you lack the other. When one is in being, being-doing proceeds whether the body is active or quiet. It may or may not express through the body. The body may or may not contribute its experiences to the total experience. The inter-relationship between being and body may enhance both but it hinders neither.

This is what it means to be body-free. One knows that bodily action is not the only kind of action, nor is it the most important. One does not equate doing with physical doing, or with mental doing. One knows that there is being-doing, and that both physical and mental doing have meaning just in proportion as they are impelled by and infused with being-doing. One is not dependent upon the body for one's experiences. One is able to let body have its life because one has one's being-life.

Curiously enough, though body-free I did not *feel free* of it. It was as if I had never been bound to it. I say curiously enough, but there was nothing unaccountable about it. When a man walks through the prison gate and knows he is at liberty he feels free because he has just come from confinement and emotionally remembers how he felt when confined. He has a basis for emotional contrast. I had none. I had no remembered sensations of the body-bound condition. It was as though that condition had never existed. Besides, the man set at liberty from a jail is the same man who was confined, with much the same consciousness. He who was imprisoned is now free. There is a continuity of "he." But I was in a different being. There was no continuity of "me." It is questionable if the being of my present experience had at any time been body-bound. More likely it had always been "free." Now I was in its native condition.

When body finished its job at the sink it strolled around the living room, pausing at the work-table. I looked at the pile of manuscripts. Those papers! What labor had gone into them! Out of curiosity I picked up a page, read it, put it down. Could it be possible that I, for months past, had tried to function by that means? Had I really believed that those words would convey something of worth to other human beings? Truly the blind try to lead the blind.

I took up a book with a bit of paper in it for a marker. I, in that other condition, had been reading it only the day before. Doubtless it had meant something to me or I wouldn't have marked it. Neither did this seem possible. Near the book was an ash-tray filled with cigarette stubs. That fellow had smoked, doubtless feeling he needed to smoke. Close by stood a comfortable chair, showing signs of having been used by the same fellow. It was like coming upon a man's room left just as it was before he died.

Here was a situation! These were his belongings, not mine. Yet not his, for he was no more. He had gone, leaving neither will nor heirs. To whom then did these things belong? The laws of men were hardly adapted to handing down a decision in a case like this.

The phone rang. I talked briefly with someone who thought he had business with the "me" that I knew to be among the departed. A woman came in to clean the rooms. Body got out of her way. I continued being.

VIII. LET BE

* * * While free of the body and of the personal self I was, in consequence, free of the internal condition that gives rise to wrong external relations. So complete was my liberation that I had to make effort even to remember that I had ever coveted, or willed not to covet, the goods of the earth. I let things be. Since the rooms were furnished, let body use what it needed. Let me appreciate things as materials. For the rest, I was non-related. It was an absence of both positive and negative attitudes, an absence of relationship. Had someone come in and said he wanted everything that I, according to his belief, owned, he could have gone off with the entire outfit, from pots and pans to cash.

Neither was there anything in me to make my hand reach out for distant things. No prospect of earthly wealth could make my heart rise hopefully. Out there in the world, as I knew when I thought of it, people were going after things. Were they doing anything else? How much was necessary labor? How much unnecessary manipulation? How much for use? How much for misuse? The scheming, competing, fighting, killing. The ever increasing labyrinth of laws governing the getting and keeping of things—laws troublesome to make, as troublesome to enforce, evade, break, change.

I was so out of that world that it was only by effort that I could understand what motivated people in their mad pursuits. It seemed incomprehensible that *beings* could be the victims of such a mania. I was as astonished by this aspect of the human situation as you would be to see eagles scratching around the barnyard like chickens.

Possession? To me it was an obvious fact that no one *can own* anything—not a pencil, not a fortune, not his "own" body, not even his "own" soul. The things of the earth are of the earth. The things of man are of man's commonwealth. All things are of God.

All that we can do is to use or misuse. We can appreciate or take for granted or violate. The belief that things can be made "mine" and "yours" is an illusion of people who are neither completely asleep nor completely awake. What a ghastly illusion. Those in deep sleep are free of it. Those in high consciousness are free of it. Those in the so-called waking state are under its spell.

Since I was being, it was only natural that I let body be. But why did it let me be? What had happened to render it so undemanding, content to move quietly around the rooms or sit motionless for long periods? I suddenly recognized that though I had beheld the processes of my transformation, I had had no insight at all into the changes going on within the body itself. I focused on body with new interest; and as I did so I became quite aware of certain features of its condition only half-recognized up to this time.

What remarkable well-being! Body seemed purified, as though a deep-seated illness had been cured. Now it was recharged with tender vitality. If walking, it seemed to flow. If seated it seemed to rest in perfect equilibrium. What unity, what serenity! Body was singing. It knew something about itself that I did not know, and what it knew made it happy.

I would have given a good deal to see inside of it, to know precisely what had happened. In general it was doubtless true that the Power which had worked wonders in me had also worked wonders in it—but what? What changes had occurred in its organs and functions? The only clue was an impression that came again and again. A weight has been lifted. A weight has been removed. Presently I asked—What weight? All at once it dawned on me. The weight of that-me! Of course; what else? The event that had liberated me from the personal self had also liberated body from that self. Both of us were free of that self and, to whatever extent, of each other.

Not bearing the burden of that self, body was buoyant. No longer driven and made ill by that self, body was at peace and well. Not cramped and congested by that self, its vital currents circulated unimpeded and unimpaired. Now body could be and move as was natural to it, because relieved of burdens not rightly belonging to it. It was itself as I was myself. I recognized that there is reason for referring to the body as the physical being. Body too was being—and this was why it let me be.

Physicians and psychiatrists daily verify the fact that mental and emotional factors are involved in and frequently cause bodily disease, and therefore, must be effectively dealt with if there is to be a cure. My findings go a step further. They indicate that the entire ordinary self oppresses and deranges the body; and that, therefore, this entire self must be overcome and eliminated if there is to be total health.

The overcoming of the self is as necessary to bodily well-being as it is to social and spiritual advancement. Right-circulation, I am convinced, is the key to health and wholeness: right-circulation within the body, within the being, between the two, and between the being-body and the larger world. Right-circulation is impeded and sometimes critically arrested when the personal self obstructs the way between the being and the body. Right-circulation is restored when that self is removed, and just in proportion as it is removed.

I believe that were people to become free of the self, the following results would be immediately evident in the body. Minor disorders would disappear at once. Major disorders of long standing would readily yield to treatment. Bad habits formed by cravings for stimulants and sedatives would pass away. Most of the drugs now used would be dispensed with. People would enjoy health of body, pliability, sensitivity, to a degree beyond anything ordinarily dreamed possible. It would be as if a miracle had been wrought.

IX. ANONYMITY

The adventure of discovering myself and moving within an ever expanding inner world, was in full progress. Another, that of exploring the Earth to which I seemed newly come, of finding out about earth-beings and their life, was more in prospect. Though in no hurry to pursue it beyond what happened within the precincts of the rooms, my anticipation of it grew livelier as the morning advanced.

Said I to myself: Here I am on Earth—and I'm the only one who knows it! No one witnessed my landing. As yet, not a soul suspects my presence here. I've come out of the blue. In due course I'll sally forth, in body as well as in consciousness, and have a look at this place and its beings.

A feeling that had been there all along now came fully into my awareness—a profound and free and happy sense of utter anonymity. Going abroad in the world would not alter my status. People would see my body, but not me. I would remain invisible, unknown. Even in a literal sense I felt anonymous, for the name that had been applied to me when in that other condition seemed unrelated to me now.

Had I ever at any time anywhere had a name that referred to my being? It did not seem so. If in some other place or world I had had a being-life among beings, and a name by which I was called, that was forgotten. In my sense of it, I had always been nameless.

Now anonymous-I went to the window to obtain through body a view of the city. There it was—the real world, as people called it. The street with assorted pedestrians, street cars, truck traffic, a row of flat-faced brown houses across the way; and, above, a patch of blue sky with a moving white cloud. Could I have looked at this scene for months past? It seemed quite improbable. This was a street on Earth, now in daylight, that I had viewed for the first time only the night before.

A stranger from Europe or Asia would have regarded this scene as American or Occidental. Its typical features would have stood out in contrast to those of his home. To me it was an earth-scene—and it might as well have been anywhere on Earth. I had no remembered home with which to compare it.

That this was New York had no particular meaning for me, one way or another. It was simply a section of earth-life to which I was neither oriented nor disoriented. It seemed quite accidental that I had landed on just this part of the globe. That I had ever felt myself to be part of it, that I had struggled to make my way in its life, that I had had particular attachments to some of the inhabitants—yes, I knew it, but the memory was remote and unreal.

Had my body been in a city completely strange to it—Dunedin, or Punaka, or Tomsk—I could not possibly have felt more strange to myself, more unrelated, in any personal sense, to the world out there, or more elated by the feeling that when I ventured forth I would be exploring the unknown.

Observing the passersby, I saw them as earth-beings. Each and all seemed equally strange, equally familiar. People were people, stripped of the labels and classifications they foist on each other, stripped too of the ratings they give each other. I saw an earth-being, not an American or a New Yorker or a foreigner. I saw an earth-being, not a white or a colored man. I saw an earth-being, not a street-cleaner or taxi-driver or a salesman.

One large truth I knew, and if momentarily forgotten, it soon returned. The people who walked the streets and rode in cars and looked out of windows, each and all were beings, as I was. Though I could not yet feel it, I was sure that as beings of the same Universe we must be basically alike. It seemed likely, therefore, that if I went out and met with any of them, some kind of real contact would be established. Just what this contact might prove to be I could not imagine.

For the rest, I felt other. My world, it seemed, touched theirs yet did not mingle. Without egotistical stake in the human situation, neither did I yet have a being-function, a work that would connect me with the life of people. For the present, then, I could only feel: Here they are, let them be. This too was a non-relationship in every respect except one: I wanted to understand human beings. This desire steadily increased until it became intense.

My observations began as any man's would. I saw bodies first and foremost. The bodies of people were prominent, though I knew that their beings were primary. This recalled the ride on the "L" train the night before, the man who had looked at my body and taken it to be me. Of course; what else could he do? He saw the body; he had no basis for knowing that I was being. What could be expected of him when I, who had basis for knowing that people are beings, found it no easy matter to make this knowledge outweigh the visual impression that people are bodies only?

Of bodies, what my eyes saw were the features that any pair of eyes would see: the sex, skin color, facial features, gait, etc. I looked. My eyes told me all too little. What bearing did the fact that bodies were of male and female sex, of various colorings and conditions, have on the central puzzle, namely, why the consciousness of people is so inadequate, why people are beings but do not realize it? Apparently, none whatever.

I tried to see with something more than the physical eye, and seemed to move closer to people, so that I beheld their bodily features in sharper light and discerned something of the individual character of the person who inhabited the physical frame. What I saw fascinated me.

Each feature of each face—the nose, the jaw, the brow—was a perfect masterpiece, perfectly modeled and articulated with the others to comprise just that face as a unique face. Each body was just that body, not to be mistaken for another. Each character was just that character. Yet, as unmistakably, each and all were of the one kind, the kind called human. What countless variations of the common mould!

Each man's uniqueness showed forth strikingly. Each one was himself and none other—and so should be met, valued, treated. The membership of all in one kind was just as evident. All were vital interrelated parts of an unimaginable whole—and so should be rated and appreciated. For a moment I felt so near to the reality of that whole that I seemed about to embrace it.

Presently my memory of certain things, inactive till now, began to stir. Said memory, "After all, this is New York, not just somewhere on Earth."

Said I, "Maybe so. What of it?"

"You have lived here off and on all your life."

"But it's not real to me, that past life."

"You have friends here. You must have; in fact you do have."

"Friends? Have I? You may be right, but it doesn't seem possible, or important."

Memory mentioned names. Each name evoked a picture of a face, an idea of a definite human character. There was recognition but no special response.

Nevertheless the thought persisted, "In this city are the friends with whom you lived and worked. Call one up. Tell him what's happening. Go out and see him. Communicate what you can. He'd be as interested as you. He'd understand some of it. He may have had a similar experience. He may understand what you don't. He may have gone far beyond what you are experiencing now." True, but it didn't click.

"You have relatives on this Earth, bodies related to your body by blood. You know people all over the country. Look here—" It was fact, but might as well have been fiction.

Yes of course, in another condition I had been on the Earth long enough to have met with all sorts of people and formed many friendships—and a few antagonisms. All of that had not changed simply because I, within myself, had changed consciousness. It existed in its world, but there seemed nothing for me to do about it.

An idea came to mind, however. Although I might not be moved to get in touch with those whom memory singled out as my particular friends, they no doubt would be moved to get in touch with me. What then?

Here was an entirely new prospect. I sat up and took notice. So far, to be sure, the outside world had let me alone, as if giving me time to become acquainted with myself and reach a certain stage of this new growth; but it was hardly likely to continue to do so. Wherever else I might be, here I was right in these rooms where others knew I lived, as available as ever. Those friends and I were bound to meet, and I would welcome it—not because we had been friends but because we were beings. * * *

X. RESTAURANT*

That in men which limits them in other ways, also limits them in regard to time. The little self condemns us to a miser's view of hours and years, shutting us out of a sense of the eternal. We give authority to clocks and

*[Chapter XI in original ts.—Ed.]

calendars, and they rule us. We feel pressed for time and must rush, unknowing that in the Universe hours are countless, years innumerable, and life continuous.

In Being, time seems unlimited. I knew with certainty that there is time to do whatever we need do.

Though the time signals of the everyday world exerted no pressure on me, I took notice of them on occasion and was sufficiently in touch with the habits of my body for all natural purposes. On this first day, for example, when the time came for body to have its midday meal, we went to lunch.

As an explorer I went out upon the street. More vividly than ever I had the sense: This is the Earth. These are people. This is what people do on Earth. The Earth and all its beings are in the vast and radiant.

A restaurant was around the corner. Many a time I, in that other condition, had gone there and fared rather well. So there we went now. It amused me to see my body smile greetings to the proprietor and head straight for the table at which it usually sat. I heard the waitress being kidded by—was it myself? And just who looked over the menu and ordered what was usually ordered?

I looked around. Here were earth-beings. The Universe was all around them, and within them, but they were not in it. God was all around and within them, but they were not in Him. They were in their little selves, and enclosed by these walls. Yet were they? I observed them more carefully. What I saw sent a question racing through me.

These people were not like the ones I had seen on the "L" the night before, nor like most of those upon the streets. These appeared more as I felt beings ought to look. Everyone was well-conditioned and seemed at least as wide awake as I. Was it true? Could it be that these people also were in Being-Consciousness? Could it be—and this was the question that startled me—that these people, and many more, had been in their real beings all along, whereas it was only I who recently had awakened? If true, how extraordinary!

I sort of shook myself and looked again, and listened too. Across the way a good-looking young woman had a book propped on the table so that she could read while eating. Now I recalled having seen her often. She always read during lunch, in lieu of other companionship. Would a being in Being-Consciousness feel lonely because she was alone?

Near enough for me to overhear their conversation were two ruddy and vigorous middle-aged men, talking business. How absorbed they were! Nothing else existed for them. What energy, what enthusiasm! And all about prices, profits, and an intricate deal, the fine points of which escaped me. No prayer-life was there, no practice of the presence of God. Beings in Being-Consciousness, those two? Beings, yes. But they, who looked as awake as I, who showed ever so much more force and verve, were evidently among the exiles, as I had been the last time I had come to this place.

Body developed a lively appetite as the food was brought in. Not much was consumed. A relatively small amount seemed to satisfy all needs. Taking notice of this fact I said to myself: Body enjoys its food as never before, but wants less of it. Not until I had observed the same thing at meal after meal did it strike me that this was a fact of some significance.

Body and I were in our proper conditions, freely circulating. In consequence, so it seemed to me, two things had happened. Body was able to extract more nourishment from less food. Consumption was decreased; the value derived was increased. Body fared better on less. Both body and I were obtaining sustenance and energy from sources other than physical food. This surmise was supported by the fact that body skipped meals without missing them in the least. It seemed probable that it could easily have fasted for quite a while.

For the first time in my life I saw that there might be literal truth in the words,

> Therefore I say unto you, Take no thought for your life, what ye shall eat, or what ye shall drink; nor yet for your body, what ye shall put on. Is not the life more than the meat, and the body than raiment?

> Behold the fowls of the air: for they sow not, neither do they reap, nor gather into barns; yet your heavenly Father feedeth them. Are ye not much better than they?*

This possibility opened up a new aspect of the revolution that would occur in man's life if more and more people were to come into their proper condition. No longer would men's lives be bound up in the production and consumption of vast quantities of physical foods. Human beings would be liberated from the endless chain of eating to live and living to eat. Man's bondage to his belly would be broken. Broken too would be his slavery to the commerce and the institutions that thrive on that bondage. The energy now spent in slaving would be released for development.

*[From the New Testament, Luke 12.22–24.—Ed.]

XI. SIGHT-SEEING*

Lunch finished, body and I stepped forth into the open world of the sunlit city. As there was more to be seen on 23rd, I wandered along this street of the Earth, looking in shop windows, reading signs, watching people. As never before or since, I was a sight-seer.

Arrived at Fifth Avenue I took an uptown bus and found a seat on top in the open. Up the man-made canyon we rumbled, and that ride was impressed on me indelibly. Years after I had fallen from Being and the experience had been all but forgotten by my conscious mind, I would be reminded of it every time I rode on the top deck of a Fifth Avenue bus.

High above the skyscrapers was the blue sky. I seemed to be up in that sky. Down on the street was the thick traffic. I seemed to be down on that pavement, closer to people than they were to themselves. And now, as on the previous night, I was aware: Above me arches an incredible Universe. Below me spreads a living Earth. Within me is a wonderful being.

People moved to and fro, all in a rush, some running, some dashing across the street at the risk of their lives—where to? Why? They brushed elbows, squeezed past each other, sometimes bumped; but they were not together. Bound—yet separated. Each wedged his separate way, bent on his exclusive business. Each was so wrapped up in himself, so cut off from the rest of life, so tight in his little self that I felt sure it must be painful.

Because of the pain, each and all must want release from that condition. Because they were beings, each and all must want a larger and more real life. How could they be interested in money-profits? Why didn't it strike them that the only profit to be gained in that separated condition was the progress made towards liberation from it? Why did they not stop each other and ask the only important question: Have you found the way out?

Instead, they were simply "going ahead," as if their condition were quite satisfactory. If they suffered, they apparently thought the cause to be something outside of themselves, a cause to be overcome by busyness and worldly success.

Yet it couldn't be that way with them, whatever their outward behavior. They *had* to want to be free of their ego-prisons. They *had* to want to be beings. Of a sudden the essential core of people seemed to emerge, so that it stood out, more real to me now than their myopic preoccupations. All that had made me feel other than them fell away. There was a swift contact of essences, a mingling of being with beings. I felt completely

*[Chapter XII in original ts.—Ed.]

with them. I felt We, unqualified. The feeling became radiant. How wonderful! We were beings, together in life, co-workers in a sacred work.

Then we seemed to separate. My sense of kinship vanished; the feeling of otherness returned.

The bus swerved to avoid a car. A car jerked to a stop to avoid a pedestrian. Cars and people, in that world, seemed in constant danger of colliding. Crowded into a tiny space and moving rapidly, they but dimly saw each other, never foresaw. I seemed not to share that danger. I felt I could have made my way on foot in the thickest traffic, through it, not into it.

Each object was seen with stark clarity. There was no filter between myself and things, no buffer between myself and men, but an amazing immediacy. I was stripped bare. Sight and feelings were exposed. Impressions penetrated to the quick, so that something like pain mingled with the thrill. Each contact had an electric quality. Life crackled, and I enjoyed the sting of it.

I was present. The vivid sense of myself as a receiver of experience was matched by an equally keen awareness of myself as a source. Within me, I knew, was a boundless store of everything that constitutes the life of man. I was present in the source of thoughts, feelings, and actions, able to govern what issued from it. Able to control, and therefore responsible. This realization broke in upon me, and I knew it was true. Self-responsibility was in the very core of my being.

My basic experiences issued from me, and returned to me, affecting me first and last as they affected no other being. I was building myself. The causes of my actions were in me. Their consequences would inevitably be in me. I would reap what I sowed. Not God, not others, I alone was responsible for my life, for my inner as well as outer actions, even for the almost imperceptible thoughts and desires that would never be recorded anywhere in the Universe except upon the malleable substance of my mind. This was what it meant to be a being, to be a real "I."

My eyes lighted on a fellow passenger. Seated up front, his back was to me, his head bent forward, in his hands a newspaper. The man's head, newspaper, arms, and back seemed to form a closed circuit. It was as though his vital currents followed a course from his head to the newspaper, from it up his arms into his body, and through his head back to the paper, round and around. Nothing else existed for him. But was even the newspaper real to him?

Was *he* reading it? True, his eyes saw the print. Some part of his mind followed the words. Pictures were evoked, emotions perhaps. But was the "I" of that man present and active? Did what was read really enter him?

Did what was thought and felt really issue from him? Had he any sense of himself as a responsible-I? That man, I was sure, was absent-I'd.

Sitting next to me was a woman-being. Now she opened her purse and she—or what?—rummaged through its contents for something that eluded her. Was *she* looking for whatever it was? Or were her hands taking orders from a desire or a fear that acted on its own without reference to the "I" of that woman?

Across the aisle was a man who, by all appearances, was alert to his surroundings. At any rate his eyes were open and looking around. His fingers nervously tapped a brief case held on his lap, and now and then he glanced down as if to make sure that it was still there. The more I looked the more I felt that he was concerned exclusively with the papers in that case, with an event in which they would play an important part. Though apparently awake to the world, he was in fact inwardly committed to a focus as narrow as that of the woman with her purse, the man with the newspaper. Had he so committed himself? He or something in him would feel acute loss were the papers to stray. Yet in that man himself was a reality of incomparable value, and he felt no loss though he lost it every day.

The bus driver, the pedestrians, the traffic cops, the millions of beings on Earth in the slums and mansions, in mines, in factories, on farms, most of them doing active work, some doing skilled work—it could not be that all of them, all the time, were absent-I'd, yet it must be that most of them were like the people on this bus, so thoroughly in that strange condition that they could not recognize it.

Neither active sources nor active receivers. Life sort of washed over them instead of flowing within and through them. The surrounding world merely pattered on their bodies. The experiencer was absent; and so, though the means of experiencing were at hand, there was no one to use them.

Yes, but the situation was not that simple. There was something else. The experiencer of joy and meaning might be absent. The experiencer of pain? Present, I was sure. Always available at any rate. Strain, protracted anxiety, disappointment, bitterness—these were experienced, and not passively either. You could see it on people's faces. Something in them actively received and gave hurt, suffered and made suffer. How strange. The experiencer of happiness, absent. The experiencer of misery, present. How unjust. How diabolical. What was the meaning of it? Who or what was to blame? More to the point, what was to be done about it?

Understand it. The words rang out as if they had been voiced. Examine it, search for the meaning. This is the most important and indeed the only thing that you or anyone can do, first. People are living. Life may not be real to them, but that they exist is a reality. Therefore they exist for something. There is purpose in the human situation, and it is being worked out day by day in the very conditions people find themselves in.

Here was a possibility and it was worth exploring. If the outer behavior of people was as automatic as it seemed, and as disconnected from the inner being, then I did not see how there could be meaning in the daily round. But suppose the outer were somehow connected with the inner, what aim might be served by apparently commonplace experience? If the experiencer of pain were unrelated to the experiencer of meaning, what purpose in suffering? But suppose these two, though seemingly separated, were actually linked. Then what? I could think of one and only one purpose. The meaning of man's life was a developmental meaning. The purpose of human life was human development. We are here to grow up to God.

What I was witnessing as the bus continued up the avenue, what everyone was engaged in was a drama of development in which even the most apparently trivial action played a part. Human beings, without their conscious minds knowing it, were putting themselves into situation after situation the real function of which was to make each individual meet and contend with, and in some measure overcome, the very things in himself that blocked the way to his real being and proper consciousness. Each would remain in just that complex of situations until he had outgrown the need of being there. Whereon he would pass into another complex, calling forth still other impediments.

People were inclined to live for their pleasure rather than for development. A function of pain and suffering was to jolt them out of that inclination, shock them awake, spur them to ascend. If and as they undertook their real work, pain would diminish because the need for it would become less. If and as they ascended, suffering would fall away proportionately. Meanwhile, the experiencer of pain had to be present, for a minimum development was required of each being in each life. No matter how asleep, or how reluctant, each had to lop off something that impeded his growth. But how small that minimum was, compared to what might be. How slow the progress, how devious, how tortuous. If people would only undertake their development consciously, voluntarily. If they would only awake enough to realize that the work of growing is their chief work and the only basic meaning of their lives. If they would only put their heart and strength into meeting all situations for the sake of the development to be gained thereby, using all obstacles and handicaps and difficulties as opportunities for creative struggle leading to new birth. If they would see that the only way out is to develop out. Then indeed would their progress be speeded. Then indeed would they become great in growing.

Suddenly it occurred to me to ask: Can I help them? Can my discoveries be of use to them? I who have awakened, what can I do to aid these inward kin of mine also to awaken, that we may better serve each other and our Creator?

And the answer promptly came—Not a thing.

Such help, it seemed, was not within the ability of the newly born. It rested with the Life and Power that were in all beings, as in me. Not a thing could I do to help the woman-being at my side, the man-being with the newspaper, the crowd on the avenue—except to continue being and growing. What happens to a unit of the whole affects the whole.

I was suddenly filled with a burning sense of what might be communicated. An unspoken testimony flowed from me, not as a man speaks words to another, but as an inner communication of a common consciousness.

People, you can awake and be. You can outgrow the condition you are now in, and what you now think to be real will cease to exist, and you will stand in newness. I bear witness that what you believe to be you is not you. You are other than that. But in each man there is Man. In all beings there is Being. In Being there is God who designed man to fall and to ascend perfected.

XII. HERE WE ARE*

At 57th Street I got off the bus and began walking down the avenue. The idea seemed to be that body and I were heading back to the 23rd Street rooms. Why? Central Park or the river front or anywhere would have done just as well. Life was everywhere—and when you are in the whole you have no need of a particular part or place.

Now I was in the midst of the pedestrians—walking bodies, sleeping beings—moving through them. Life in that world, broken into innumerable separate currents, was a tangled wash over the pavements. And all the while the great Universe looked down at this small globe and its beings.

The impression of walking-bodies–sleeping-beings was so sharp that I had a sense of moving in a crowd of somnambulists. A sort of awe arose in me. How did they manage to get about? Where had they come from? Where were they going?

I singled out particular people, trying to make a contact with them

*[Chapter XIII in original ts.—Ed.]

which would again evoke a feeling of kinship. Though I failed, I knew the basis was there. The radiant seed was in that boy swinging along whistling a jazz tune. The Power was in that bent old man. The Life was in that doorman, and in that business man, and in that smartly dressed woman.

Presently I found myself yearning towards these people, asking that they be quickened to the essential work at hand. It was a prayer to the Nameless to lift these beings to Life.

And then I had a vision of it actually happening. I saw the Power rising in them, claiming them right in the midst of their occupations, transforming them as it had transformed me.

People hurrying along the streets, window shopping, buying, selling, I imagined them stop and become still. The city would be hushed, waiting. The human world all over the Earth, silent, wondering.

And then, in each one, the perfectly quiet, the quietly perfect awakening.

I saw each one make the wonderful discovery in secret, then find that all the others were making the same discovery. I saw them, bright in wonder and new beauty, join hands and give thanks.

The vision expressed my wish. Was it anything more? Might it have been a glimpse of an actual event towards which mankind is tending?

Later that afternoon, standing at the window of the room on 23rd, I looked down at the front yard where the miracle of new life would soon show in the grass of the lawn and the single tree. Shortly the sun would disappear behind the palisades on the other side of the Hudson, and, in due time, bring another day to China. A soft light was in the world, an invitation to feel loveliness, which I could not accept. Deep in me there was a gathering gravity.

Implications of existing, charges laid upon me by my own being, the commands of a superior necessity—into my consciousness these came, and I felt: I did not make my being; I cannot unmake it. No power of my own, no power on Earth or in the Universe, can cause me to cease to be. I am—and I am in for it.

Here I am, *an irremovable reality*. I exist in the Universe, and cannot not-exist. I live because I have to—not because I desire to. Not my wish nor will, but a Will greater than the wills of all beings put together, is back of it. He who is called God has made it imperative, for *His* purposes, that beings come into existence and stay in existence. There is no escape, no appeal.

I felt pinned by reality. A noble but terrible truth was burning its way into my heart, steadily thrusting into my vitals. I wanted to draw back, to get away. I wanted to turn to someone, call on someone. I squirmed, as a living thing upon a spit.

God help me, was the cry uttered by a voice I did not know I had. The cry did not seem fitting. If God had placed the charge upon me, it was not for me to ask Him to relieve me of it. This was something for me to face and handle.

Now I was awake in a new way, and I trembled. It was solemn, awesome, to touch what I was touching. Existence, an unending progression, myself inescapably in it, without appeal. On my own, no sleeping, no forgetting, no dallying, forever responsible. Starkly in me the undimmed realization that I exist, and for a purpose that *will be* served.

The thought of death popped into my mind. There was no comfort in it. Some day, to be sure, death would come. What then? I would pass from *this* life, but not out of existence. Death would not deliver me. It would not close the accounts. It would not remove me from the Universe, nor terminate my responsibility.

I saw clearly that what is called death is not a condition, but an event in time, of brief duration. It is an event of unending life. By it the being separates completely from the physical body. The separation puts an end to that partnership, to that particular phase of existence. The being continues being.

By the way in which the thought of death came to me, I understood why it comes to others, why so many people believe that death will put an end to them. They want it to! They would rather be destroyed utterly than to continue bearing even such responsibilities as they are aware of having. They would rather be annihilated than to continue living as they are, and they know of no other possible life. The protraction of their present kind of life is an intolerable prospect. Seeing no escape whatsoever except by death, they fasten on the death-event and interpret it according to their wishes.

How easy it would be if death wiped the slate clean. How comforting if death offered a permanent escape; if, no matter how we lived, what suffering we heaped upon others, we could look forward to complete deliverance in a few years, and without any special effort on our part. This pleasing but deceptive fancy appeals with equal persuasiveness to those who believe that death causes utter extinction and to those who believe that it will release them, once and for all, into paradise. Both are escapists, and to no avail.

Those who are in the Universe are going to remain in it. The death-event was not designed as a boon to the lazy, the wayward, the criminal, but as a needed change of condition. There is no means of escape. There is only progress—or its opposite. There is only progress towards an ultimate liberation to be attained through growth and transformation.

In existence before we came into this life, we are in existence now, and will so be after we leave this life. Forms and conditions vary. We change consciousness. The essence of a man continues until it has made full use of its manifold equipment. The being remains in the created world until it has fulfilled its destiny. Somewhere in the living Universe we shall live until we have accomplished the long-range purpose of our creation.

The starkness of my own presence in the Universe threw a sharp light on the presence of other beings and things. *Here they are!* There was this vivid cognizance, this inward exclamation. Not why, not how, not what for; simply the sheer existence of each thing: a windowpane, a tree, an iron fence, a human being, a car, a house, the Earth, the Sun. I accorded everything special attention, a kind of salute.

What a contrast between this electric recognition and the usual casual acceptance. Those in the waking state simply do not see and feel enough to realize the existence of surrounding presences, and salute them. To say that they take things for granted is true, yet it isn't. They do not *take* a thing.

Ask a man if he realizes he exists. His indignant answer will be that of course he does. When challenged—but not otherwise—he really believes he does. Suppose he is on a liner crossing the ocean. Ask him if he realizes the existence of the ship, the other passengers, the sea. Of course he does. What do you take me for, he'll snap back.

Midway across, something happens to the ship, and to the man in consequence. The ship is wrecked and sinks. The man suddenly finds himself in the water, struggling to keep hold of some floating stuff. There he is—neither more nor less in existence than when safely on shipboard—but how much more aware of it! Now his sense of himself as a living reality is so keen that it may be painful. Now he as vividly perceives what's around him: the wood he clings to, the vast swelling ocean, heads bobbing in the water, a lifeboat. And the ship itself, though it has disappeared, is ever so much more real to him than when it was afloat and he on it. In short, the emergency has aroused him from his habitual torpor and made him almost a conscious man. * * *

XIII. KINSHIP*

Sometime during the morning of the second day the phone rang. Answering it, I heard a voice I recognized. Now I was at least in speaking contact with a particular person who felt he had a special relationship

*[Chapter XIV in original ts.—Ed.]

with me because of past experience. My first response was a sense that the world I had left, that I seemed never to have been in, was catching up with me. My second was a wondering what this would lead to.

I was aware of my body at the phone, and had a vivid picture of his at the other end. As if I were a third person, I saw the two speaking to each other, on the Earth. At the same time I had a broad impression of beings on other planets, in other spheres of the peopled Universe, communicating with one another, carrying on their many occupations, while we here on this globe were using an invention of earth-beings called a telephone.

How strange to hear a man talking to me as to an old acquaintance, assuming that he knew me. Stranger still, I heard myself talking as if I were my former person. The voice that came out of my body was, it seemed, the voice of that person. Something in me accepted that person's interests in things, commitments to people. That self, then, was somewhere in existence? It could be called to life, if addressed? It still lived, if only as a ghost?

Presently I began to recognize that at the other end of the wire, there was a living reality—not merely a voice, not simply a body, not only a man with whom I had been friends—but a being, a being of the Universe, we together in a cosmic process.

We talked for a while and made a date to meet for lunch. Later, on the way to the meeting place, I felt that something extraordinary, unimaginable, might happen when we met in person. I must have expected our former closeness to each other to open the way for a meeting of beings more intense than had yet occurred between myself and anyone. But when I walked up to him, it did not happen.

We met as bodies, friendly bodies. We met as people who were accustomed to each other's ways. With unspoken consent we headed for the restaurant where we usually went. We gravitated towards the same table, ordered what we usually ordered. Now I felt that the pattern of that past relationship had quite caught up with me. It was familiar enough, and most interesting to watch as it unfolded; but in my sense of it, it had no connection whatsoever with my present being. Yet I was not playing a role; it happened naturally.

The self that was meeting my friend might be ghostlike to me; it was, to all appearances, sufficiently authentic to him. He accepted it as me. He accepted me, without question. By no look or word did he give sign of sensing that I had changed. I wondered about this. I suppose I must have expected that this man, of all people, would feel something different. I must have anticipated, and perhaps hoped, that a question from him would give me a chance to mention my experience. It would have been good to have communicated, in words, with this human being.

When nothing of the sort happened, it became clear that my new condition simply did not register with him—and if not with him, then with whom? If it did not in any noticeable way affect this friend, who not only had known me intimately but was more aware than most of my other acquaintances, it was not likely to be sensed by anyone. Nor was it. I may as well say here that when I did meet with others, not one of them seemed to perceive anything unusual. But why not? If I had lost my mind or otherwise changed for the worse, that certainly would have been noticeable. Then why not this radical change for the better, this transformation which had restored me to my real being? There are accounts of transformed men acting as catalysts, deeply moving others simply by their presence. I can only say that it was not my good fortune to be one of these. For the rest, I am at a loss to explain it.

Though my friend seemed unaware of the change in me, I looked for change in him. I was alert to the possible, mindful that transformations may occur in any human being at any time. But would I recognize the signs if I saw them? Would a deep change in him be communicated to me, seeing that mine was not communicated to him? How would I know if a man had awakened from the ordinary consciousness—unless he told me? How would two beings, both in their real beings, behave towards one another?

Presently something happened in me, and I no longer asked such questions. Neither did I attend to the exchange between my revived self and the self of my friend. New feelings awoke, and I ceased seeing his body as an object out there, the man as a separated entity. I discovered him as he might have discovered himself had he entered his real being; and I knew that the so-called conscious part of him was unaware of this meeting. It was happening behind his back! Yet he was looking straight at me!

Suddenly he, the being, was with me and I with him in a life that had centers of being and functioning, but no fixed boundaries and no barriers whatsoever. It would have been impossible, now, for me to break apart and experience myself and himself as separated. As during my bus ride but now more concretely and with much greater warmth, I felt *we*. I lived *we*. This being and I were together in an indissoluble existence where divisions not only did not exist but were unthinkable.

I knew that he and I were kin—not because we had been friends, not because our body-minds were of the same nationality, spoke the same language, shared similar interests—but because kinship is the fundamental relationship between beings.

My awareness of the truth of kinship had come of a sudden, and just now; but it was perfectly evident to me that neither I nor he had just brought this kinship into existence. It was a reality existing from the unimaginable beginning. All I had done was to realize an already established bond, to become conscious of an ancient and enduring unity. Had it not been there, nothing I could do would have made it so. Since it was there, nothing I could do would negate it. Kinship, clearly, was the work of our Common Creator, and was woven, never to be unwoven, into the very fabric of our essential existence.

What was true of this being and myself is true of all. All men, as beings, are kin. Our task is not to make it so, but to try to realize that it is so.

Men as bodies are separate, but not as separated as they appear to the eye. Like the leaves of a tree they are distinct as forms, but each and all are organically related to one another through their connection with the one tree. Men as egotists are mutually repellant. Men as beings are joined. The several conditions coexist.

It is not possible to join bodies beyond their given interrelationship. It is not possible to force egotists to behave as brothers. But when the consciousness of men is lifted out of the body and out of egotism and centered in being, men thereby discover that they are joined as beings—and bodily behavior expresses the new consciousness. Brotherhood is realized kinship.

The beauty that could be in the human world, the unceasing wonder! I beheld something of this beauty, and into my heart came a love so tender, so magically potent and extending that it seemed to reach to all the people of the world, and to all life, and I felt—If only the will of this love could be done on earth, what a world there would be, and what people!

My attention returned to the particular friend sitting with me at the table; and now it seemed that I was not only joined with him but that I was in the place of his being, so that I felt as his being may have felt. From that vantage point I saw his personal self, as if I were connected with it from the inside, as his own being was. There was a visual element in this. I seemed literally to see that self. I saw it as a coil, a creeper around a tree. Though the being was larger than it, it was wound around the being. Though the being would outlive it, it seemed to be squeezing the being to death. So this was what wrapped a man up, cut him off from other beings, prevented consciousness of kinship! This was the thing itself, the very form of egotism—a mortal coil. Of a sudden I wanted to cry out to my friend—Struggle against it, fight it, throw it off!

I wanted to call to all men—There is your enemy, right in yourself! Fight that, conquer that, and you will be delivered.

If ever I had been vague about it, vagueness was dispelled now. I starkly realized that a being is first, last, and all the time up against the egoistical self that is part of his own human totality. He is constricted and thwarted by his own egotism as by nothing else in the whole world. Therefore his main sustained effort should and must be to overcome that self. Only secondarily and occasionally need he contend with the personal selves of others. And when he struggles against those selves of others, he should keep in mind that the beings of others are always to be affirmed and cooperated with.

At first sight the coil seemed an alien and evil parasite that had somehow gained root in human life and was destroying that upon which it fed. But presently I realized that it is an intended part of the human totality. I understood that it is designed to perform an essential function!

A being develops by overcoming difficulties. The personal self provides them. And this is their joint proper purpose! The personal self is meant to be limiting, to provide resistances and obstacles that are always at hand. A being is meant to struggle against these impediments. If and as he does, he develops as a being, and the personal self functions as intended. It is only when a being does not so struggle, but becomes passive or actively abets the self, that the self misfunctions, thwarts, and in extreme cases virtually strangles the being. In this case, a developmental opportunity becomes a paralyzing handicap. The man defaults— and all other faults and defeats of human life stem from this primary failure.

The coils and their ramifications are meant to be points of application for our being-efforts leading to being-development. They are what we are working on and working out in this life—if we are. And this is the purpose and the meaning of this life.

What is true of the individual in relation to himself is also true of individuals in relation to their world. The world is simply a larger coil— and is meant to be. Small coils within us, large coils without and all around us—here it is, a sufficiently varied workshop, a well-equipped gymnasium, providing daily opportunity for our individual and collective developmental efforts.

Limitations, though necessary at this stage of human development, are not designed to be forever limiting. When overcome they cease to exist. They are to be used as means to the limitless. Ego-prisons are not meant to imprison forever, but to serve as means to permanent liberation. Separatism is not an externally fixed condition, nor need it continue to breed the maladies of men. It can be used as a means to the discovery of the kinship of beings with one another, and the fatherhood of God.

Let us make good use of this life and these conditions. Let us make greater developmental use of everything at hand and of everything that comes to pass. This is the life for a man. This is the life for the human beings of this Earth.

That first meeting with one of my friends seemed to start the ball rolling. That afternoon I took the initiative and called up another. That evening I went to a gathering. From this time on I circulated among the people I had known when in that other condition. My former relationships with people came to have a place in my transformed life; and these remained, on the surface, much as they had been.

But wherever I went, whatever I did, whomever I met—former acquaintances and those called strangers—I was aware of kinship in being. I did not have to try to remember it. It was impossible to forget it. The reality of *We* was ever present, outshining the separation of bodies, the divisions of personal selves.

My body did not feel kinship for all other bodies. As before, it seemed to have its likes and dislikes; but its inclinations did not bias my essential response as a being to beings. Nor did its visual separateness from other bodies dim my realization of spiritual connectedness.

There was something in me that liked certain qualities in people and disliked or was indifferent to others. To this extent, personality entered into my relationships. I did not experience an unqualified love of people in their entireties. Yet these personal matters were unimportant. They did not pull me out of being nor prevent me from meeting with others as beings.

I knew that people did not realize their kinship to me or to each other as I realized mine to them and theirs to one another. But their lack of realizing did not stop me.

People-as-egotists pitted themselves against each other, each trying to wedge his way, each striving and often scheming for what he or she believed to be to his own advantage. Ugly things were said and done. One day I saw a brutal street-fight between two men. All over the city of New York and throughout the Earth, men-as-egotists and separatistic groups were clashing. These facts contributed to my understanding of the human situation. But neither did they stop me. The power of realized kinship made way for me to enter.

These people were beings, as I was. This was the firm basis on which I met them, every one. Under the surface was a sacred seed awaiting a sacred growth. Their visible behavior was but the distorted reflection of a radiant reality. Even to glimpse this reality was to have faith in men. I had faith and felt a pure personal-impersonal kind-ness. I had a gladness for these beings, and a sorrow too, a gravity, a glowing and boundless goodwill.

[1937–1946]

III

The Negro, the Blue Man,
and the New Race

Editor's Note

The writing in this part reflects the abhorrence Toomer had for rigid classifications of people. He felt that especially in America, it was a distortion and a limitation of the individual to define him or her solely according to ethnic background and race. He had personally experienced the force of such limitation after writing *Cane*: Critical pressure urged him to continue writing from the viewpoint of black life, while he thought that that perspective was now used up for him, a dead end, and he wanted to pursue different literary projects in his continuing search for meaning and personal growth and wholeness.

The three short introductory pieces express Toomer's repugnance toward prejudice. The opening statement on prejudice is an undated, handwritten note in draft material for the essay "The Negro Emergent," which I have included in the next section of this part. "The Negro Emergent" comes from an undated typescript draft that Kerman and Eldridge (*The Lives of Jean Toomer*) estimate was written around 1924. "Germ Carriers" is my title for an excerpt from "Preface #3," a second-draft preface to "Book X," one of Toomer's autobiographical works. "Preface #3" is dated March 13, 1935. In the third section of this part, "The Blue Man," I have used much of the rest of "Preface #3" in the essay I have titled "Not Typically American." "The Fable of a Creature" (1930) comes from the third typescript of "Essentials," a collection of writings not to be confused with *Essentials: Definitions and Aphorisms*, privately printed in 1931.

The second, third, and fourth sections of this part represent Toomer's thinking about the state of African Americans in the United States in his time, his feelings about his own racial identity, and his ideas about the future racial situation in America. Toomer used the term *blue man* in his long poem "Blue Meridian," published in *The New American Caravan* in

1936. The blue man was an amalgamation of the black, white, and red races of America, and as such represented the people of the future. I have chosen "The Blue Man" as the title for the third section because it is a representative term for Toomer himself, who felt, with his racial mixture, that he was a blue man.

Toomer's essay on *The Emperor Jones* is undated. The play was produced by the Provincetown Players in 1920. Sherwood Anderson's story "Out of Nowhere into Nothing" (letter of December 29, 1922) is part of *The Triumph of the Egg,* 1921. Toomer's comment in this letter about Anderson's "London acquaintance" refers to Anderson's letter to him of December 22, 1922, in which Anderson wrote that he had met a woman in London he felt to be "a bit too negro [sic] . . .—that she was inclined to over-estimate everything done by a negro [sic] because a negro [sic] had done it."

In his letter of September 5, 1923, Toomer is reacting to Horace Liveright's request in a letter of August 29 that he not "dodge" his "colored blood" in the biographical sketch he had sent to Boni and Liveright to be used in advertising for *Cane.*

In "Fighting the Vice" (my title), the poem Toomer says he showed Waldo Frank may have been "The First American," which Toomer wrote during the winter of 1920–1921. This was the prototype of "Blue Meridian." "Fighting the Vice" is part of a fifteen-page draft of an undated typescript titled "This May Be Said/The Inside Story." Internal evidence in the original essay indicates that Toomer wrote it in response to the media reaction to his marriage with Margery Latimer, his first wife, in the fall of 1931.

The absurdity and viciousness of forced and false racial classification became especially palpable to Toomer at that time. Latimer was a white author, and their marriage received national coverage, including an article in *Time.* The press couldn't resist titillating the public with a juicy story of miscegenation. "A New Race in America" (my title) was a handwritten statement that, Toomer noted parenthetically at the top of the page, was "written for publication a few days before my marriage."

In the July 11, 1930, letter to James Weldon Johnson, Toomer explains why he could not honor Johnson's request to include Toomer's poetry in the update of his *Book of American Negro Poetry,* published in 1931.

"The Americans" comes from an undated typescript draft of what appears to be an introduction to a proposed book with the same title. Among the notes to this proposed book is an undated, untitled handwritten essay that I have named "Oppose the Force, Not the Man."

"Mankind Means Brotherhood" is an undated typescript by "Nathan

Jean Toomer." For a few years, beginning in the late 1930s, Toomer used this name. At his birth in 1894, he was named Nathan Pinchback Toomer. In 1896, after Toomer's father deserted the family, the name *Nathan* was replaced by *Eugene*. Toomer took the name *Jean* in 1920. The reference to a fight between a Nazi and an Englishman in "Mankind Means Brotherhood" suggests that the essay may have been written around 1940. A slightly longer and different version of the poem at the end of the essay appears in *The Wayward and the Seeking: A Collection of Writings by Jean Toomer,* edited by Darwin T. Turner (1980), and *The Collected Poems of Jean Toomer,* edited by Robert B. Jones and Margery Toomer Latimer (1988).

Introduction

Prejudice

It is a mistake to believe that most of those who feel prejudice do not want to feel it. On the contrary. They want to feel it. It serves their ends.

If to change, they must change so that they desire ends, other ends, in relation to which prejudice will be seen and recognized as an impediment.

Weapons will be discarded for tools only when we cease desiring the ends that weapons attain and begin desiring the ends that only tools can achieve.

[1924?]

Germ Carriers

Words were the original germ carriers of the majority of our prejudices. Without words it is doubtful that we would contract the prejudices—or that they ever would have started and multiplied. How without words could prejudices be passed on and worked up from generation to generation? Seal the mouths of all of us, prohibit writing, destroy all printed matter, and when those who are now infants come of age they would have acquired from us only those antagonisms communicable by gestures. (Much else too would be lost, but this is another matter.) There is no doubt that we, being what we are, would strive with might and main to make gestures talk and convey our hatreds. But also there is no doubt that, for all our ingenuity in the way of circulating poison, our children would be affected but comparatively little.

[3/13/35]

The Fable of a Creature

I see a tiny moving creature.

I say to myself, "Hello, I wonder what this is."

And then I begin, as it were, thinking about the creature.

I say, "It is a baby beetle. No, it is a small ant. I am not sure. No, I think it must be a flea . . . I wonder what it is."

I call my colleagues to look at the creature.

We procure a magnifying glass, put our heads together, follow its movements, and discuss among ourselves whether it is a beetle, or an ant, or a flea, or what.

No, it is something we cannot recall or find a name for.

We get the dictionary and a book of synonyms. We pour through these and out of one eye watch the creature.

There is quite a debate.

The tiny moving creature moves along.

Suddenly, one of us declares authoritatively:

"I have it! It is a limebug!"

"So it is!" we all exclaim. "It is a limebug of the family of cockroaches!"

At last we understand.

We shake hands and look knowingly at the thing we understand.

The tiny moving creature goes about its business, being what it is.

[1930]

The Negro

Negro Psychology in The Emperor Jones

The Emperor Jones has already been explained, criticized, and accepted as an achievement in experimental dramatic form. Likewise, its significances for the Negro have been recognized. There remains, however, one aspect of the play which I find to be of unusual psychological interest, namely, the means employed by Mr. O'Neill to particularize the general emotion of fear in the Negro. It is obvious of course that a distinct racial flavor is created by having a Negro act the part of Brutus Jones. But this has to do with presentation, and not with the actual construction of the drama. In this construction, Mr. O'Neill first establishes fear by means of suggestion and association. This original feeling is increased by physical circumstances: a forest, and the beating of a tom-tom. And then, as fear intensifies to the point where it overpowers Jones, it successively unlocks chambers of the Emperor's unconscious. Now the contents of the unconscious not only vary with individuals; they are differentiated because of race, by social conditions due to race. And in fact Brutus Jones lives through sections of an unconscious which is peculiar to the Negro. Slave ships, whipping posts, and so on. And because these things are actually real and present for him, his fear is at once expressed, intensified, and colored by them. In a word, his fear becomes a Negro's fear, recognizably different from a similar emotion, modified by other racial experience. In this way then, Mr. O'Neill achieves his purpose. And *The Emperor Jones* is therefore a section of Negro psychology presented in a significant dramatic form.

[n.d.]

From Letter to Sherwood Anderson

1341 You Street, N.W.,
Washington, D.C.,
29 Dec 1922.

Dear Sherwood Anderson,

In your work I have felt you reaching for the beauty that the Negro has in him. As you say, you wanted to write not of the Negro but out of him. "Well I wasnt [sic] one. The thing I felt couldnt [sic] be truly done." I guess you're right. But this much is certain: an emotional element, a richness from him, from yourself, you have artistically woven into your own material. Notably in Out of Nowhere into Nothing. Here your Negro, from the stand point of superficial reality, of averages, of surface plausibility, is unreal. My friends who are interested in the "progress" of the Negro would take violent exception to such a statement as, "By educating himself he had cut himself off from his own people." And from a strictly social point of view, much that they would say would be true enough. But in these pages you have evoked an emotion, a sense of beauty that is easily more Negro than almost anything I have seen. And I am glad to admit my own indebtedness to you in this connection.

The Negro's curious position in this western civilization invariably forces him into one or the other of two extremes: either he denies Negro entirely (as much as he can) and seeks approximation to an Anglo-Saxon (white) ideal, or, as in the case of your London acquaintance, he overemphasizes what is Negro. Both of these attitudes have their source in a feeling of (a desire not to feel) inferiority. I refer here, of course, to those whose consciousness and condition make them keenly aware of white dominance. The mass of Negroes, like peasants, like the mass of Russians or Jews or Irish or what not, are too instinctive to be anything but themselves. Here and there one finds a high type Negro who shares this virtue with his more primitive brothers. As you can imagine, the resistance against my stuff is marked, excessive. But I feel that in time, in its social phase, my art will aid in giving the Negro to himself. In this connection, I have thought of a magazine. A magazine, American, but concentrating on the significant contributions, or possible contributions of the Negro to the western world. A magazine that would consciously hoist, and perhaps at first a trifle over emphasize a negroid ideal. A magazine that would function organically for what I feel to be the budding of the Negro's consciousness. The need is great. People within the race cannot see it. In fact, they are likely to prove to be directly hostile. But with the youth of the race, unguided or misguided as they now are, there is a tragic need. Talent dissipates itself for want of creative channels of expression, and encouragement. My own means are slim, almost nothing. I have had and am still having a hard pull of it. But as I write these lines there are two young people whom I am barely keeping above surface by the faith and love I have for them. I would deeply appreciate your thoughts in relation [to] this matter. * * *

Do you ever come down this way? For Negro life, its varying shades, its varying phases of consciousness and development there is no better place. I would be glad to share with you whatever I possess.

The Negro Emergent

Where life is conscious and dynamic, its processes naturally involve an extension of experience and the uncovering of new materials. Discovery, in one form or another, is provided by nature for most of us. For the larger part, however, it is reserved to childhood and is attended with no more than a child's concern. Beyond this phase the range of experience is quite limited when seen in terms of human possibilities. Even so, experience may and often does yield isolated moments of discovery. And, rarely, these moments come with such frequence and intensity as to constitute a state. It is then that the fortunate individual undergoes an inward transformation while all the world about him is revealed in fresh forms, colors, and significances. He discovers himself, and at the same time discovers the external world. One may, of course, uncover new facts by means of old modes of thought, feeling, or conduct. This is partial, often false discovery. For it means, simply, the extension of a given organism to novel ground. But real discovery means precisely this: that new facts, truths, realities, are manifest to a transformed state of being. In one sense, these new realities themselves may be nothing more than new illusions. And discovery may be seen as a process which merely substitutes a fresh appearance for an old one. But if this fresh appearance is related to a deep inward change, and the state of being approaches wonder, then one may rightly term this act discovery.

If it were possible to glance at will about the human world and accurately see it in its varied phases and conditions, it would doubtless be seen that the state or process of discovery is constant, that it is always operative in some place, individual, or a group of persons. This glance, for the present, wherever else it rested would be certain to observe the impulse at work within the Negro in America. For the Negro is discovering himself. I refer of course to individuals, and not to mass.

The Negro is emergent. From what is he emergent? To what is he emerging? An answer to these questions will define his present status and suggest his possibilities.

Generally, it may be said that the Negro is emergent from a crust, a false personality, a compound of beliefs, habits, attitudes, and emotional reactions superimposed upon him by external circumstance. The elements of this compound are numerous. I shall consider what appear to me to be the most outstanding. These fall roughly into two distinct groups. First, there are those factors which arise from the condition of being a black man in a white world. Second, there are those forms and forces which spring from the nature of our civilization, and are common to Americans. I shall treat of these in turn.

Because of external pressure, the Negro, unwittingly, has been divorced by attitude from his racial roots. Biologically, the Negro sprang from what he sprang from: a Negro, or a Negro and white stock. These bloods are in him. No attitude can change this fact, else it would have the power to deprive him of his physical existence. But since he himself has wished to force his slave root from his mind, and since his white root denies him, the Negro, psychologically and spiritually, has been literally uprooted, or worse, with no roots at all. From the anemia and chronic invalidism produced by this condition, the Negro is emergent.

Closely connected with his blood is the matter of his birth; not his birth in this generation, but the possible manner of birth of his great grandparents. Perhaps they were illegitimate. At any rate, he has been called a bastard. This charge has provoked feelings of shame or murder. When not openly expressed, the supicion has been that it might exist in the white man's mind. Hence the Negro has closed himself and erected barriers, resistances, aggressions, for his own protection. But these things really enslaved the Negro, for, as the old saying goes, a wall restricts the city it surrounds. From this wall and reaction the Negro is emergent.

Then there are the factors which have to do with a century and more of slavery. The practice of using the Negro as slave laborer and concubine, and the consequent attitude of white men toward black women. The assertion that the Negro is inherently inferior, that he is a slave by nature. The Negro's child-like reliance upon the whites. The free admission of white superiority; the forced admission when the free type did not come naturally. The split within the Negro group due to difference of color and economic preferences, often stimulated by the white group. Disdain and contempt on the part of those of lighter color and better position;

distrust and jealousy on the part of the others. Economic poverty. Reactions from [these?] factors.

The effects of the Civil War upon the Negro and the Negro problem are as yet to be accurately known and balanced. Certain of its influences, however, are clear. It freed the Negro nominally; it increased the Negro's bondage to white resentment and white fear, (and, in a large measure added political exploitation to the already existent forms, while doing but little more than modify these forms). For the white southerner resented the Negro's forced liberation. Because of the unrest stimulated in the Negro by abolitionist propaganda and the legal paper-fact of freedom, the white man had additional cause to fear him. Nor will the South forget the sporadic dominance of Negroes during Reconstruction. From such factors as these the modern insistence on what the Negro's place is, the emphatic and sometime brutal measures taken to keep him in it, have their source. And these in turn give rise to the Negro's need for defining his own place and attempting to establish himself therein. In a word, the whole question of social equality, with its mutual bitterness. From this question the Negro is emergent.

But the Civil War and the mock-freedom which followed it, caused a more subtly unfortunate condition. Prior to the war, the Negro, though in slavery, had his roots within the soil. He had an emotional allegiance to the soil and country which he sprang from. I am aware that such a picture of the Negro lends itself to poetic exaggeration, but that it is not wholly fanciful is evident from the folk-songs. Since the war the Negro has been progressively divorced from both. For a time, he could not hear beauty even in his own spirituals; white southerners were often closer to his heritage than he was. He could not love the soil when those above him tried to force his face into it—and then allowed him no real possession. He was too well aware of the fact that he could not generously partake of America, to respond to it. He felt himself the least of aliens, though he knew himself in essence to be native. He might be patriotic. But patriotism is a lean substitute for poetry. The Negro is finding his way to them.

And, ever since emancipation, well intentioned white men, aided by Negroes, have been trying to plaster a white image on a black reality—to superimpose Boston on Georgia. This has led to an over-valuing of academic study; a prejudice against hand-training. It became a matter of shame that the men whose muscle had built the South could not read Caesar in the original. But, that the image is white is secondary. That it is an *image,* is primary. Because of it, the Negro has become a victim of education and false ideals. In terms of mastery, the results have been both ludricrous and pathetic. But this is true of most educational attempts, though it is less apparent in white examples. For Negroes had a special cause for their submission and desires: the white man claimed that the Negro was mentally inferior. Here was a chance to disprove that statement. The Negro would cram his brain with theories, dates, the Greek alphabet, and become equally civilized. He has done so; he is beginning to question the profit of his efforts. For he now seeks a balanced life, based upon capacity, wherein *all* faculties are given the necessary usage. He is beginning to discard the image for reality.

I think particularly of the illusion that the white American is free in fact, that he is actually free. Because the white man is not racially oppressed, the Negro has tended to picture him as existing in a state of perfect freedom and happiness. Economically, all sorts of avenues and opportunities are imagined to be open to him, so that, if he but wishes and works for it, the fruits of the earth will come into his possession. Every white boy has a *real* chance to become a millionaire and land in the White House. There has been a strong tendency to think of the white man as being psychologically free: he can think, feel, and do just what he pleases. It is assumed, among other things, that the white man *voluntarily* oppresses the Negro, that he freely hates him, that white mobs are acting from free will when they lynch a Negro. In brief, the white man is seen to exist above the laws of necessity and determinism. Indeed, he is believed to sit beside the throne of God, already. This attitude, more than any other, has stimulated the Negro's wish to be like the white man, to be white in fact. It is now being realized, however, that the mass of whites, save in the single instance of racial oppression, are as bound and determined as the mass of blacks, that the fundamental limitations are common to humanity, and that their transcendence demands something more than the mere possession of a white skin, or of a white psychology.

There are, in addition to factors already considered, several other quite important ones. But for the present I will do no more than mention them. A painful self-consciousness, which makes it difficult for the Negro to meet even the well disposed of another race. A suspicion that he is being patronized. An emotionalism on the one hand, an emotional sterility on the other. The list could be continued.

Nor is it necessary that I give a detailed account of those forms and forces which arise from the nature of our civilization and are common to Americans, for these have received extended treatment: their features and effects are familiar to every one. The chaos and strain of these times, the lack of functioning religion, religious pretense and charlatanism, the reaction from these to materialism, industrialism, the ideal of material success, a devitalizing puritanism, herd psychology, the premium placed on individuality, the stupidities, lies, and superstititions that Mr. Menken has warred on, and so on, and so on. In general, all these elements can be grouped under the head of environmental influences as opposed to essential nature. From these, as I say, the Negro is emergent.

Precisely what, however, do I mean by emergent? Do I mean that the Negro is escaping or trying to escape from these things, that he denies their existence in him and is seeking to forget them? On the contrary, for the first time the Negro is fully recognizing that they do exist in him: this constitutes one aspect of his discovery. The Negro can no more leave them behind than a gull can leave water—but in both cases detachment is possible. The Negro is emerging to a place where he can see just what these factors are, the extent to which he has merely reacted to their stimuli, the extent to which he has been controlled by them. In a sense, he is adjusting to this feature of his reality. Further, he is discovering a self, an essence, interior to this crust-compound.

It would be premature to seek a final definition of this essence, for the act of discovery is only recently initiated, and, moreover, it is for the individual himself to reveal it in his own way and time. Nevertheless, I have already suggested certain of its features: it may be seviceable that I now bring these together and tentatively expand them.

The Negro has found his roots. He is in fruitful contact with his ancestry. He partakes of an uninterrupted stream of energy. He is moved by the vital determinants of racial heritage. And something of their siprit now lives within him. He is about to harvest whatever the past has stored, good and evil. He is about to be released from an unconscious and negative concern with it.

He is discovering his body. "For no man ever hated his own flesh; but nourisheth and cherisheth it."* These words are beginning to have real meaning. Save that it shares the derivation and genesis of things created, what matter who made it, the manner of its birth, the outward conditions that its parents were subject to? Here is it, this amazing instrument. It is strong and pliant, capable of work and lovely movements. In color and type it seems to include the varieties of humanity. Artists and anthropologists have been drawn to it. Now the Negro is finding it for his own experience. Let others talk about it if they have a mind to.

Beneath the reactive type, the Negro is touching emotions which have to do with the primary facts of existence. These flow with that lyricism which is so purely Negro. Sometimes they come in jerks and spurts, yet more powerful than a merely modern rhythm. Rarely, they suggest no strain or time at all, having blended with the universal. Liberated from past excess and recent throttling, love and passion may now pass in joy between man and woman. Pain is seen to be of the texture of life; not due

*[From the New Testament, Ephesians, 5.29.—Ed.]

to racial oppression, only. Likewise with fear, conflict, frustration, and tragic circumstance. Above all, the Negro finds that the poverty of creed has not killed his religious impulse. He is on earth, so placed; somewhere is God. The need to discover himself and the desire to find God are similar. Perhaps that strange thing called soul, hardly an existence, rarely mentioned nowadays above a whisper, the Negro in his search may help uncover.

The Negro is led through himself outward to the surrounding world. He feels his own milieu to be desirable; its beauty, ugliness, passion, poverty, rhythm, and color. There is truth in the statement that Harlem differs from other communities in shade merely, but not in pattern. But it should be remembered that this shade appeals to something more than the eye of a Negro. He wishes to generously partake of it; he wishes to press beyond its boundaries, for he knows that neither his nor any similar group provides the range to satisfy a large capacity and keen appetite for experience. He is frank to recognize the advanced status of the white creative world in the matters of discovery and experiment. He wishes to learn from it. But now he does not meet it as a white world, for he recognizes there his own impulse, gone farther, more matured. He meets it as a world of similar values. While he is uncovering the life of Harlem, he is exploring New York. While he finds out things about himself, he learns what other men have found out of themselves. In short, he is emerging to the creative level of America.

But more rapidly than he emerges toward it, the white world of America takes steps towards him. The Negro is being studied in relation to the general economic problems. The problems of population. He challenges attention from those who are sincere in their democracy. His social and educational aspects are being investigated and aided. Pschoanalysis has interesting data concerning him. Articles about him are appearing with increasing frequency in the leading magazines and newspapers. Books are coming out, and publishers are receptive of Negro material. Clubs, societies, and forums wish to hear about the Negro. All this is indicative of a certain type of discovery. I had in mind particularly, however, the discovery of the Negro by creative America.

Speculations as to the Negro's genius, whether or not it was distinct, if so, what would be its contribution, how best to aid its growth—questions such as these foreshadowed direct contacts. And then they came, men who had rid themselves by search and struggle of what the Negro in his efforts toward creation is now contending with. Men who are relatively free to meet life in its own terms and respond to it, not merely through the conventions of thought, emotion, or of conduct. The influence of this discovery is mutual. It is deep-seated. It may prove to be profound. For each brings the other an essential complement: a living contact made from different levels of experience.

Thus far, the most striking evidence of discovery is the change in Negro life as expressed by attitude. To himself, the Negro says: I am. Need it be pointed out how many centuries of struggle bear their fruit inviolate within this affirmation? The Negro says: I am. *What* I am, I am searching to find out. Also, what I may become. When he faces these mysteries the Negro is humble. It is permitted that he be so; for by this act all racial factors: black, white, birth, slavery, inferior, superior, prejudice, bitterness, resentment, hatred, aggression and submission, equal, reactions, patronage, self-consciousness, false shame and false pride—gravitate to conscious placements. The crisis of race becomes a fact within a general problem. Hitherto, the Negro has been utilized by this crisis for its purposes. The question is, How may he use it for his own? And the concern is with new values.

Discovery itself is such a value. It is the first, for all higher ones depend upon it. But it may not be pursued unattended by dangers. To these, the Negro is now subject. To say, I am. To search to find out what I am and what I may become. This is the true state and temper. But it is all too easy to substitute for this, fanciful excursions and pride oneself for real achievement. Likewise can a feeling of the exotic be mistaken for wonder. One may be thought by others to be novel, and incur no risk. But if one feels himself to be exotic, then the chances are that he will never advance beyond infantilism and inflated personality. Discovery is accompanied by respect for materials. For by means of it one becomes conscious of what a thing really is. One could not touch sand in such awareness, and not respect it. * * *

Discovery implies receptivity to all things: the rejection of no single one, save it be unreal. Prior to the present phase, because he was denied by others, the Negro denied them and necessarily denied himself. Forced to say nay to the white world, he was negative toward his own life. Judged by appearance, he considered appearances seriously, and had no time to find out what lay beneath the creature that America had made of him. And since he rejected this creature, he rejected everything. Something has happened. I have tried to suggest the nature of this happening. An impulse is at work within him, transforming rejections to acceptances, denials to affirmations. It is detaching the essential Negro from the social crust. One may define the impulse; it would be premature to name the substances that may be revealed by it. I think it best not to attempt it. For should there be set up an arbitrary figure of a Negro, composed of what another would have him be like, and the assertion made that he should model himself after it, this figure, though prompted by the highest interest, would nevertheless share the false and constricting nature of all superimposed images. Rather, I would be receptive of his reality as it emerges (being active only by way of aid to this emergence), assured that in proportion as he discovers what is real within him, he will create, and by that act at once create himself and contribute his value to America.

[1924?]

The Blue Man

Letter to Horace Liveright

Box 651,
Ellenville, NY
5 Sept 23

Dear Mr Liveright,

Your letter of Aug 29th on hand. First, I want to make a general statement from which detailed statements will follow. My racial composition and my position in the world are realities which I alone may determine. Just what these are, I sketched in for you the day I had lunch with you. As a unit in the social milieu, I expect and demand acceptance of myself on their basis. I do not expect to be told what I should consider myself to be. Nor do I expect you as my publisher, and I hope, as my friend, to either directly or indirectly state that this basis contains any element of dodging. In fact, if my relationship with you is to be what I'd like it to be, I must insist that you never use such word, such a thought, again. As a B[oni] and L[iveright] author, I make the distinction between my fundamental position and the position which your publicity department may wish to establish for me in order that *Cane* reach as large a public as possible. In this connection I have told you, I have told Messrs Tobey and Schneider to make use of whatever racial factors you wish. Feature Negro if you wish, but do not expect me to feature it in advertisements for you. For myself, I have sufficiently featured Negro in *Cane*. Whatever statements I give will inevitably come from a synthetic human and art point of view; not from a racial one. As regards my sketch-life—it was not my intention or promise to give a completed statement of my life.

94

It was my intention to give briefly those facts which I consider to be of importance, and then to allow your publicity department or the writers on the various papers and magazines to build up whatever copy seemed most suited to their purposes. I expect, therefore, that you so use it. With this reservation: that in any copy not used for specific advertising purposes the essentials of my sketch be adhered to. I mean, for instance, that in copies of *Cane* sent out to reviewers (these are not advertisements)— that any pamphlets included in these copies should follow the essential lines of my sketch. All of this may seem over-subtle and over-refined to you, but I assure you that it isnt [sic].

I shall go over the sketch and revise it as near as possible in accordance with your wishes.

And I'd be glad to have dinner with you at New Rochelle.

ever,

Toomer

From Letter to Waldo Frank

[no date]
[1922?]

* * * The only time that I think 'Negro' is when I want a peculiar emotion which is associated with this name. As a usual thing, I actually do not see differences of color and contour. I see differences of life and experience, and often enough these lead me to physical coverings. But not always, and, from the stand point of conventional criticism, not often enough. I'm very likely to be satisfied with a character whose body one knows nothing of.

It is true: Spartanburg (how curiously, painfully creative is the South!) gave us each other perhaps as no other place could. A bond that is sealed in suffering endures. And one finger of life can do more weaving than a thousand spindles of literary buzz-buzz. * * *

Not Typically American

* * * Though my life has been lived as it could have been lived only in America, it is, for better or for worse, not typically American.

Naturally, I am by no means the only untypical one. There are other individual exceptions, many of them. Without these others of my kind I would never have happened. Thanks to them I have happened. Without them I too would have become typical, or I would have left the country, or I would have been destroyed, perhaps landing in a mad house. Yes, there are thousands of exceptions, men and women who have more or less individualized themselves, scattered all over the country in every section, with the gods of a new America dwelling in them. But I am thinking now, not of the exceptions, but of the general rule, of those who are of the country's past and present, but not of the future.

The typically American thing is for a man, if he is white, to live all his life as a white man, and to have queer unreal views of the people of other groups; if colored, to live all his life as a colored man, and to have queer unreal views of people of other groups; if Jewish to live all his life as a Jew, and to have queer unreal views of the people of other groups; if an Indian to live all his life as an Indian, and to have queer unreal views of the people of other groups. If of English descent to live among people of English descent, if Scotch or Irish or Welsh or German or French or Italian or Spanish or Greek or what not, to live amongst those of similar descent all his life. In the typical view, matters of genesis overshadow matters of Being.

Thus it is, among other things, that when a citizen of this country uses the word American he tends to use it either with reference to his own group to the exclusion of others, or else with reference to some other group to the exclusion of his own.

The attitude of the typical white man is that he and his group are Americans whereas Jews, Negroes, and "foreigners" are in this country but not of it organically and integrally. This typical white attitude is underlaid by typical subattitudes which show that the members of the white group are much more conscious of their descents—English, German, or what not—than of their present American-ness. Americans to outsiders, they are Irish or Swedish or what not amongst themselves.

The attitude of the typical member of any minority group is a reflection of the attitude of the dominant white group. The white group says he is not an American. He says he is not an American. The minority person believes and feels that he and his group are Jews and Negroes or Indians or what not whereas the Christian white people are Americans.

In short, the typically American thing is for people to group themselves (or to be grouped) and adhere to racial or religious or nationalistic separatisms. Though in ideal one country, united and indivisible, though our biological actuality approaches this ideal (we are undoubtedly forming an American race) we are, sociologically, a replica of Europe's mutually repellent nationalisms with the red man and something of Africa and the Orient thrown in for good measure. Our social psychology lags far behind our spiritual ideals on the one hand and our physical realities on the other. Indeed as a nation we resemble one of our own sandwiches—two slices of good bread with questionable matter in between.

If the old world fatherlands of our new world citizens were to feed their respective children in this country with inflammatory nationalistic propaganda they could stir up in no time a world war within the borders of the United States. Technically of course it would be called a civil war. Whatever called, it would be explosive evidence of the fact that though we are citizens we are not yet a people—and we are not yet a people owing to two main causes: first, that there has not yet been time enough for such a consolidation; and, second, because the natural process of consolidation has been artificially checked by certain powers in this country who, for their own profit and with characteristic shortsight, have maneuvered to divide us and keep us divided.

There are, however, some members of the minority groups who want to get into and become members of the majority group. Thus we have what is known in this country as "passing"—and this too is a typical phenomenon of the American world. The attempt to pass can be looked at from two points of view. From one point of view it signifies an absence of a view of the country as a whole, the presence of the belief that the majority group is all of America and that it holds all the advantages of privilege and superiority. From another point of view it could be held that passing is one of the means by which America is becoming America, in the sense that the majority group will in time absorb all minority groups.

Some members of the colored group pass or try to pass into the white group. Some members of the Jewish group pass or try to pass into the Christian white group. At the time when America was fighting in the World War no few people of German descent changed their names and wanted to be taken for any white person other than one with German heredity or affiliations. Similar "passing" phenomenon would appear should this country declare war against some other European power. If war were to be fought with England then some number of those with English descent would want their descent forgotten.

And, of course, there is quite a bit of passing with respect to classes. Some of the lower or middle class want to pass to the upper class. With the increasing strength of Communism and the class struggle it will become more and more desirable or expedient or compulsory for increasing numbers of the middle class to pass to the proletarians.

There are people with Negro and Indian blood in the white group. There are people practically white in the colored group. There are roughnecks and bounders among the socially elite. There are aristocrats and artists among day-laborers. There are those who pass for writers or artists among the intelligentsia. There are bourgeois among the communists.

Social passing, however, has not the stigma attached to it that racial passing has. The identical impulse is behind it, namely, the impulse to improve one's lot; a similar characteristic marks it, namely, the desire to be rid of an actual or an imagined hindrance or handicap; but since so many people are involved in social passing of one kind or another, public opinion is more tolerant of it, public opinion sometimes affirms it. Nor are the social lines drawn as hard and fast as the race lines.

All of us have something in our past that we want to forget and pass beyond. A case could be argued in favor of passing. Whether commendable or not, wise or stupid, daring or cowardly, justified or unjustifiable, it is a human thing. Where harm is done the harm hits the passer far more than anyone else. A real service might be rendered by an analysis of passing, leading to a discrimination between well-guided and misguided attempts to improve one's lot. Here, however, it is not my intention either to argue the case or to attempt such an analysis. I simply want to state in brief certain of the features of American life that are typical; and, to summarize, these are racial, religious, class and social separatisms, and passing.

Now let me put in a few words about prejudices, and then I will go on.

In my view there are two kinds of prejudices, one I affirm, the other I deny. One kind of prejudice is conducive to a sharpened perception of reality: it increases the ability to discriminate and select, it spurs the mind, it operates to place you in creative opposition to what you consider, judged by human values, a hindrance or a blight to human life. The other kind of prejudice discolors and distorts perception, paralyzes discrimination and critical selection, is a drug to thought, and it operates to place you in futile conflict with its objects whatever they may be. I not only affirm the first kind of prejudice, I have it. For example, I have a prejudice against the second kind of prejudice. I generally use the term prejudice to mean prejudice of the second kind.

I began by saying that though my life has been lived as it could have been lived only in America, it is not, as you will be able to judge for yourself, typically American. Having indicated certain typicalities, I can now proceed to indicate how my life has differed.

I have lived in the white group but I am not a white man according to typical standards, nor have I remained in that group exclusively, nor have I formed queer unreal views of the people of other groups. I have lived in the colored group; but I am not a colored man according to typical standards, nor have I remained in that group exclusively, nor have I formed queer unreal views of the people of other groups. I have lived in the Jewish group but I am not a Jew according to typical standards, nor have I remained in that group exclusively, nor have I formed queer unreal views of the people of other groups. I have lived adjacent to Indians but I am not an Indian according to typical standards.

I have lived as an American, which I am. I have passed from one American group to another American group, in search of the fundamentals and also of the vain fulfillments desired by man ever since he reached the stature of a somewhat civilized three centered bisexual product of this planet, its sister planets and sun.

While I lived in it, each group became mine—which means that in a spiritual sense the total world of America has become mine. This identification with the entire country is most untypical—and I have had to pay for it by suffering a variety of strains, stresses, counterpulls, and misunderstandings, in the process of which I have individualized myself and crystalized my kind of American-ness.

I have been called a negro [sic]. I have been accused of passing. Pimples of men have alleged that I "quit the flock." I have been called white. I have been accused of nigger love. Doughy parasites have said all manner of things, alleging, among others, that some of my friends sought my company only because of their "thirst for the exotic." I have been called a Jew. Said to be a half-breed I have been thought to embody the tragic villainy attributed to such fellows.

For saying that no blood was any too good, that all blood contains possibilities far in excess of any yet realized, that there are both good and bad blood in all races, I have been suspect. For saying that my race is the human race I have been called a hypocrite and a traitor. Some of my best friends, in moments of lechery, have gone out of their way to persuade women that the women would become involved in my "tragedy" if they married me. Certain other of my best friends, in moments of jealousy, have tried to shunt me into a channel of concern with negroes [sic] and negro [sic] material exclusively, so as to insure themselves against my rivalry in the general field of American life. At the time of the first national outbreak of publicity about me, some number of respectable citizens were tickled and gleeful to have newspaper authority for believing that the "developer of men," the "teacher," turned out to be, after all, just a little pickaninny.*

At various times in varying places I have been taken for no less than the following. I have been taken for an Englishman, a Spaniard, a Dutchman, a Cuban, a South American, a Russian, a Japanese, an American

---

*Toomer is probably referring to his Gurdjieff teaching in Chicago and Portage, Wisconsin, and his 1931 marriage to Margery Latimer, which received national press coverage in 1932.—Ed.]

Indian, a Hindoo, an Egyptian, a Frenchman—all of which goes to prove, among other things, that as my life is, so my looks are, untypically American. And my looks have determined my life and my life has determined my looks—and both together have brought about the growth and crystallization of the values, the beliefs, the faiths and the visions that mean something to me.

Such a life it has been, and still is, and will be until I die and sink to that peace.

Though we have cleared ground there are still more woods than men, still more bipeds than human beings.

My kind of Americanism—I have wondered if it were of value only to myself and to a few others or if it also had value for the country at large. I now wonder if, though untypical of American life today, it may not characterize the American life of the future.

More than three hundred years were required in order to consolidate and blend a mixture of stocks into the present day English people. More than three hundred years will be required to consolidate and blend the mixtures existing here into an American people.

I say my kind of Americanism; not my life. My life is the life of my individual person, as it existed in the time of America from 1894 to 19__. But the results of my life, what I call my Americanism, perhaps this will be typical of people years hence. The view that America is America, that its citizens are Americans, that its people are the American people, that people are human beings, that the human beings of this continent have fundamental points in common with the people of all continents, that human life should be lived, that human society should operate and cooperate on the basis of the primary common factors of mankind in its existence and plight upon this planet of the universe.

Or may be it will befall my vision as it befell Walt Whitman's in that, just as I today can see no large signs of the country developing along his lines, so an individual one hundred years hence will see no large signs of the country having developed along my lines.

There are, we will say, two main views, views of man which amount to commitments. One view I call bipedism. The other view I call humanism. A man afflicted with bipedism sees only himself, and of himself he sees chiefly his legs, his sex organs and his belly. Not so bad, but not enough. A man developed to humanism sees all that a biped sees and in addition he sees others, and of himself and others he sees chiefly their human attributes, the most important of which is the spiritual mind. The extension of bipedism gives rise to racialism, classism, creedism, narrow nationalism. The extension of humanism gives rise to a proper valuation of race, of nation, of religion, and it moves on to a view and a feeling for the total human world. When I say I am an American I mean I am a humanist, born and formed in this country.

My Americanism is not only untypical of the America of today, it is untypical of the human world of today, this world being split and torn asunder by ancient separatisms and rivalries, by contemporary forces leading to militant nationalisms on the one hand and to international class struggles on the other. Yet perhaps that which is untypical of the human world of today will be characteristic of the human world tomorrow. * * *

[3/13/35]

Fighting the Vice

* * * When I wrote *Cane* I was viced in a set of circumstances more terribly than any I had ever known. I need not detail these circumstances here. For my present purpose it is enough to say that *Cane* was projected from this vice; and I had the desperate hope that its publication would release me into a different life. The conditions under which it was published and advertised were of minor importance; the main thing was to obtain its acceptance. Nevertheless, realizing that it would [be] my first appearance before the public, I had a natural desire that I should be presented in my true light. Waldo Frank had championed the book with Horace Liveright, and Frank had agreed to write the introduction. To insure his knowing of my position—as well as for reasons of friendship—I asked him to visit me in Washington, where I was then living. He came. He met and saw my family. I told him my views as regards myself as a member of the American race of the American people. In brief, I told him of myself just as I am writing of myself in this paper. I even showed him a poem I had written on the matter. He seemed to agree with me and to understand. I had hopes he would put this understanding in his introduction. He left me, and before long his paper arrived. His appreciation and response to *Cane* as a work of literature, and to myself as an artist, filled me with deep gratitude. His statements [implications?] as regards my racial position dismayed me; but in consideration of all he had done [and] was doing for me, I simply could not take him up on this count. Even now I find it difficult to do so—for it was because of his championship that *Cane* appeared, and *Cane*'s appearance did in truth open the way for me into a new and different life; and all that [I] most value has happened to me since then. I owe very much to Waldo Frank; and I

would do nothing to obscure this fact. Yet, in justice to myself and others, I must now state and clear up the matter which I did not clear up then.

I let his introduction stand. Liveright published *Cane*. Meanwhile I had left Washington for New York. I was in a new life, and this was the thing that mattered most to me. It was of no major importance that the book was circulating and becoming known as the work of a Negro author. In New York, with Frank, Munson, Hart Crane, Kenneth Burke, Paul Rosenfeld, and Stieglitz, I was in the life I wanted to be in. Let me be called Negro. I was experiencing the life I wanted to experience. Nevertheless, when one day Liveright wanted me to push the Negro feature I refused. He then wrote me to the effect that he did not see why I could not accept my race. This angered me, and I doubtless said something that angered him. Neither could I see why I could not accept my race; but what I meant by my race and what he meant by my race were two different things. And so it went on.

Time passed. I became interested in a way of life which took me far away not only from the race question but from literature and from my New York life. And not only what I was called did not matter, but even many of the things which formerly I had deeply valued did not matter. My new values were in another world, and into this world I had placed myself completely.

Then began the events which rapidly grew into the New Negro in literature movement. Though *Cane* had to some extent made it possible, perhaps even given it some of its impetus, I personally knew nothing of it until it was well under way. When I did see it, I was impressed by certain of the values I saw. Countee Cullen wrote and told me of a collection he was editing, asking for permission to use certain of my poems. I gladlly gave it to him. Soon, however, I began seeing two things I did not like. I did not like the boosting and trumpeting and the over-play and over-valuation of the Negro, of the products of Negro writers, which were springing up. I refused to have any part in this kind of displaying. I did not like the anthologizing which was springing up. Everyone seemed to want to edit an anthology. I received requests. I refused them, because I did not want *Cane*, which is an organism, dismembered, torn to bits and scattered about in the pages of anthologies.

One day Alain Locke came to see me. I admired his taste and intelligence, but when he said he wanted something from *Cane* for a book he was preparing I refused him. I told him I would give him an article I had recently written. But he did not want the article. And the matter, so I thought, rested there. Before leaving, however, he suggested that Winold Reiss would like to do a portrait of me. Well, having not the slightest idea that the portrait was going to be used in Locke's book, I sat for Reiss. When *The New Negro* came out, there was a short story "Fern" from my *Cane* book, and there was the Reiss portrait.

Later on Locke again used without my consent one of my pieces for a new book of his, the book in which are collected Negro plays and dramas. Years before, I had submitted this sketch, "Balo," one of my early attempts, to Locke and Gregory when they were running the Howard University players. They had done nothing with it. I had forgotten I had written it. I had forgotten they still had it. Imagine my surprise, then, and my anger years later suddenly to see this naive attempt appearing in a collection.

My resistance against anthologizing increased; but, after all, it was of no great moment. I was still mainly completely absorbed in another world.

Then I went to Chicago in pursuit of the aims of my world. Little by little, however, I began discovering that the anthologies had preceded me. Not my own book *Cane*. No, but few people knew of *Cane*. Some, though, did know of the collections, and they had formed pictures and feelings about me based on their impressions of my work and name appearing in these collections. Finding that these pictures and impressions tended to hinder my work, I began destroying them. When the occasion arose, which it did now and again, I destroyed the notions in my close acquaintances, and conveyed the facts about myself and my life which would enable them to see me in this respect as I was. These friends, in turn, conveyed the matter to others, and to others. And so the number of those who understood my position increased; and the way was cleared for me to do what I had gone to Chicago to do.

But the fact that I had at first been somewhat hindered made me realize how widely the misunderstandings of me had spread, and made me realize, too, that I had best set about correcting them wherever and whenever they arose. I did just this. I set up a general counter movement.

In line with my new intention I had to do, among many others, one thing which, in other respects, I regretted having to do. I had to refuse James Weldon Johnson my consent that certain of my poems appear in his revised anthology—which is one of the best. * * *

I wrote him stating in brief my real position, and saying that in order to establish it, I was finding it necessary to disassociate my name from Negro, and that to effect this latter, I was having to take, for a time, a stand more extreme than I really wanted it to be. In reply to me Mr. Johnson affirmed my individual position as an American, but said, in substance, that he doubted that the time was ripe for the projection of such a symbol for a general movement towards a fundamental Americanization of all American people.

I, however, felt that the time was ripe. Already I had written quite a bit on the matter, and now I began gathering my materials and set about definitely to produce a book on America in general with the racial vision given what in my way of thinking is its proportionate place and value. * * *

[1932?]

The New Race

A New Race in America

There is a new race in America. I am a member of this new race. It is
neither white nor black nor in-between. It is the American race, differing
as much from white and black as white and black differ from each other.
It is possible that there are Negro and Indian bloods in my descent along
with English, Spanish, Welsh, Scotch, French, Dutch, and German. This
is common in America; and it is from all these strains that the American
race is being born. But the old divisions into white, black, brown, red, are
outworn in this country. They have had their day. Now is the time of the
birth of a new order, a new vision, a new ideal of man. I proclaim this new
order. My marriage to Margery Latimer is the marriage of two Americans.

[1931]

Letter to James Weldon Johnson

1447 North Dearborn St
Chicago Ill
July 11   30

Dear Mr Johnson,

My view of this country sees it composed of people who primarily are
Americans, who secondarily are of various stocks or mixed stocks. The
matter of descent, and of divisions presumably based on descents, has

been given, in my opinion, due emphasis, indeed over-emphasis. I aim to stress the fact that we all are Americans. I do not see things in terms of Negro, Anglo-Saxon, Jewish, and so on. As for me personally, I see myself an American, simply an American.

As regards art I particularly hold this view. I see our art and literature as primarily American art and literature. I do not see it as Negro, Anglo-Saxon, and so on.

Accordingly, I must withdraw from all things which emphasize or tend to emphasize racial or cultural divisions. I must align myself with things which stress the experiences, forms, and spirit we have in common.

This does not mean that I am necessarily opposed to the various established racial or sociological groupings. Certainly it does not mean that I am opposed to the efforts and forces which are trying to make these groups creative. On the contrary, I affirm these efforts. I recognize, for example, that the Negro art movement has had some valuable results. It is, however, for those who have and who will benefit by it. It is not for me. My poems are not Negro poems, nor are they Anglo-Saxon or white or English poems. My prose, likewise. They are, first, mine. And, second, in so far as general race or stock is concerned, they spring from the result of racial blendings here in America which have produced a new race or stock. We may call this stock the American stock or race. My main energies are devoted and directed towards the building of a life which will include all creative people of corresponding type.

I take this opportunity of noting these things in order to clear up a misunderstanding of my position which has existed to some extent ever since the publishing of CANE. I am stating the same things whenever opportunity allows to everyone concerned. I feel that just now the time is ripe to give a definite expression of these views.

My best wishes for your anthology; and my warm regards to you and Mrs Johnson.

Sincerely,

Jean Toomer

The Americans

The strength of a country can be measured by its ability to digest, assimilate, and transform all the diverse materials present in it. The health of a country is dependent upon the right flowing of its digestive processes. The achievement of a country occurs when it has transformed all of its food into blood, a blood unique to itself, and when, from the life of this blood it produces people, bodies and souls, and customs and culture special to it. This is true of the individual members of a nation. It is true of the nation as a whole. A country is like a huge stomach into which enters all kinds of materials, some unusable, some usable; and its existence is maintained, it is nourished, it grows and develops by subjecting these materials to the processes of digestion and assimilation, rejecting unusable matters, incorporating usable materials into its structures and functions. * * *

There must be death before there can be new life. The materials themselves need not die, but the forms in which they previously existed must be broken down before these materials can enter as elements of new forms with new life. When we pick and eat an apple that it [sic] is the end of the apple. The apple dies. But that is the beginning of us, in so far as we are embodiments of the elements which previously existed in the apple-form.

Some foods, in relation to some eaters, do not noticeably resist dying and being eaten. The apple does not noticeably resist us. But certain foods, such for example as race-forms, though entering the stomach of a nation, do resist. This resistance both retards and stimulates the appetite, it both retards and stimulates digestion and assimilation. But the nation eats them. The race-forms die. They must die before there can be new life. In America, the white race, the black race, the red race, the brown race must die before there can be a new race. They are dying. America is eating them. They are dead. America has eaten them. This is the tendency. The tending here is to break up all old racial forms and incorporate their materials for the forming of a new racial form with new life.

It has been said that America is a melting-pot. Rather I would view it as a stomach. Rather I would view it as the place where mankind, long dismembered into separate usually repellant groupings, long scattered over the face of the earth, is being re-assembled into one whole and undivided human race. America will include the earth.

There is a new race here. For the present we may call it the American race. That, to date, not many are aware of its existence, that they do not realize that they themselves belong to it—this does not mean it does not exist; it simply means it does not yet exist for them because they, under the suggestion of hypnotic labels and false beliefs, are blind to it. But these labels and beliefs will die. They too must and will die. And the sight of people will be freed from them, and the people will become less blind and they will use their sight and see.

This new race is neither white nor black nor red nor brown. These are old terms for old races, and they must be discarded. This is a new race;

and though to some extent, to be sure, white and black and red and brown strains have entered into its formation, we should not view it as part white, part black, and so on. For when different elements come together in chemico-biological blendings, a new substance is produced, a new substance with new qualities in a new form. Water, though composed of two parts of hydrogen and one part of oxygen, is not hydrogen and oxygen; it is *water*, a new substance with a new form produced by the blending of hydrogen and oxygen. So the blending of different racial strains, taking place in the geographical setting of the American continent, has given rise to a new race which is uniquely itself. Save in the case of those who only recently have come here, it includes *everyone* in this country.

The biological process has already taken place. And, despite sociological resistance, it will inevitably continue to take place. Our views and our conscious are far behind and often untrue to the physical facts. We often speak as there were only white races, black, red and brown races here. True enough, on the sociological plane, that is, in terms of our social groupings, there are what we call white, black, red and brown groups. But I am speaking now of the biological actuality which underlies these social groups. There is white and red and brown blood in the so-called black group. This is generally recognized. There is white and black blood in the so-called red group. This too is recognized. There is red and black blood in the so-called white group. The red blood in the white group is somewhat recognized. The black blood in the white group is not. At the present time our psychology is such that it would be more painful than drawing an eye-tooth to draw from people this recognition. This is the American racial neurosis.

People with, as it is said, black blood in their veins, have been entering, passing into the white group for several centuries. So true is it that there is black blood in the white group that if the entire black group were to be destroyed, the black blood already present in so-called white people would continue circulating throughout the future history of the country, thinning out but spreading wider and wider as the years rolled on. And, on the other hand, should the white group be destroyed, the white blood already present in the so-called black group would continue circulating through America's history, similarly thinning out but spreading wider and wider as the years rolled on.

So much has the biological process taken place, so thoroughly are the various strains mingled and blended, that no living American knows but what he has all the various strains in him. If he has not, it is more than likely that his progeny will have.

Only, as I say, these strains do not exist in unblended parts. They are organically combined more closely than hydrogen and oxygen are in water. When we thoughtlessly say of a person that he is half white and half black, or part Jewish and part Gentile, it sounds as if we thought or believed that white blood was in one half of his body and black blood in the other half, that Jewish blood was in his right side while Gentile blood was in his left. But this is only a manner of speaking. And we speak in this manner only because we have not thought about it, only because we speak loosely and inaccurately, and only because our psyches are in parts and in chaos and we unconsciously assume that our body is as unintegrated as our psyche. In this person of so-called mixed blood, in his body, the bloods have combined to form a new uniform blood. It is not white plus black, or Jewish plus Gentile. It is itself, a third thing, a different and unique substance with unique attributes. Moreover it is a mistake to speak of blood as if it had various colors in the various races. All human blood is the same. When we use color adjectives what we really are referring to are skin pigmentations. This is one of our main troubles. We see a surface and assume it is a center. We see a color or a label or a picture and assume it is a person.

The above fact, namely, that blood blendings give rise to new blood need not alarm anyone, not even those who have prided themselves on racial purity. For just this purity, just the uniqueness which they cherish, has itself come about as a result of a blending of various strains. The present day English people are, according to some students of the matter, the product of the blending of fifteen or more different strains. From the point of view of descent, we all are mixed blooded. No one knows, or can possibly know, all of the different racial elements, entering through his millions of ancestors, which he now, in a manner of speaking, embodies. From the point of view of our present existence, we all are pure blooded.

There is only one pure race—and this is the *human* race. We all belong to it—and this is the most and the least that can be said of any of us with accuracy. For the rest, it is mere talk, mere labelling, merely a manner of speaking, merely a sociological, not a biological, thing. I myself merely talk when I speak of the blending of the bloods of the white, black, red and brown races giving rise to a new race, to a new unique blood, when I liken the combination of these strains to the combination of hydrogen and oxygen producing water. For the blood of all the races is *human* blood. There are no differences between the blood of a Caucasian and the blood of a Negro as there are between hydrogen and oxygen. In the mixing and blending of so-called races there are mixtures and blending of the same stuff. When members of the human race, whatever their skin pigmentations, whatever their labels, whatever their different psychological behavior, meet and mingle there can only result other members of the human race.

So what I really mean by the American race is the human race—again the human race. The real and main difference between this new American group and previous groups will be found, necessarily not in blood, but in *consciousness*. Be of "white" blood, purely so; be of "black" blood, purely so; be of "red" or "brown" bloods, purely so; or be a blend of them. It is all the same stuff. And the same stuff added to or combined with the same stuff results in the same stuff. In America we have a new body. And, having recognized this, let [us] forget it. Let us forget that. Let us be born above the body. The important thing is consciousness. Here, in this country, among the people I refer to, the human essence, *humanness*, is again to be realized and emphasized. After having for years been hypnotized by labels and suggestions to believe we were less than human, merely Caucasian, or Mongolian, or Negroid, merely African, Russian, Italian, Spanish, French, English, or American; after having been identified with these surfaces, we are emerging from these limitations, we are waking up, we are nonidentifying from surfaces and from the preferences and prejudices associated with them, and we are realizing our basic human stock, our human essence, our humanness, our fundamental and universal humanity. Those who have or who are approaching this [sensing?], this realization—these are the ones I mean when I say Americans. These Americans are not of America only; they are of the earth. And, with various [titles?] in various countries they of course exist in other national groups. These are the [natural?] conscious internationalists.

[no date]

Oppose the Force, Not the Man

I have heard Negroes protest that they are held down by white people. I have heard white people protest that they are held back by Negroes. The common factor of both statements is that each and both feel they are held. It is precisely this common factor that, in my way of thinking, is to be realized by both. Though they are held in different ways, they are bound in the same way. If you and I come to grips you may be stronger and have an advantage in the tussle, but the central fact is that both of us grip and are gripped and so remain as long as the fight lasts, powerless to stop, powerless to really separate and go our ways, powerless in short to do anything else.

Let us note, moreover, that Negro and white or whoever is so held, both feel that they are being held to their detriment. Both feel the damaging effects of the binding force. But neither, of course, understand [sic] that it is precisely a force that is holding them. Therefore they do not and indeed cannot truly get together to overcome their common enemy. No, each separatistically [sic] blames the other. The only solution that occurs to them is also cast in the mould of separatism. The white man would break away from the Negro, or further suppress him, or, in extreme cases, murder him. The Negro would fight the white or undermine him in some way. Such measures are evidently doomed to failure. You cannot resolve the problems of separation by operating within the force of separatism. Nor can you genuinely break from slavery by opposing people who are as much its victims as you yourself are.

Oppose the force, not the man. Oppose, both in yourself and in the other human being, that part of yourself and that part of him which acts as the agent of the force of separation and the force of binding. Cooperate with, both in yourself and in the other man, that part of yourself and that part of him which represents the good man, the decent human being who desires to be friend, who wants companionship, understanding, development, and some measure of real freedom. Let the other man do the same thing for himself and towards you. The forces of separatism and binding could not long withstand such a league of human beings, so dedicated.

[no date]

Mankind Means Brotherhood

By Creation we are brothers in being. By Nature we are brothers in the flesh. We *are* this way, even though in all too many of our habits we act as if we were not. Human Being means brotherhood, and will forever mean brotherhood, even though in our lives we continue to distort, pervert, and do violence to this meaning.

The reality is not wanting, nor is it at fault. We are wanting. We are at fault for not realizing the reality.

Mankind is one kind. Those of one kind are essentially brothers, whether they know it or not. Our knowing, or our lack of knowing, does not affect the reality. But knowledge or ignorance on our part does vitally promote or impede the manifestation of the reality.

We were designed, and now are designed, to be moved and related each to the other by love, faith, and conscience. It is our faulty conditioning, coupled with the devil which we permit to remain in us, that so often moves us to hate, distrust, and violence. Thus moved, it is not only that we fail to practice what we preach, it is that we defect from and violate the structure and functions of our own reality.

Kinship is the enduring reality. Separatism is the habitual actuality. Disunion is a tragic make-believe. Enmity is a delusion. We call ourselves human beings. This is true to fact. We are human, every last one of us. We are beings, including the least of us. No one is excluded, though we in our conceit may act as if we were excluding all those against whom we happen to feel prejudice.

We call ourselves man-kind. Many of our terms are not true to the reality. This term is profoundly true. All men *now*, in reality, *are* kinsmen. There is no need for us to be re-made into kinsmen. Kinship already *is*. There is no need for anyone to try to bring us together on the deep level of spiritual reality, for on that level we *are* together, though there is great need for efforts toward unification on the behavior level.

There is no need to "make" the reality. Nor is there need to unmake it. The reality need not be changed in any way. As it is, it is right and good, it is beautiful and far more marvelous than words or ideas will ever tell.

All we need is to *unmake* our fictions and false beliefs about the reality, is to overcome and cast aside the *barriers*. All we need do, and this we must do, is to affirm and enact brotherhood with all our heart, is to deny and oppose on every occasion the obstacles to brotherhood.

It can be done. It can be done by patient work implemented by effective means. Also, by what we call an act of grace, we can be lifted in an instant into the realm of unity. For if the spirit itself works in a man, that man for that time is transported. He is transported out of his ordinary self, out of his ordinary world. He experiences the essential oneness of mankind and knows, by an authority deeper and more valid than thoughts and ideas, that it is so.

Life does not demand the impossible of its members, and we are life-members. We are integral members of Life and we continue being integral members of Life even while we behave as if we were disintegral outlaws. Nor can any conceivable power by any conceivable act put us out of Life. We simply cannot be expelled, not by death.

Life itself in the very beginning established kinship as a basic reality even between men who murder each other. It is therefore all the more terrible that men do murder each other.

It is not for us to do what Life has done. It is for us to undo some of the things that we have done, and to do some of the things that thus far we have left undone. It is for us, each one for and within himself, all helping all, to purify ourselves, to rid ourselves of ignorance, and to open our eyes as to what Life has done and we have not. It is for us, in fine, to *awaken,* to *realize.*

There are foundations and fountains. There are principles. There are laws. There are people. There are Nature and the Earth. There is the Universe. There is God. Our task is to open our consciousness so that it receives and comprehends *the reality that is.*

An awakened sense of *being* must arise to overcome our already too active sense of egotism. An alert mindfulness must overcome our heedlessness. An awakened religious feeling must enable us to transcend the apparent evidence of overwhelming evil. Salvation is as real as sin, and so it must become for us.

Some deep and abiding intuition of the brotherhood of man does now already exist, I am convinced, in the subconscious of all men. This is no glittering generality. It arises from particular experiences with men of practically every race, color, class, and condition. I have yet to find a single person in whom this intuition does not exist. Yet, just as surely, I have yet to know a single person who at some time, usually many times, has not violated this intuition. We do commit crimes against each other, and every crime that men commit against men is done against the reality of kind-ness and in violation of our subconscious knowledge of and feeling for this reality.

Time and again our narrow thoughts, our disjective [sic] emotions, our irrational reactions get the better of what we really know and feel because we, to use a popular expression, are asleep at the switch.

But does sleep cancel reality? Does crime destroy law and justice? Does hate in hell destroy love in heaven? Sleep merely closes the sleeper to reality. Crime harms the criminal. Hate banishes love from the heart of the hater. Ugliness may cover the Earth and close out beauty for those who dwell in ugliness, but beauty exists nevertheless and all the while. We have it in our power to exist in the one. We have it in our power to exist in the other. We have it in our power to wake up.

A Nazi and an Englishman engage in a fight. Their *enacted* relationship is that of enemy to enemy. Their *created* and enduring relationship is that of kin to kin. Even as they fight they *are* brothers. Fighting does not destroy the basic kinship of these men. Nothing that man has ever done or ever will do can destroy this fundamental relationship. What the fighting does is to blind these men, is to prevent them from acting as kin, is to commit them to act as if the good of each depended upon the destruction of each other.

Do not you and your blood-brother remain blood-brothers even though you quarrel? Do not you and your spiritual brother remain spiritual brothers even though you behave as enemies? All of us *are* blood-brothers. All of us *are* brothers in being. No winds of false doctrine, no torrents of hate, no murders, massacres or wars will ever change it.

No matter what we do to the contrary, we cannot in reality disconnect ourselves from the great body and being of mankind. No matter what is done to us, we cannot be pushed out of humanity. Not even lynching can destroy the kinship that exists between the man who suffers torture and the man who suffers degradation. Not even the wars that rage in the world today can nullify, much less annihilate, the essential brotherhood of those who fight and die.

Men

Workers in the flesh
Kinsmen in spirit
Brothers in being

Antagonists in egotism
Companions in good will
Friends in understanding

Separate in bodies
Many in desires
One in ultimate reality

[no date]

IV

Caught in the Machine

Editor's Note

For about ten years, beginning in 1924, Toomer was a disciple of Georges I. Gurdjieff, the mystical philosopher who was popular among some intellectuals and writers in the 1920s. Gurdjieff believed that people's minds were cluttered with destructive notions because they lived in negative social environments. Most of what people heard and read gave them distorted or false views of the nature of the world and themselves. This negative environment prevented people from developing full and harmonious lives. Gurdjieff believed that most people were like machines, mechanical and efficient but asleep, with no consciousness of their real potential as human beings.

Many of the pieces in this part reflect Toomer's great interest in Gurdjieff's philosophy. The fiction describes negative and mechanistic societies containing human automatons, some of whom are groping for freedom from their rigid, programmed, and often lonely lives. The nonfiction discusses the problems with modern society that have created a less than human world.

"To Dike" and "To Sleep" are part of an unpublished collection, "Essentials: Prose and Poems," that Toomer put together in 1930. "Selling" is undated. F. Scott Fitzgerald's play *The Vegetable* was published in 1923 to mixed reviews. Its being a satire on the American Dream and American politics probably explains Toomer's interest in it. His unpublished critique is undated. Toomer wrote his statement on the Scottsboro Boys in an undated letter to Langston Hughes. On November 17, 1933, Hughes had written to Toomer requesting a financial contribution and a statement for the press in support of the nine young black men who had been sentenced to death and were awaiting a new trial.

"American Letter" was published in French as "Lettre D'Amerique," translated by Victor Llona, in *Bifur*, May 1929. At the end of his typescript, Toomer jotted some fragmented notes, which I have not included here. "Man's Home Companion" was written in 1933. "The Spoken Word" is an untitled typescript from a collection of notes and drafts for lectures that Toomer was preparing in 1933 under the title "The Psychology and Craft of Writing." The typescript of "Winter Road" is dated February 26, 1937. The untitled typescript of "George Washington" is dated November 8, 1932. "Atomic Energy," handwritten, comes from a collection of rough notes and drafts on New Mexico that Toomer entitled "Sequences." It may have been written around 1947, the year of Toomer's final trip to New Mexico.

"Drackman" and "Love on a Train" were part of a collection of stories that Toomer proposed for publication in 1929. "Lump" may have been written around 1936.

To Dike

A number of our means of communication and influence, such for example as our educational, religious, and literary systems, have been used on occasion to pull people by their noses, or, to use the term coined by me, to dike people, with the aim of compelling them to act according to the desires of the manipulators.

To dike means, in the particular, to pull people by their noses, and, in general, it means to manipulate things towards one's own ends, and usually to be applauded for doing so, even when the manipulation is counter to the real interests of those who applaud.

A most obvious form or means of diking is provided by our advertising system. For, as is well known, advertisers and advertising frequently pull people by their noses: the pulling is paid for and applauded. And so, from this point of view, advertising, along with newspapers, politics, and other systems, is an excellent example of an organized play upon the property of suggestibility.

This property is so deep-rooted and widespread that should all outside suggestion be removed, given people are [sic] they are, each one would continue as he now does to dike himself.

[1930]

Selling

Advertising and selling assume that people do not know what they want, that people are without taste, without experience, without formed needs or wishes, without a sense of selection, without thought and judgement; but that they have dollars, and that you can and must make them spend not only what they have but more than they have. In short, advertising and selling see a human being as a potentially responsive automaton with money. The idea is to induce this characterless organism to spend its money in a given way.

Thus, if a person goes in for a suit of clothes, the salesman acts as if the prospective buyer had never bought a suit before. The salesman's job is, as it were, to clothe this hitherto naked and ignorant body. If a person wants, or does not want, an apartment, a house, a car, a book, music, and so on, the case is the same. A young upstart of one year's sales experience in a book store will attempt to tell a seasoned literary man what he wants.

Whoever sells assumes that the prospective buyer knows nothing and is nothing.

It used to be that a salesman might assume that though you knew of other similar goods, you did not know the special and unique virtues of his goods. Or, if his line was a new line, he would of necessity describe it to you. This was legitimate and serviceable. But now, with a decrease of respect, with an increase of the urge to gouge people, it is assumed that you need someone to superintend your wishes, tastes, and the spending of your money. Salesmen are such superintendents. They are, in fine, a strange kind of parent.

This attitude and practice, specialized and organized in advertising and selling, is fast becoming a marked characteristic of all our relationships. In most fields of life it is more and more assumed that you have no mind, no feelings, no tastes of your own, and that, consequently, you must be told what you want and then sold it. We are fast becoming sellers and buyers of pleasure, health, love, friends, marriage, homes, government, education, professional services, art, religion, science, philosophy. This is indeed a new thing under the sun; and it is not in vain that we have progressed and prospered.

[no date]

A *Comment on* The Vegetable, *by F. Scott Fitzgerald*

Of the various pestilences known to attack vegetable life, the literary, operating through the agency of Mr. F. Scott Fitzgerald, is at once the most distressing and the most negative. The distress is caused by the spectacle of what was once a genuine talent, now reduced to the state where it can find satisfaction in such trifling. It is a commonplace that Mr. Fitzgerald's promise has failed to achieve an acceptable fulfillment. Therefore, let the bare statement of this fact suffice. The negative feature is included in the criticism, that in this play the pest sets in before the vegetable is fairly sprouted. Jerry Frost does not come to life. The thin sophisticate disillusion of Mr. Fitzgerald begins, as it were, to eat away at his character before he is created. Hence one finds here nothing more than an attitude edited by means of a dialog which, at least, is quite appropriate to it. This attitude doubtless springs from a recognition of the poverty of American middle-class life, of its absurd ambitions and its cheap pretense. It is so general, however,—unless informed by some unique thought or emotional power—as to be commonplace. *The Vegetable* is wholly lacking in qualifying features. And since there are no flashes of prose brilliance or beauty to in any way lift it, one finds it, at best, tedious and trivial; and at its worst, vulgar.

[no date]

Drackman

One morning, a usual New York business morning, Daniel C Drackman was being driven to his offices. His friends called him the Iron Man. He liked this title, but accepted it with impersonal reserve. A powerful figure, he sat back in his Pierce Arrow limousine with a robe about his limbs and a silk scarf showing above the collar of his overcoat. His handsome black derby and superior nose-glasses emphasized the polished, self-contained, dominant expression of his entire person. So accustomed was he to controlling the world's affairs that he took his role as a matter of course. This was a morning of several large financial deals.

The day was cold and flat, grey, smokey. The sun, struggling unheeded to break through, seemed like an imperfect and discarded artificial light. Save, however, that the car's heater was not working there were no signs of unusual happenings. Drackman, as they say, was in the prime of life. He looked in the pink of condition. Together with several million of his countrymen he was fond of repeating that he had never felt better in his life. And to him, as to most of its inhabitants, New York appeared normal. Yes, traffic, as he saw and experienced it, was an acute problem. It imposed upon the motion of his car a series of unpredictable abrupt stops, starts, twists, and irritating delays. Once, only the skill of his chauffeur avoided an accident. And it was true that each new skyscraper meant more congestion and danger. But new skyscrapers had to be built. Let human beings adjust to them. He told himself that the city engineers, physical and psychological, would soon solve this problem. If they did not, he, Daniel C Drackman, who knew their business better than they did, would.

Drackman's life had moved regularly; yes by leaps and bounds, with no correspondence between personal efforts and material results, with no adequate development of a sense of responsibility, but in strict accordance with the rules of business and within the authority of upper-class conventions. So that now, at the age of forty-eight, he was eminently successful financially. He had palatial offices downtown, and an expensive apartment uptown Park Avenue where, during the winter, he kept his wife and three children.

These children were the promise of America. They were marvelous lovely creatures who seemed to have direct contact with the world's sunshine. Their bodies were exquisite, blending high sensitivity with robust plastic strength. Their intuitive intelligence was phenomenal. Though they were obviously the children of Drackman and his wife, though one could see physical resemblances, their spiritual difference was so marked that they gave the impression of belonging to a new emergent order of human beings.

Drackman's wife, Martia, was ten years younger than he. At the time of their marriage eighteen years ago she had been a forerunner of the postwar combination of debutante and serious critical youth. She was slender of body with large brown thoughtful eyes. Popular in her social set, a good dancer. Head-strong, impetuous, yet she could be patient and considerate. She felt she had greatly matured during the period of her marriage to Daniel; and she attributed this growth, in part, to motherhood, in part, to his influence. For Drackman, the Iron Man, was a different person within the form of his home: he was no less a force, but a force of a different order. Here, his affections, his generosity, his human intelligence were liberated and became active.

His mind, of course, was largely factual and rationalistic, somewhat crude and hard-boiled, unshakably given to materialistic views. He believed he believed in nothing save what was tangible to his senses. Man, according to him, was an accidental complex combination of chemicals, a swift combustion, a transient flash in eternal oblivion. Man was what you could *see* of him. All else was fancy and delusion. He often felt a duty to impress his notions on other people; but for some strange reason he withheld mention of them to his children. Indeed towards them he was secretly inexplicably shy and diffident.

But within the limits of its materialistic frame, Drackman's intelligence was active with a wide range of interests which led him to explore the worlds of ideas and of art. He had, in fact, made of himself something of a practical philosopher and critic of the arts. He read a great deal, visited the art galleries, and went regularly to the theatres and to concerts at Carnegie Hall.

And whatever he may have thought, in feelings he was hearty, jovial, and often affectionate. Though he had no pity, he sometimes did things which led people to call him a humanitarian. In private life these qualities were liberated. He managed to bring the results of his interests not only to his wife and children but to a large circle of friends, and even to outsiders whom one would not have thought him concerned with. So that, all in all, Drackman, idolized as a business force, was also esteemed as a good husband and a good father, a generous and cultured individual.

This morning, as he lay back in his limousine, his appearance was that of a hard cold dominant business man. To anyone less well placed than himself, his expression, as he looked out of the car, as his glance cut through human flesh, his eyes and face of steel—his expression seemed to ask: "What right have you to live?"

His car, having passed as usual down upper Park Avenue, was speeding southward from Grand Central Terminal.

The first unusual sign was a sharp pain which shot through the base of his head. Drackman sat bolt upright. His heart beat suddenly with fear. His heavy dark eyebrows contracted ominously. His bulldog jaw thrust forward. He held himself prepared against a recurrence of the pain. His neck tightened. But he felt nothing more; and when he worked his head from side to side his stiff neck seemed to yield and relax. So, after a brief period of troubled questioning, he lay back against the seat, gave a strange grunt, and crossed the experience from his mind.

Not long after, however, of a sudden he heard a voice speak to him. The voice sounded queerly like his own; yet, its source seemed so removed from him that, when he answered, as he did, it was as if he were holding conversation with a second person.

In a tone used to a child, the voice asked: "What do you see out there, Daniel?"

Daniel ground his jaws, as he did when emotionally stirred, and answered with anger: "What business is that of yours?"

"Do not try your temper on me," the voice commanded. "Answer what I have asked you."

Drackman's eyes flashed, but he replied: "New York."

"Of course," said the voice. "What a stupid, commonplace remark. Must I be specific? What are those great towering things you see?"

"Skyscrapers," he shot out.

"Obviously," said the voice, satirically. "But what are they?"

"The greatest buildings man has ever erected," said Daniel with authority. "Do you not know, my dear sir, that they are greater than the Pyramids, and that no civilization has ever produced their equals?"

The voice replied: "Mr. Drackman, you would make an excellent mouthpiece for a sight-seeing bus. What you say is evident to any American. But I want to know what you, what you yourself call them."

Of a sudden Drackman expelled the words: "Giants' tombstones."

"Precisely," said the voice. It seemed to be pleased. It seemed to belong to a face which grinned, almost leered at Daniel. "Now do you see the point?"

"No, I do not," growled Daniel.

"Tombstones . . . giants . . ." the voice insinuated.

"Well, what of it?" asked Drackman.

"Do not you own one?"

"What if I do?" he snapped out. And then he quickly smiled and added: "Ah, I see! My tomb!" he exclaimed. "But that does not matter, does it? The tomb is not the point. The point is the giant. The important point is that Daniel C Drackman is a giant!"

"Right!" the voice agreed. "The tomb is the measure of Drackman. Daniel C Drackman is a giant!"

Both Daniel and the voice were satisfied. There was silence. Then Drackman felt a swimming of the head, a strange nausea, a swift on-rush of blackness, as if the world were whirling and dissolving. This state was brief; but it was soon followed by a far more alarming condition. Of a sudden, he had a gripping shivery sense that he was going to run amuck. He felt helpless and impelled by powerful swirls of irrational urges. So he might have felt had he accidentally swallowed a potent drug.

Indeed it was as if a swarm of chemicals, germs of egomania, of self-assertion, existing, like influenza germs, in New York's atmosphere, had suddenly entered him and effected a radical change of his chemical composition.

Drackman felt so utterly unlike himself, his sense of the change, actual and threatened, was so acute, that he experienced a terrifying pang of self-uncertainty. He felt panic. His habitual confidence in himself and in his world quivered, and momentarily broke. To himself he seemed on the verge of disintegration. To counteract this, the muscles of his face and body contracted in an effort of self control. He clenched his fists. He ground his jaws. Fires of energy leapt up in him. And then, feeling like a powerful locomotive about to jump the tracks, he ordered the chaffeur to turn about and drive home.

His appearance was but little changed when he entered his apartment, so that his wife, though surprised at his return, sensed no special strangeness. He curtly explained that he had decided to spend the day at home, doing whatever necessary business over the telephone. He asked to be left alone until lunch time. As he removed his overcoat, the build of his body could be seen. It was a business man's athletic body over which the clothes fit snugly, showing powerful posteriors, broad shoulders, and deep chest. His stomach tended towards corpulency. It was held in check by regular golf.

Once in his room with the door closed, he walked slowly to the window, twenty-one stories above ground, which opened southward and from which he could see in the distance the towering forms of several sky-scrapers. One of these, a comparatively slender form, stood erect and mighty against the sky, with no competition from surrounding buildings. It was his. It bore his name. The Drackman Tower.

It caught his eye, and then his fancy. With hands clasped behind his back, with face glowering at it, the more he looked the more the form fascinated him. Before long, he was unable to take his eyes from it. He gazed at it as if it were crystal. Then, after a time, he managed to jerk away. He strode about the room in a strange, intense, animal sort of way. Soon the skyscraper drew him back to it. With a wild glaring of his eyes he again stood before the window. Again he gazed as if at a crystal.

A strange thing happened. As he looked, the building gradually lost its rigidity and became plastic, almost palpitating, as though it were no longer a thing of steel and stone but a great towering mass of human flesh. And then this flesh, at first formless, took human shape. It took the shape of a man. The shape of himself! The shape of Daniel C Drackman! His head, an exact duplicate of his head and face crowned the body of what had been a skyscraper.

The eyes of the head were looking directly at him, over the roofs and through the murky atmosphere of New York. The head bowed. The face smiled. Drackman bowed and smiled back. The figure, gazing intently at him, a giant figure, raised one arm and removed its derby. He made as if to remove his derby. The hat was cast aside. Daniel repeated the gesture. The figure sharply clicked its heels and brought itself to a military salute. Drackman brought himself to the same salute. The giant looked sternly, commandingly at him, as though it were a superior officer rebuking him for a failure of office. He gazed back and reprimanded the giant. Then the figure relaxed and smiled and began swaying softly to and fro like a coy young girl. Drackman did likewise. The figure kicked up its heels in a sort of fandango. So did Daniel. The figure stopped dead, and glared at him with the eyes of a demon. Drackman, demon-like, glared back. Again it swiftly softened and this time raised one arm, in the manner of an aesthetic dancer, skyward. But instead of imitating the gesture, Daniel raised his eyes aloft; and there he saw a marvelous diaphanous female form pleading with him to follow her. He moved forward impulsively, threw up the sash, and was about to step out the window—when the form disappeared and in its place there shone a great lambent star. It cast over the world a lustrous silver light that dazzled him. In wonder and amazement he stood arrested, and then drew back. Then, suddenly, the entire vision vanished. The giant resolved into the skyscraper. The window showed only the commonplaces of New York.

The expressions of Drackman's face underwent marked and rapid changes from bright flush to ashen grey. With an abrupt turn, he left the window and walked towards his favorite arm chair. His movements were slow. He almost dragged his feet, like a beast with a bullet in its rump; and yet, there was a stealthy wary precision in each step he took. He eased into his chair. And there, without sign or change of expression he sat for upwards of half an hour. On his face were the same dual aspects: the lower part seemed rigid, semi-paralyzed; but his eyes, set in their deep sockets, glared with animal canniness. The entire room was like himself. It too was intently silent, immobile, yet charged with invisible forces.

Just then a round of child-laughter, gay and impetuous, came from another part of the apartment; and not long afterwards his young daughter with curls dancing and cheeks aglow suddenly burst into his room. She romped in to show her father the queer animals drawn in a picture book. Aware only of her own joy and wonder, not sensing the change wrought in him, she climbed upon his lap as was her custom and began turning the book's pages enthusiastically. She wanted him to see and share her delight over the queer animal creatures.

The instant of her entrance, an automatic centre of control had taken Drackman's external behavior under its direction. It made the muscles of his face contract so that his face smiled. His muscles smiled at his child. It made his head nod yes and no to her running comments and questions. It made his eyebrows lift so as to express appropriate curiosity and amazement. It raised Drackman's left arm so that his hand rested on the crown of her head. His hand stroked her hair. It moved down the back of her head till his fingers felt the warm silken skin of her neck. His fingers toyed with her neck.

This gesture, though also automatic, connected with his caged intelligence and stimulated the thought that simply by pressing hard he could choke this bit of life to death. How extraordinary! How frail, how mortally weak life was! How powerful, Drackman! He had power by pressure to cause the mystery of life to cease! As his fingers toyed with her neck, his mind played with this idea. He felt no impulse to exert the pressure; it was simply the idea, the lucid recognition of the fact, that engaged him. It was quite impersonal, as if a disembodied unit of consciousness were observing the frailty of a breathing body.

Before long the child was called to get dressed for lunch. The children were going visiting that afternoon. Drackman permitted her to go.

Soon after she left, he sprang to his feet, rushed into the hall, grabbed his hat and coat, and, without word to anyone, slammed the apartment door behind him.

He made straight for the office of his lawyer whom he greatly disturbed by ordering papers drawn so that he could settle a large portion of his wealth on his wife and children. The lawyer was an old friend of his, but Daniel offered no explanation of his actions. Aside from stating, with evident lapses into strange mutterings, what he wished done, his sole expression was impatience with the slowness of legal procedure. This business started, and, for the time, completed, he went out on the street and began walking about.

Happening to find himself on the corner of Fifth Avenue and 42nd Street, he walked east on 42nd to Madison Avenue, then south on Madison to 40th Street. He turned west on 40th and walked to Fifth Avenue. Then south on Fifth to 38th, east on 38th to Madison. He walked north on Madison to 40th, then west on 40th to Fifth, and north on Fifth to 42nd Street. And then, having thus arrived back at his starting point, he again strode off to go over the same route. He knew he had cut a figure 8, and he wanted to cut it again because the cutting of it gave him a strange satisfaction. So Daniel C Drackman cut it again. Down 42nd, south on Madison, west on 40th, south on Fifth, east on 38th, north on Madison, west on 40th, north on Fifth—and back again! He gave a grunt, smiled, tipped his hat to the Lenox Library, and was off again.

After the third lap he felt hungry; so he went into the first restaurant to catch his sight. It was small and cheap, crowded at the noon rush hour with clerks, stenographers, salaried office people. Had the largest table been vacant it would have been too small for him. Four men were occupying the place he wanted. He took twenty dollars from his pocket, gave five to each of them and told them to treat themselves to a swell lunch elsewhere. With smiles and shakes of the head the men got up and left. The entire restaurant then turned to serve and stare at Drackman.

Towards the middle of the afternoon he returned to the apartment. Martia was greatly worried. Upset by his abrupt leaving, she had been further alarmed by a phone message from the lawyer. Before he had time to remove his coat she approached him, impulsively threw her arms about him, buried her head on his broad chest, and then, after a short while, raised her eyes. He could see tears glistening on the surface of her pain and fear. Martia was very beautiful when she suffered.

"Why, Daniel?" she asked, her eyes searching his face.

He held himself muscular and aloof. His brows contracted and his powerful voice told her: "For your good."

"For my Good? I don't understand." For a moment she looked stunned, bewildered. She clutched him and asked: "Why, why, oh tell me Daniel? Has something happened?"

"Nothing," he said.

She felt him repulsing her. He disliked seeing her weakly feminine.

Remembering this, she stepped back from him and tried to collect herself. In a voice stronger and steadier she wanted to know: "Wouldn't you like to tell me about it?"

Drackman's eyes suddenly leapt forward, glaring. "I'll tell you this," he said savagely, "I never want to hear of money again! Don't ask me, don't question, don't mention it!"

Martia recoiled as though he had struck her.

Then his face broke into a strange grin. He spoke to her amiably, but with a queer chill tone: "You know, dear Martia, you are growing too soft. It does not become people to grow soft. To become soft, soft, softies. To lose confidence in themselves. To disintegrate. Ah, you see what I mean, dear Martia? You are growing too soft. Our children are growing too soft, too soft and silken, too weakly mortal. Ah, you see? A mere pressure on the neck—and where is life? Like the cat and the fiddle, it has jumped over the moon!" He raised his brows archly. Then, sternly—"We must be sturdy, yes, powerful and hard and sturdy! We must be a trifle assertive, self-assertive. For who can tell what day the Iron Man goes smash? For who can tell what day the engine jumps the tracks? Softies cannot cut figure 8s in New York. No, no. No, no, Martia," and he wagged his finger at her. "No, no, not in New York!" He kicked his heels in a fandango.

Before she could adjust to her fear and amazement, Drackman had suddenly wheeled about and left the apartment. She was too spellbound to try to detain or even follow after him. For some moments after the door slammed she stood rooted on the spot. And then, giving way to an on-rush of conflicting emotions, she sped to her room, banged the door, threw herself on the bed, and sobbed and sobbed. Now and again she would jerk erect with startled eyes, as if seeing a horrible figure in a nightmare.

Towards evening Daniel returned. This time, he let himself in quietly. With as little noise as possible he went to his room, put on a dinner coat, and, after securing a bottle of Johnnie Walker from a locked cabinet, again quietly slipped out. Martia heard his movements, but dared not approach him.

He went downtown and took a room in a hotel in the Vanderbuilt Avenue section. Once in his place, he uncorked Johnnie Walker and began drinking toasts to himself. It was his intention to sally forth later on to some night club and tear the lid off. Toasts were interrupted for dinner in his room. As soon as the table was removed, toasts began again. There were only two mirrors; one on the bureau, and a long one on the inside of the bathroom door. Daniel swung this door open so that the mirror would be in the room. Then, alternately standing before the long one, and sitting before the short one, he drank toasts to himself.

As the whiskey loosened him he grew loquacious and witty. He began speaking out loud, with appropriate changes of tone, so that anyone passing would surely have thought several men were in the room. He grew hearty and boisterous. He roared and rocked. He made more hilarious noise than ten men at a stag party. A neighbor complained. The office telephoned the request that he and his company modify their conduct. Drackman flew into a rage and told the whole hotel to go to hell. He dared them to come up and try to do anything about it. But after this, he grew more sober. A glance at his watch told him that it was still too early for the club. So, finishing the bottle, he lay back in a chair. A heavy, drowsy feeling came over him. Lest he go to sleep he got up and began pacing the room. And then he remembered that he had not had time for a bath at home. Immediately he drew one. He let himself into a warm tub. The warmth felt good. He wanted the water hot. He let in hot water, hot as he could bear. He stayed in quite a while; and when he got out, he felt so clean, glowing, relaxed, that he decided to luxuriate on the bed for a short time. A minute later he was dead to the world.

Early the next morning Drackman awoke, saw the strange room, and felt in full possession of his senses. His mind was clear, active. His emotional state quiet and normal. Nor were there hang-overs from the bottle of Johnnie Walker. Realizing that he had been out all night, his first act was to telephone Martia. Her tone was strained, nervous, anxious, sounding as though she had had no sleep. Daniel, with a gruff hearty voice, seeming to have forgotten his odd behavior of the day before, made light of her worries, tenderly joshed her for being a lovely child frightened without warrant. Then, as quickly as he could, he left the hotel and took a taxi to the apartment.

Martia was standing near the door awaiting him, not knowing what to expect. She made ineffectual attempts to control her twitching nerves. Her face was lined and drawn. It appeared aged. Under her eyes were dark circles. The minute he entered she threw herself into his arms and buried her head in his overcoat. She wanted to hold and to be held by him; she also wanted that he not see her face.

To her great surprise Daniel folded her with tenderness, petted, caressed her, and continued joshing her for being a frightened child. He lifted her head and kissed her; then rubbed his face, bristly with a day's growth, against her cheek. With rumbling laughter he made fun of her dark circles and kissed them away. To each of her attempted questions he gave a jocose turn, making it appear that her concern had been caused not by his conduct but by the circumstance that she had been left alone in the apartment for one night. He was so like the usual Daniel that

Martia's apprehensions soon gave way to a deep-felt relief and a low cry of joy.

The family had breakfast together. Daniel was natural with the children. With them also he was hearty and jovial. Indeed the general atmosphere was so bright and familiar that though she could not help secretly looking for signs of strangeness, Martia was compelled to half-believe that it was she who had just awakened from a nightmare. In any case, she decided to pretend that nothing unusual had happened. She would drop the matter and try to forget it.

Drackman went down to his offices; and for a week thereafter he moved about the world much like his normal self.

Then, however, he again began acting queerly. Again his behavior evidenced an acute change. But this time the signs were less fantastic, more subtle and psychological. They arose, as people sensed, from an increasing wish to assert himself, exhibit his exploits, win praise, and feed his ego.

His change of attitude towards business was quite obvious. Formerly, Drackman had taken his various feats as a matter of course, not even a single triumph going to his head. Now he brought his conquests home and paraded them. At the dinner table—he saw to it that each night there were a number of guests, Martia being insufficient audience—he would dominate the conversation and draw all attention to himself; and then, after telling of his projects or achievements, he would lay [sic] back and glow and purr like the cat who has swallowed the canary. Daniel was a big cat. His ego-hunger had a strange subterranean intensity. Martia and whoever was with him were compelled to feed it. They were drawn into praising him. They could not help it. But she and they began resenting him.

As his pride in himself increased, his regard for other business men diminished. One Sunday morning Martia handed him the paper and called his attention to a picture showing a group of the country's leading men of industry. Daniel gazed at the picture. With a burst of anger and contempt he spat at it, exclaiming that these men were nothing but soft timid little shopkeepers made to appear big and bold by the conditions of big business. His pinky-finger could bowl them over.

Old friends of his began realizing that he was a different Daniel. Towards them he was closed, and gave nothing. He appeared to be open, he tried to act as if he were. He indulged in generous smiles. He encouraged conversation. But they could not help but feel his false self-centeredness. He had grown intensely selfish. He was so avid for assertion and praise that they could clearly see these motives behind all his behavior.

Or if, for a time, he failed, if someone else happened to make a praiseworthy remark, Daniel might pretend to receive and value it, even thanking the person, verbally. Inwardly, and in fact, he would hate him and cut him to pieces.

He grew destructively critical of his favorite authors, calling them imbeciles, charging them with stupidly misleading the public mind.

More and more it became evident that, to him, no one could do anything, feel anything, think anything, no one save Drackman. There were only three things he wished to do: assert himself, win praise, destroy competition.

However much his acquaintances, through fear, outwardly yielded to him, inwardly they drew away and, when possible, found good reasons for avoiding his company.

He did a number of odd things. For one, the matter of tailors, shirtmakers, and haberdashers. Ever [sic] so often he would stay at home and have these people come to him. Several who had served him for years, who were accustomed to giving him the very best impersonal attention, were curtly dismissed without explanation. The new ones called in, if they were clever, soon caught the idea that Drackman wished them openly to admire him, his build, his taste, his sense of materials. They put it on as thick as they dared; but if they, poor fellows, fearing lest they over-flatter him, reduced their tones, he would dispense with them. If their praise grew flat, or too repetitious, or if he tired of hearing anyone's voice, the same thing happened.

He wanted his barber to tell him how handsome he was.

He bought several new cars, with the wish of having the salesman say that now he possessed the finest car in the world. "But how about the other car?" he might ask, a severe, threatening frown on his face. If the salesman were quick witted and replied, "That *was* the best car in the world—until you bought this," all would be well. Drackman's hard expression would give way to a roguish smile—"Ah, that's different!" But should the man fail to say the right thing, not only would the sale be lost, but Daniel might lodge a complaint against the service.

Then, the matter of chauffeurs. The driver who had been with Drackman fifteen years was suddenly discharged. Daniel placed an order with an agency. One after the other these new chauffeurs were tried and fired. One day, however, with a new man beside him, Drackman barely avoided, by brilliant driving, collision with another car. The man was forced to exclaim, "That was great, Mr. Drackman!" Whereon, to his amazement, Daniel turned with a huge smile, clapped him on the back and shouted, "You know it was!" Thereafter the man would have been indeed dull not to have seen what his master wanted. He gave it to him, thick and heavy. With the result that the agency received no more calls, and the chauffeur's salary was raised twenty-five dollars a week.

It was just about this time that one of his friends saw Drackman striding down 42nd Street. The friend spoke to him, but Daniel did not hear. So, moved by a queer impulse, he began following. He followed Drackman south on Madison, west on 40th, south on Fifth, east on 38th, north on Madison, west on 40th, north on Fifth—and back again to 42nd. In short, he discovered Drackman cutting the figure 8.

The spectacle shocked him. It gave him the feeling of seeing a powerful engine jump the tracks. Something warned him not to accost Daniel; but, impelled to speak to someone, he got in touch with Martia. She in turn, badly shaken by the news, arranged for an immediate conference between herself, the friend, the lawyer, and the family physician.

They concluded that since Drackman was not dangerous as yet it would be inadvisable to take direct action. For should anyone approach him on the matter, he would be sure to fly into a rage, aggravate the condition, and become stark mad. They would pretend not to see his oddities. They would humor him, and, at the same time, keep a strict watch, perhaps hire a man to shadow him and report. They did worry, however, lest people and the newspapers get hold of the story that Daniel C Drackman was cutting figure 8s in the centre of New York.

Martia, anticipating a sudden outburst, sent the children away to visit relatives, and temporarily dismissed the servants.

Meanwhile, Drackman himself was growing more and more preoccupied with an idea which fascinated him. Towards outside affairs he became increasingly indifferent. Often he would stay at home, as he said, to think. Or, if he went to his offices, he would close himself in his private place and give orders that no one was to disturb him. The slightest interruption made him furious.

He began writing. Sometimes he would sit and brood for an hour or more, then grab pen and fill pages. Sometimes without preliminaries he would suddenly seize paper and write away for unpredictable periods. He set his private secretary typing manuscripts.

Soon he insisted on showing his stuff not only to Martia and those of his close friends who still remained, but to his employees, anyone. He almost dragged them in to read or listen. He was avid that their responses feed his sense of self-importance and achievement.

When read, the pages were felt to contain a powerful, a demonic force. But the ideas, the images, though highly provocative, were wild and disordered. He seemed unable to put down just what he meant to write. Beneath this chaos there was, one sensed, a single dominant idea. He wrote around it, never touching it, never explicitly expressing it. Scien-

tific facts about animals, facts and fictions about man, fictions and phan-
tasies about God—all tumbled on, streamed onto and spread over his
pages.

Things came to pass that everyone who could deserted him. They
shunned him as they would a mad-man.

For some while he appeared not to notice their withdrawal. But in
truth he did. Inwardly, he was hypersensitive. He saw what they were
doing, and he hated them. He tried to compel company. When he found
he could not, he began interpreting everyone's behavior in terms of
jealousy. He told himself they were jealous of him, jealous of his ideas, of
his writing. Martia also was jealous.

Indeed, one day, in a fit of rage, he openly accused her. She was wise
enough not to oppose him at the time. She watched her chance, and, at
the first opportunity, in a quiet but firm tone told him he was mistaken.
She tried to explain just what had caused people to avoid him. She also
mentioned that for all his writing neither she nor anyone knew what he
was driving at, it was all so jumbled.

To her surprise, this remark crumpled him. Of a sudden he collapsed,
and looked like a big overgrown boy who has been unjustly scolded.

For several days he sat around the apartment gloomy and depressed.
He would not go out. She could not get him to move. His meals had to be
brought to him. His body seemed huge, large and heavy as a ton. His
deep eyes smoldered. He wrote nothing.

Martia was more fearful of this state than of the previous one. She
could not tell what was happening inside him.

Then, one afternoon after long brooding, Drackman suddenly leapt
from his chair with a roar. His eyes gleamed with mad triumph. His
entire frame vibrated. He shook his fist at an invisible foe who, presumably, was retreating in terror from the roused Iron Man.

"Martia!" he yelled.

She came in quickly, shaking all over.

"Martia!" he shouted, "I have it!"

"Yes, Daniel," she said meekly.

"I have it! You thought you could floor the Iron Man, did you? Listen!
Tell this to the dogs and insects who thought I was beaten. Tell them, I
say!" he roared the command.

"Yes, Daniel, I will," said Martia, "but they are not here now."

"Get them! Get my friends! Get my dogs and insects! Take a net and
catch them!"

"But, Daniel, you haven't told me what it is yet."

"Haven't I?" he asked, with a surprised frown. He made a strange self-
satisfied smile. "Haven't I? Then you listen. I'll tell you first. Wives,

especially good wives, should be told first. Do you remember the old legend telling how the Gods, jealous of man's power, fearful that man would dominate them, deliberately cut man down and took away his force? Well, no matter if you remember or not. You get the idea. You do, don't you?"

"Yes," said Martia, fearing what would follow.

"Then get this idea also. If man has been cut down, our job is to rise up again. Our job?" he asked. *"My* job," he said with great emphasis. "My job! I don't give a damn what others do, so long as they don't interfere with me. My job is to assert myself. Do you get that? My job is to assert myself! I've got to win back dominion over the earth. I've got to conquer the skies. I've got to rule earth and heaven!"

"But Daniel," she nervously interposed, "you already rule thousands of men."

"Not enough," he told her. "Not enough. What are a thousand men? Napoleon ruled an army. Daniel C Drackman is greater than Napoleon!"

Of a sudden he softened, twinkled his eyes, and asked: "Do you remember what I told you not so very long ago? It was when the idea first came to me. I can repeat it word for word. You think I've gone mad, but I'll be damned if I have. To prove that I haven't, I'll repeat what I said then verbatim. Here goes!"

He did recall exactly, with a few significant additions: "You know, dear Martia, you are growing too soft. It does not become people to grow soft. To become soft, soft, softies. To lose confidence in themselves. To disintegrate. Ah, you see what I mean, dear Martia? You are growing too soft. Our children are growing too soft, too soft and silken, too weakly mortal. Ah, you see? A mere pressure on the neck—and where is life? Like the cat and the fiddle, it has jumped over the moon!" He raised his brows archly. Then, sternly—"We must be sturdy, yes, powerful and hard and sturdy! People call me hard-boiled. I am hard-boiled! I am iron! I am steel! I am the Steel Man! You see? We must be a trifle assertive, self-assertive. For who can tell what day the Steel Man goes smash? No, the Steel Man will not smash! For who can tell what day the engine jumps the tracks? No, the engine will not jump the tracks! Softies cannot cut figure 8s in New York. No, no. No, no, Martia," and he wagged his finger at her, but with force. "No, no, not in New York!" He kicked his heels in a fandango. Then he brought his feet down with a bang.

"Enough!" he yelled. "I have a book to write!"

He chased her out, slammed the door, and started writing. Now he was aware of his central idea and felt sure that he could clearly powerfully express it. No beating about the bush this time!

Not long after, he again called Martia. He brusquely took her arm and led her to their sitting-room, and there, indicating a stiff upright chair, commanded her to sit in it without moving. She obeyed him.

He himself began pacing back and forth, glowering at her each time he passed. Strange noises came from him. They pleased him. He made them louder. Louder. He was working up to a high state.

"Whist!" he hissed. He paused. He smiled.

He made Martia take and hold a difficult posture, arms crooked, head tilted at an angle, eyes looking at him worshipfully.

He stalked the apartment, from room to room, emitting the strange noises. He was like a caged wild animal.

"Whist!"

He passed Martia, severely frowned at her, jerked his head away— "Whist!" Then a sharp whistle rising to explode—"Zuy! Whist! Bang! Zip, zip! Whist, bang, bouy!"

Elation on his face he stalked quicker.

Of a sudden his face clouded. He wheeled about and confronted a table-lamp. He accused and condemned it. Then his features broke and he smiled at it mysteriously, perhaps in pardon. After all, its offense was not serious.

A burst of dynamic power seized him. Off he started about the apartment.

"Whist!" Pause, his ears listening intently for a counter challenge. Then, rapid fire—"Whist, bang! Zuy! Zip, zip, whist, bang, bouy!"

"Ah, Daniel!" in great self-praise. "Ah, my great Daniel! Daniel, my boy! Daniel, my man! Iron Man! Steel Man! Zuy, bouy! Zip! Zip! Bang! Bouy!"

And so it went on.

When he tired, he released Martia and chased her from the room. He himself immediately started writing.

At unexpected hours during the next few days he forced his wife to assist him repeat this ceremony.

Finally he turned on her and asked:

"Where are those jealous friends of mine? I haven't seen them for a long time. What's the matter? Afraid of me? Jealous? Where are those dogs and insects? I thought I told you to get a net and catch them. You haven't? Well, never mind. I have a plan. Ah, Martia, a good one! A great plan! I'm going to leave New York! To hell with New York! I'm going to build myself a fortress in a forest, or on an island! You see? Drackman's Castle! The great fortress of Daniel C Drackman. I have a tower in New York. I'll have a castle in the wilds of America. I'm going to live there until I've finished my book. Too many interruptions in New York. Too much spineless jealousy. Bad atmosphere for a great creation. Get this, my dear. I will leave next week. I'll fly from here like a bat out of hell! My friends, the dogs and insects, won't mind coming for a farewell party, will they? Of course they won't. If they know they are going to be free of me, they'll come. They'd better come, or I'll come back and break the necks of every last one of them! The dogs! The insects! Now you, Martia, my dear, you tell them my plan, and invite them to my farewell party. Get this. It will be this coming Saturday. You make all the arrangements save one. I'll make that."

She was in terror of the outcome. She felt certain that he would use the occasion to insult them and get revenge. He would contrive some diabolical way to tear the roof off. Yet, seeing that he was in earnest, not daring to oppose him, she said she would do whatever necessary, all save the thing he himself wished to do.

Drackman himself attended to the following. He had a special caterer make a special cake according to his design. It was to be a huge cake with white frosting and many candles, and, in the centre, there was to be placed a tall wax figure moulded into the shape of a skyscraper, an exact copy of his skyscraper, the Drackman Tower.

On the evening set, everything was in readiness. The skyscraper cake was on a large table, candles lit. The room had no lights save these.

Martia flurried about. Daniel stalked the reception-room, impatiently waiting the first arrival. He glowered, clenched his fists, made noises.

When the bell rang a strange smile crossed his face. Martia opened the door. Daniel went forward savagely to greet his guest. But, to his immense surprise and satisfaction, the friend looked exactly like himself. He seemed to be a small edition of Daniel C Drackman. Daniel shook hands cordially. The next person, and the next, all looked like Drackman. He was in high spirits. He carried on a vigorous, hilarious conversation with these friends, these duplicates of himself. When all were assembled, he, the father of this flock of Iron Men, Steel Men, Daniels and Drackmans, led them with pomp to the dining-room.

At sight of the cake they went into ecstasies.

Then, while their gaze was on it, with one great blast he blew the candles out, and at the same time pulled a concealed switch. Lo! Lights shone from all the windows.

All the Drackmans uttered Ah! The spectacle well nigh overcame them.

Drackman himself gazed intently at it. As he gazed, the wax began to move, to change. It became a towering mass of human flesh. The flesh took shape, human shape. The shape of a man. The shape of himself!

His head, an exact duplicate of his head and face crowned the body of what had been wax.

The eyes of the head looked at him. The head bowed. The face smiled. Drackman bowed and smiled back. The figure clicked its heels and brought itself to a military salute. So did Daniel. The giant rebuked him. Drackman rebuked the giant. It relaxed and began swaying to and fro like a coy young girl. He did likewise. The figure kicked its heels in a fandango. Daniel kicked a fandango. The figure stopped dead, and glared at him with the eyes of a demon. Drackman, demon-like, glared back. Then the figure began talking to him. It spoke rapidly with great power. It argued. Daniel argued back. It got enraged and shouted curses. He, enraged, cursed it. The figure insinuated. It said that Martia had been unfaithful to him, that he, Daniel, had been unfaithful to her. Drackman shouted and denied and said the figure lied. The giant, furious with hatred, reached up, clutched a ball of dazzling light, and hurled it. The ball struck Drackman between the eyes. He saw a blinding whiteness. Then all went black.

After a week of special treatment such as given those suffering from influenza, Drackman was convalescent. It was as if the germs of egomania, having run a critical course in him, were being rapidly expelled back into New York's atmosphere. Medical men and psychiatrists, specialists of long experience, marvelled at the speed of his recovery. It was due, they said, to his phenomenal constitution.

Before a month had passed, Daniel C Drackman, the Iron Man, now the Steel Man, was up and about, doing business as usual.

[1929]

The Scottsboro Boys

Those who have been caught in a machine will sympathize with the plight of the Scottsboro boys. Those who have freed themselves will realize how much they owe to the help of others. So let us help these boys in every way we can, for surely their suffering is greater than our own.

Justice aids life; law often takes it. That we need less law and more justice has never been so true as it is today. It would be an amazing thing for the world at large and for the nine S[cottsboro] boys in particular to have justice prevail in their case. Those who have been caught in a machine, who have gotten free, realize how much they owe to the help of others. I for one feel that I may in some measure pay my debt[.] I feel I must help these boys in every way I can.

Then let us, who are free today, help liberate these boys who are caught.

Most of us at one time or another have been caught in a machine, though few have been in so painful a plight as the S[cottsboro] Boys. How did we get free? Partly by our own merit, largely owing to the help of others. The help of others. So let our realization of this arouse us in turn to help liberate these boys who merit to be as free as any of us, who need our help.

[1933?]

American Letter

The election of Herbert Hoover to President of the United States was and is, in my opinion, the most important election in the history of this country. Its significance is three-fold. First, it was more than a political event; it was an experience which involved the entire life and direction of America. Second, it was an emphatic decision made at what may well be the most critical period of America's history. Mr. Hoover, in all probability, will be President for the next eight years. He will not be a figure-head; he will be an active centre of influence. Those whom he represents, namely, the dominant American type, a practical, factual, business, rational type, will be in control of the nation's affairs for the next eight years. During this period the fate not only of America but of western civilization will probably be decided. Third, the election solidified both the best and the worst features of our national and personal life. It gave us opportunity to see ourselves more clearly and more surely than ever before. No thinking person is now in doubt as to the general characteristics and tendencies of the American people. In short, an analysis of this election would lead to a fairly complete and accurate understanding of our psyche. In this letter I will do no more than suggest certain of its meanings.

It is interesting to note that before the election almost everyone, whatever his party, whatever his social class, whatever his temperament, knew without doubt that Hoover, a successful business administrator, would be elected; that Smith, a successful politician, would be defeated. This simply means that most of us, consciously or unconsciously, understood the dominant forms and forces of our country. We understood that Hoover corresponded to them; that Smith did not.

Herbert Hoover is a symbol. He is a symbol of Business, Efficiency, Prohibition, Protestantism. He represents the practical, capable, unfeeling, unimaginative type. He assures us that we have definitely passed beyond the phase of social idealism, that we are ready literally to get down to business. No longer need we be disturbed by attractive but unprofitable dreams, feelings, aspirations. He promises us continued Prosperity. And Prosperity is a term which includes all that is desirable in life. Woodrow Wilson proposed to make the world safe for democracy. Hoover convinces us that the world is for business.

In Alfred Smith the old idealism, the former manner of emotional appeal, still lingered. He spoke, so to say, of a finer and better society. He was, therefore, a source of disturbance. We did not want him. He was behind the times. At any rate, he was not of this time.

Some years ago Sinclair Lewis wrote *Babbit*. Even then, all the Babbits wanted a business administration. Now they have it.

In barber shops before the election you often heard: "We will see whether America wants for president a business man or a politician." We have seen.

Thomas A. Edison said, in effect: "The United States Government is the greatest business in the world. Herbert Hoover is the man best qualified to run it." We had no doubt as to the first part of Edison's statement. By an overwhelming majority we have shown our belief in the second part.

In short, Hoover evoked the support of typical American business. His election solidified our dominant commercial forms. It gave impetus and assurance to all things associated with this field of life.

It means that the direction we have taken since the World War will be continued and accelerated. Personally, I think this is a hopeless direction. From the standpoint of creative national life and culture it is, of course, open to severe criticism. From the standpoint of world harmony it is open to severe criticism. Here, however, I am basing my opinion on the testimony of those who outwardly support this direction and appear to profit by it. For these same people, in their sincere inner lives and feelings, reject it and know they are not profiting by it. Yes, any number of business men like business as a game. It is good sport. But there are many who feel that it is a dirty game, a burden, a thing to be rid of as quickly as possible. Thousands of them accept the present with distaste and eagerly look forward to the time when, having accumulated sufficient wealth, they can retire. Thousands of business men impatiently await the day when they can quit. They aim, as we say, to make their pile and pull out. This is not the attitude of one who values a thing. On the contrary, this is the attitude of one who hates a thing. Much of the talk about the greatness and glory of business is "bunk" and "boosting" of the worst kind. However . . .

The election also means that Business will increase its domination over all other forms of American life. The arts, sciences, and professions, will be even more constrained to take the tempo and technique of commerce, industry, finance, and advertising. Advertising is the great American vice.

Bernard Shaw has pointed out that business in its proper sphere is, as it were, quite all right; but that when it assumes the role of governing, as in America, it is a source of destructive behavior. Well, we are on the way to seeing business not only assume the role of governing, but be the government, more, be America. Soon we will say, America is Business.

We have some literature. We have great quantities of literary-business. We have some art. Quantities of art-business. We have some excellent physicians and dentists. We have a great deal of medical and dental business. And so on. Education, science, religion, philosophy, in short, all professions and all forms of culture are coming to be but branches of Big Business.

The majority of the American people appear to wish just this.

Also, it seems, the majority of us wish another war. At any rate, we are not willing to risk the loss of five dollars in order to avert another war. We know quite well that we are over-producing. We also know that over-production, together with a surplus of capital, leads necessarily to the establishment of foreign markets; and that competition for these markets brings nations to war. But over-production is, it appears, an inevitable part of our Prosperity. At all costs, we must have Prosperity. Hoover was elected to continue the reign of Prosperity which Coolidge or Harding, or somebody Republican, is supposed to have started. What do we care about life and the creative future of our country, if only we get a raise of salary and are able to buy a bigger motor-car and reside in a better part of town?

We fail to see and realize the large vital issues. This is because of faulty leadership. America's trouble lies not with the American people but with our rulers and their agents. We have sharp eyes for seeing petty issues and trivial gains. From the day we are born we are educated to see, and only to see, petty issues and trivial gains. We want these small things to get bigger and better. Bigger and better, always! This is the American slogan. There are things right at hand, already gigantic and important. We ignore these. We seek and find little things. We devote ourselves to magnifying them. This is characteristic of the American psyche. This is a ridiculous aspect of our character. Also, there is a serious and valuable aspect.

As to this latter . . . We are a nation of builders. A living need compels us to start with almost nothing and increase it. We find a wilderness and make a nation. We take a swamp or a prairie and build a city. Chicago, for example, is a city of this kind. It is built on the prairies at the side of Lake Michigan. There are men still living who recall the time when the region now occupied by it was what they call a "hog-wallow," that is, a region of mud-land. Today, it has a population of over three million people, people come from all quarters of the earth; and, next to New York, it is the most important city in America. Chicago is more American than New York. It is, I think, the typical American city.

People who dwell elsewhere hear much of the negative aspects of Chicago. They hear of its crime and gangsters, its racketeers and gunmen. Also, they hear of its stockyards and slaughterhouses. They hear of its vaudevillian politics. These reports are exaggerated; but there is truth in them. But Chicago also has a positive aspect. It gives rise to and maintains the finest qualities of American character. In this very juxtaposition of extremes of bad and good it is typically American. For America is a land—and we are a people—where and in whom the good and the bad, the beautiful and the ugly, the sincere and the hypocritical, intensified, magnified, exist side by side. No European nation is as enslaved to money-making, to mass standards, to standardization, to machines, as we are. Also, no European nation allows such opportunities for varying from the standard. The history of America is full of unique and even exceptional individuals. Ever [sic] so often one of our writer[s] gives us, to our surprise, the biography of one of them. Without understanding this, as it were, duality, it is difficult to understand America. And, I might add, without knowing Chicago, where this duality is most strikingly embodied, it is difficult to know the country of which it is typical. In any case, this great city, in less than a hundred years, has sprung up, has been built up, from a flat-land.

Our best business men have indeed started at the bottom and climbed up. Lincoln was born in a log cabin. Our best writers and artists work with crude stuff, without help from tradition, and, as in the case of Whitman, build it into imposing forms.

We like to plant seeds and see them grow. We are planters. In this we are creative. We are indifferent cultivators, indifferent harvesters. We are poor and sometimes criminal users. We tend to misuse the finished product. Here is our trouble: we have no feeling for the things we build. We put them up. We tear them down. We buy and sell. We live in a place for a short time. We move out. We tend not to value things. We are attached to less and less. Soon we will be attached to nothing. We respect less and less. Soon we will respect nothing. This trend is evident not only in the field of material products but also in the sphere of human relationships. We respect ourselves and each other less and less. Husband and wife, parents and children—decreasing respect. This is, of course, one of the main reasons why marriage and the home are dissolving.

Those of us who inherit a structure already made, whether it be wealth or culture, are likely either to make no use of it or squander it and dissipate ourselves.

We need to feel the resistance of crude materials. We need to see signal additions to America resulting from our efforts.

Our best feeling for President Hoover is associated with the belief that he can and will contribute notably to the intelligent organization and direction of the nation's affairs. He too has been and is a builder. We respond to him as to a symbol which represents our need and faith.

The election brought into bold relief the dominant American type. We may call this type the factual type. It is interested in facts, in tangibles. It is literal. It is practical. It is interested in doing things. It is extroverted. It is shy of emotions. It tends to inhibit feeling. It is prohibitive. It is unaesthetic, unimaginative. It is indifferent to art, religion, and philosophy. Or, if it is interested in these things, it tends to treat them rationalistically.

Of this type there are two sub-divisions. One sub-division covers the field of business. The other covers the field of literature and the professions. The majority of our best men and women fall into one or the other of these two general classifications. Those in the business world have, at best, practical ability, technical skill, inventive and administrative talents. At worst, they are futilely active. They bustle about, must bustle about. They waste time and energy, and accomplish nothing. Those in the literary or professional worlds have, at best, clear eyes and clear minds for seeing and thinking about the various aspects of factual experience. At worst, they reduce all things to a dry literal pedestrianism.

They may be liberal or conservative, vital or feeble, rich or poor. They have in common the factual approach and response to life. Also, they are similar in this: that they are not particularly concerned with the inner content of existence.

In the business world this type of person tends to become, as we say, "Hard-boiled," that is, so-called realistic, without feeling. He prides himself on being hard-boiled. Beneath the hard-boiled exterior you will usually find one or the other of two states: either cynicism or sentimentality. Some hard-boiled Americans are thoroughly hard-boiled. They are cynical towards themselves and towards life. They have belief and faith in nothing save in dollar; save in the power and pleasure to be had from making and spending money. Our literature contains very few examples of this kind. Babbit is authentic. But Babbit is basically sentimental. And, moreover, he is a minor character. Some of our big business men are major characters.

Other hard-boiled Americans are soft and sentimental underneath. During the day, when they have to be, they are realistic business men. At night, they like the weak sentiment of the movies, the radio, cheap novels, and popular songs. And, on Sundays, they may grow moist-eyed over the minister's sermon. This kind of business man is numerous. Here we come nearer to the Babbit type.

The psychology of the business American is the psychology of buying and selling for profit, with the help of salesmanship, propaganda, and advertising. If you come to him, he expects that you have come to sell him something, perhaps to "put something over him," that is, cheat or trick or swindle him. If your approach happens to be in terms of ideas, he thinks you are trying to "sell" him your ideas. He is on guard lest, by means of clever salesmanship, you will make him "buy" unprofitable or question-able opinions. In any case, he demands that your brand of ideas be well-advertised, and that it has the backing of a large established firm. In short, any kind of true intellectual exchange with him is difficult if not impossible.

If your approach happens to be in terms of art, he suspects that you are trying to sell him art. If in terms of life, of simple human relationships, the case is the same. And, on the other hand, if you have nothing to sell, you are indeed a suspicious character. In brief, his psyche is automatically closed to everything save business, it tends to reduce all things to buying and selling for profit.

Of course, this tendency to reduce things to the terms of one's own specialty is not peculiar to business men. A similar mechanism is present in artists and scientists. With artists it is art, art. Nothing but art. They want [the] entire world reduced to art. They tend to reject whatever is not art. With scientists it is science, science. Nothing but science. All things must meet scientific requirements. Whatever is not scientific they tend to rule out. Business, business, art, art, science, science—the psychology is similar.

I should mention that I make these statements not against the business man, or against business; not against artists, or against art; not against scientists, or against science. They are descriptive of a feature of the psychology of some business men, of some artists, of some scientists.

In literature the factual American produces the literal, so-called realis-tic novel. He transcribes this or that aspect of everyday experience. His work has points in common with the newspaper. He himself has points in common with the journalist, the news reporter. At the same time, the majority of our best novelists fall into this class. Sinclair Lewis, Dreiser, Booth Tarkington, and so on. Many of our younger writers though drawn towards the emotional, the intellectual, the imaginative, the symbolical, are nevertheless so dominated by the prevalent factualism that they either cannot or dare not free themselves from it. Waldo Frank is our one well-known writer who has tried to do so. His works do approach the symbolical. He would be more of a force amongst us if his manner of presentation were less irritating.

Mr. Frank, by the way, has just published a new work titled: *The Re-Discovery of America*. This book is just now being reviewed. The critics tend to agree in two respects: first, that Mr. Frank has made a valuable contribution to constructive criticism of America; second, that his style obstructs and diminishes the value of the book's content.

H. L. Mencken is factual.

Eugene O'Neill tends to loose his grasp and become murky and confused when he leaves the actual. His best work is with concrete dramatic matter in realistic situations. When he tries the symbolical and imaginative he tends to forfeit drama in favor of obscure tedious gestures and vague words.

Our best general magazines, with the exception of *The Dial*, are factual. They have decided political and sociological bents. They want articles, essays, stories dealing in a competent way with the tangible aspects of our world. As a rule, they are open to the formulations of advancing science. These formulations, however, must not be abstract. They must be concrete and rational. Science, in such a form, does not touch feeling. Our magazines are shy of feeling. They are closed to experiments in literature and art. Liberal in other ways, they are prohibitive of whatever strikes straight at emotions. They have little or no sense of, they place but scant value on, the aesthetic. They are strangely blind or indifferent to the potential. *The American Caravan,* a year-book, has come into existence for the purpose of encouraging and publishing the sort of things not wanted by our established organs.

In psychology, the factual type, notably represented by John B. Watson, has given rise to Behaviorism, a system of data and theories derived from observations of the facts of human behavior. Both in content and formulation it corresponds to the dominant American type. It is, therefore, the most influential of our approaches to an understanding of human nature. Just now, it is a source of disturbance in many quarters. This is because it goes counter to many of our pet preconceived notions of, and attitudes towards, life. And also, because Dr. Watson is aggressive and controversial. But soon this disturbance will die down. Behaviorism, or some modification of it, will reign without rival. It has the facts with it.

John Dewey is the outstanding contemporary American educator and philosopher. Dewey is pragmatic, that is, practical, factual.

It is, of course, a long reach from the average business man to John Dewey. And it may seem odd to group Babbit, Sinclair Lewis, Dreiser, O'Neill, Mencken, Watson, and Dewey in one class. Certainly there are sharp differences between these men. Their manners and abilities differ. But they all deal, or tend to deal with the actual aspects of experience. They are similar in that they approach the world and respond to it factually.

The majority of Americans either are, or want to be, of this type. In Herbert Hoover, whether they voted for him or not, they found an effective symbol. He addressed them practically, in terms of facts. He used the radio, and, doubtless, was glad to use it. For the radio, which eliminates the human element, which reduces man to sound (noise!), which cannot convey either feeling or imagination, is an excellent instrument in the service of the technical, statistical, factual type.

Mr. Hoover's campaign speeches were notable for two things: first, the presence of statistical data; second, the absence of emotional idealistic appeal. He stood before the American public as a commercial engineer, as a business administrator. He promised the maximum of practicality, the minimum of idealism. With his election, the factual type, already in the majority, became solidified and felt self-assurance. It received ample proof of its solidity and dominance.

There was a time when America was the proud bearer of social idealism. This was a land—and we were people—of independence, equality, and liberty. This now is altered. America is a land of business. We are business people. The election of Herbert Hoover was the decisive stroke of this change.

I should note, in concluding, that this change is not a spiritual defeat. It simply means, among other things, that human values, and the deep, moving, growing life forces, have definitely passed from the majority to the minority; that values and growing force have passed out of the keeping of the mass into the keeping of individuals. I expect to see this very circumstance give rise to solidarity among individuals. I expect to see the dominance of business cause the powerful emergence of a new way of life. There will be formed a new American type. This type will not necessarily oppose the factual type. Rather, it will balance it. It will take unto itself the functions proper to it.

[1929]

To Sleep

To sleep is neither to sense nor know what we lack. We sleep. In sleep, man, as a body, is immobile. Even the primary hungers do not animate us. We are not aware of the lack of food. We are not aware of the lack of sex. We are not aware of the lack of love. We feel no insecurity. We want neither energy nor power. We have no wishes, no emotions, no motives. Not even pride, or vanity, or egotism, or jealousy, or boredom, or ambition, not even pain and pleasure, move us. We are not moved by hope. We are inert to aspiration. We feel no need to grow. We feel no need to be. No thoughts, great or trifling, make us move an eyelid or change our rate of breathing. Save for our breathing we are like corpses. We do not see, hear, taste, smell, touch. We cannot think or feel or move.

In sleep, we are not pleasing to look upon. Sleeping people are ugly. We are sightless: we cannot see others nor can others see us. Our skin is pasty, moist, clammy. Our closed eyes have stuff in the corners. Our mouth is loosely open or grimly shut. We snore or make noises. Our hair is dishevelled. Our limbs are loose, or they are as stiff and rigid as ironing-boards. We are not pleasing to look upon; and we know it. The first thing in the morning on waking we try to arouse ourselves from a sunken ugly state and hasten to efface the signs of sleep before anyone sees us.

[1930]

Love on a Train

As if he were escaping from a thousand clamorous patients, Dr. Meron Coville rushed through the gate and boarded the Capitol Limited five minutes before it pulled out. He was leaving Chicago, on his way to New York—and then to Europe where he intended spending several months studying neurology, and, strange to say, art. A young practicing physician, interested in research, he also had a rather ardent love of art and of life, which of course included attractive women.

Barely thirty, his professional appearance and manner were such that they reassured and won the confidence of patients who otherwise might have been reluctant to place themselves in the hands of so young a physician. His work fulfilled the promise of his bearing. It was skilful, thorough, and intelligent. Dr. Corville was quite aware of his ability. He knew, indeed, that already he was well started on a brilliant career.

But to him his practice was something more than a social career, than a means of money-making. For, motivated by an active sense of decency towards others, and by feelings of responsibility and dignity as regards the medical profession, he seriously valued his work and was an out-spoken critic of those who degraded the professions by misusing them for vanity and dollars.

He was very good looking: regular featured, with dark hair and like-able brown eyes which frequently were not especially noticed because of glasses. These eyes of his never became cold and hard, not even when he was in the midst of his practice. There was always an affectionate warmth and kindliness in them. Their expression, as from one human being to another, alternated between personal and impersonal regard.

When off duty, owing to a temperament which demanded its portion of life's pleasures, he was exceedingly good company. Men liked him. Unmarried, he was accustomed to having women also respond, and, often as not, fall in love with him. As for himself—it was no discredit to his scientific interests that he felt the world lacking an essential something if there were no one with whom he was in love.

In truth, he had given much thought to the apparent opposition be-tween science and art, reason and love; between his career, on the one hand, and, on the other, his wish to experience vividly each moment, each event, purely, in and for itself. Phrasing the problem in somewhat philosophic terms, he saw it to consist of an acute juxtaposition of two dimensionally different worlds: the world of time, of becoming; and the world of now, of space, the world of being. His career placed him in the world of time. For what he did today was of value mainly only in terms of its bearing on the future. The very nature of his career compelled him to hope, and to race madly towards the fulfillment of the hope, that at some future time he would reap satisfying results from his present activities. Love and art placed him in the world of space. They permitted him to live now. They gave him immediate satisfaction and completion.

These two worlds, so different, existed side by side, doubtless inter-penetrating. Probably they were but aspects of a single higher reality. However this might be, their relationship and man's mode of functioning were such that no one could escape having a sort of dual experience, sometimes experiencing becoming to the exclusion of being, sometimes, though less frequently, experiencing being to the exclusion of becoming. Perhaps a superman could transcend them and consciously exist in one continuous inclusive state of being. Coville knew he was not a superman. For him, therefore, the practical problem was the sufficiently difficult one of making clean and satisfactory transitions from the one to the other. He rather prided himself for his ability to manage this problem.

He could, he believed, step quite well from the concerns of his career, drop them from his shoulders, wash his hands as it were, and experience the fulness of the eternal now.

True, the modern world gave him no assistance; on the contrary, it hindered him. For this world, in Coville's understanding, was largely a world of time, of becoming, a world of activity and futurities. It was a world of science, careers, and jobs. Art, love, feeling in general, had little or no place in it. It was a world of skyscrapers and transportation. Skyscrapers were vertical instrument-aspects of the time world. Trains, motor-cars, airplanes, were horizontal instrument-aspects of this same world. These aspects or forms compelled activity, but activity without rhythm, without feeling. Modern men and women, human relationships, all existed and occurred in one or the other of these forms. You were either in a skyscraper or in a motor-car. You did your job, and neither felt or loved or experienced life as beauty.

Coville recognized that he also in large measure was a modern product and that, therefore, owing both to external conditions and to internal conditioning, it was difficult for him to exist in feeling. But he had feeling, much of it. Enough to value it and to sense its absence round about him. And too, he had, or thought he had, sufficient control of himself to experience the feeling world whenever he wished.

Indeed, just at this time he was conclusively proving this. Yes, he had had to fight it out with himself. One does not easily pick up and leave his practice for a lark in Europe. Most men, instead of directing their careers, were directed by them. Most men were so enslaved by them that they could not cut free whatever the exertion. Nor had his wish to taste the joy and beauty of just living won its way without a fearful struggle with his professional conscience. However, here he was . . . Well, no, it was not exactly a lark; he was, in fact, going to put in serious work on necessary studies. But at the back of his mind Coville knew quite well that the main motive for the trip was his wish to have a gay four months in Europe where he would be free of past and future goads and responsibilities. Hence, in leaving Chicago, he demonstrated his ability temporarily to break with whatever bound him to the world of time. He still had to prove that he could make the transition and exist in the space world. The young doctor was confident that he would also demonstrate his ability as regards this latter to his entire satisfaction.

During the week prior to his leaving he had been so rushed as not to have a minute to himself. Foreseeing a sort of grim and hectic final period, he had taken one deep breath and plunged into a quantity of work which he feared he never could round off in the six remaining days. Somehow, however, his mind and body, once set moving at an unprecedented rate, had succeeded in accomplishing the necessary tasks. Twenty minutes before train time he had managed to finish the last business of an active, and, from many points of view, a very profitable year.

As he boarded the train, the momentum of his week's exertions swept along with him. He seemed pursued by a thousand clamorous patients, by all the sick people of Chicago. Hoping for a much needed relaxation, he dropped into the Pullman seat and tried to forget everything. But no sooner did his body come to rest than his nerves and emotions began to strain and roar. The plush stuffy stillness, the lack of motion, were unbearable. His face tensed. His hands trembled. He clenched them. He felt he wanted the train to start at once and race recklessly on. He wanted to be aboard something moving faster than a train ever could: a speeding rocket just shot from a powerful projector. There even came to his mind the notion of taking an airplane passage to New York.

It was a great relief to hear the conductor call all aboard; to feel the train start, slow and lumbering as its motion at first was. Once out of Chicago, it would begin speeding. This would be better.

Then, for the first time, he had a vivid sense that actually he was leaving Chicago. It gave him a feeling of power, of satisfaction, of time well spent, to glance backward at the amount of undoubtedly skilful work he had accomplished in the past year. What if some of his colleagues did consider him a bit crazy for pulling up and going abroad? Perhaps, if the truth were told, they were secretly envious. He had a sense of release when he realized that in fact he was temporarily free from the demands of his professional duties. His face lost his tenseness. He smiled. Indeed, something young and boyish and quite charming momentarily took possession of him and dispelled the doctor's serious countenance. Of a sudden he had an impulse to rush out on the observation platform and wave good-by to Chicago.

Instead, he jumped to his feet, assumed a grave important air, and made his way forward to the club car.

A number of men were there before him, some lolling, some entrenched behind newspapers and magazines. Grey curls and wreaths of smoke were being scattered by a fan. He found a vacant chair and began observing the various types round about him. Three priests. Theirs was a strange hardly to be imagined life. What did they really think of man and God? What were their sincere attitudes towards the people who depended on them for spiritual guidance, towards the people whom they guided or misguided? Several business men, obviously. And several whom Coville could not place. Again he had a sense of the number of human beings who are constantly moving back and forth across the earth's surface. Yes, here were people, himself included, locked in transportation. Having left one great collection of skyscrapers they were speeding towards an even greater collection of also skyscrapers.

There were several things which Dr. Coville wished to think over. Among other things it was necessary that he write and send back to Chicago before leaving America four or five letters of a serious character. What better place for writing them than on a train? He tried to compose them in his mind; but before long had to give up the attempt. The July heat oppressed him. And besides, he really needed a rest from close thinking.

So he ordered a lemonade, regretted that there was nothing stronger, took out his pipe and started smoking. The lemonade cooled, but also stimulated him. He crossed and recrossed his legs, shifted about in his chair, and grew very restless. Finally, unable longer to sit still, he left the club car in haste, with the intention of making a tour of the train and seeing who his fellow passengers were.

The motion of the now speeding train swayed and tossed his body. He had difficulty keeping balance. This unusual external motion caused his physical behavior nearly to correspond to the usual gyrations of his emotions.

As he rocked and progressed from car to car his eyes were observant of the curious assortment of people who raised their faces to regard him. There was a trace of eagerness, a suggestion of inquiry in his glance. Though appearing too serious and collected to obviously show it, young Dr. Coville, very good looking, could not entirely conceal that he was somewhat on the lookout for a somewhat desirable something.

Reaching the observation car, he noted that all the chairs on the platform were occupied; so he took an empty seat inside, a chair next to a well-dressed woman whose face, directed toward the rear windows, had been turned away from him when he entered.

It was not long before he began sensing that here was someone of possible interest. Wanting to get a better view of her, he was restrained from doing so by the notion that it would not do to look straight in the face of a strange woman who sat so close to him. His mind, however, started contriving a number of innocent schemes whereby with good conscience he could as it were casually glance in her direction. Then he caught himself at this trick; and was forced to smile at the ridiculous[ness] of it, and, by extension, to smile at the ridiculous general behavior of human creatures. What sound reason was there, he asked himself, why he should not openly and deliberately look straight at another human being if he wanted to? Well, it might be misinterpreted as flirting. Well, why not flirt if he wanted to? Was it going to hurt anyone? What was the matter with mankind anyway? What was the sense of all this hedging and straight-jacketing? You would think, from the way people behaved, that each one was in mortal fear of the other. That some great necessity compelled each one to hold off from the other lest the entire fabric of life be ripped to pieces. Why this shame of feeling? Why this idiotic compulsion to suppress and kill it? Besides—how absurd—in the course of his practice, how many women, perfect strangers, had he looked straight at? Hundreds. Then what was the idea? "Yes, my dear young Doctor," he told himself, "but that was strictly professional. This, my good looking young man, is strictly personal. Well, is there, in truth—let us say in the name of science—is there such an enormous difference between the two? Simply because I am myself on a train, I cannot look at this woman if I want to? Nonsense. I will do it at once."

He did.

Perhaps the same force which turned his eyes towards her, at the same time drew her face towards his—and for a flash their glances met. It was too swift, too brilliant, for either to get a good look at the other. But it was quite enough to send a current through both of them. Dr. Coville re-crossed his legs with a nervous jerk and unconsciously reached in his pocket for his pipe. She pretended to have noticed suddenly something of great interest out the window, a something which her eyes had to follow as it rapidly receded in the distance. This left her head averted. However, they retained a lively awareness of each other's presence.

Coville's impression of her, imperfect though it was, carried the conviction that she was very striking in appearance, stunning. Mature looking, but with a really young face. He had no doubt that she was proud, high-spirited, capable, self-sufficient. There remained in his mind a picture of the arch of her eyes. He told himself that it suggested the eagle, though softer than the sheer eagle quality.

Without obviously turning his head, he could see something of her figure and mode of dress. She seemed tall and rather athletic, with the build, not of an athlete, but perhaps of a person who had travelled much and used her body in difficult situations. She wore a well-made stylish tailored suit of some brown material he did not know the name of, but liked very much. Her hands were gloved. On her wrist was a finely fashioned serviceable watch. Something suggested that she was choice and exquisite in her tastes—perhaps it was the faint trace of the strangely alluring perfume she used.

Nor had she failed to receive an impression of Dr. Coville. Had some one asked her for it, doubtless she would have replied: "A serious kind of good looking young man who wants to flirt with me. I do not wish to be bothered with young men, and I do not wish to be flirted with."

In a short time his tenseness passed. He was able to tell himself: "Absurd! Asinine! If you want to speak to her why don't you? You think you can feel, and express feeling. You think you can live in the present moment. Well . . . What is the sense of this silly game? Here she is. She can do no more than cut you. It shan't be a mortal wound. You, Doctor, have inflicted graver ones. The earth will suffer no catastrophe. Neither heaven nor hell will be made or broken either way. But, by God! it would be pleasant to pass the time with her! Well, if you want to, why don't you? Who's stopping you, Dr. Coville?"

He thought of what he would say to her, what would be a good opening line. "Ask her if she likes to travel? No, my good looking young man, you can't start conversation with this young lady on such a flat note as that!"

Before he could hit upon a suitable start, one of the seats on the platform was vacated. The young lady immediately arose and occupied it.

Dr. Coville said to himself: "There now! Serves you right. Had your chance and didn't take it."

Even he was surprised at the sudden feeling of emptiness and defeat that came over him.

The train was gliding swiftly over miles of straight track, through a level wooded country, occasionally passing farms, gangs of laborers working on the road-bed, and small towns.

As Coville indulged his new-found interest in what was happening rearward of the train, never losing his young lady from the corner of his eyes, he also managed to notice that as long as the train passed through uninhabited country-side, it raised no dust, no dirt, nothing to spoil the view or cause discomfort. But let it pass through a town or village—dust and dirt, scraps of paper flew up and whirled in its wake, making people on the platform protect their eyes, or feel that they needed protection. It was not necessary to see the village; all one need do was to see the dirt fly and he would know he was passing through a place inhabited by the human species.

This observation raised in the Doctor's mind the question: Why were men such dirt-begetting creatures? Why was it that everywhere men went they marred, defaced, and often destroyed Nature? Men indeed were a horde of disintegrating agents, just the touch of whom was fatal. They touched Nature and razed It. They touched each other—and fell dead. They even glorified falling dead at each other's touch.

Coville recalled reading a book dealing with the destructive influence of men on Nature in Scotland. The facts put forth were of a startling character. This was but one example. Take the sum of man's behavior, and where could one find the slightest evidence to support man's absurd picture of himself—whether the picture were derived from theories of evolution or from the theories of scripture—that he was the lord of creation? In truth, thought Coville, the opposing facts are so glaring that the wonder is we fail to see that we are anomalies in Nature and surely pests in the eyes of a Creator, if such there be. And here I am, headed for the metropolis of pests!

Then he caught himself, and remarked that this was hardly the time for pessimism—not with a fascinating young lady within ten feet of him. But, after all, how did he know? Perhaps this was just the time for pessimism. Things didn't look any too good for him thus far.

The train passed three men working on the tracks. And then it was that Dr. Coville observed what struck him as a strange thing. His young lady raised her arm spontaneously and waved to the laborers. It was something he would not have expected her to do under any circumstance. He had judged her imperious, proud, aloof, undemonstrative. And here, on the contrary, here she was waving at a group of nonentities with what seemed to be real feeling. In comparison with her gestures, the waves of the other occupants of the platform chairs were indifferent and mechanical. He was sure some kind of spontaneous feeling arose in her. Well, perhaps it was not of any importance. But surprising, in any case. Not wishing to trust his first impression, he decided to watch carefully and see what happened the next time the train passed someone on the road.

He did not have to wait long. Sure enough, no doubt of it, she even leaned forward with eagerness and thrill as she waved. This was odd! What was back of it? What could it mean for a woman of her type? Dr. Coville smiled to himself, slouched in his chair, and began observing her with a new and somewhat more impersonal interest. Here was a piece of behavior he would like to understand the cause of.

He had one more opportunity. And then, unexpectedly, he was shocked out of countenance to see her swiftly turn, look straight at him for a flash, show unmistakable displeasure, and then avert her head with a slightly contemptuous toss.

Without doubt she had sensed his eyes on her. She never waved again.

"There now! my skilful Doctor," he told himself, "you've spoiled it, and gotten yourself in dutch. Damn observation! Damn you, my good friend Dr. Coville!"

Soon he began feeling that she wanted to leave the platform, but did not do so because she disliked having to pass by him.

"Now she'll hate me for being her jailor. A fine mess you're making of things. Well, move up front and give her a chance to escape if she wants to. At least be decent."

He did. He went forward to the club car, smoked a pipe, grew restless, tried to interest himself in a magazine, could not, could do nothing but think of her; and so, somewhat against his better judgment, with a feeling that he would not find her there, he returned with nervous haste to the observation, his heart pounding at a surprising rate.

She was gone. He was certain he had not passed her in any of the Pullman cars. Perhaps, worse luck, she was travelling in a compartment. In which case, his quest was hopeless. She could close herself in and not be seen for the rest of the trip. More, by God! he might never see her again. Not on your life! The possibility of not seeing her again, ever, left him in no doubt as to how much he did want to see her. Being a skilful doctor, he would manage it by hook or crook.

But a rather melancholy Coville took a vacant chair on the platform and felt strongly that the world left an empty space in him. "Think, you ass! it is almost time for dinner. You might have had it with her!"

When she was not to be seen in the diner, he hurried through a good meal, and, instead of going to the club car for a smoke, immediately dashed back to the observation.

Finding no trace of her there, he began to have a definite sense that she was avoiding him. If so, then he, on his part, was unwittingly caging her and cutting her off from the at best narrow range of movement possible on a train. He neither liked what she was doing, nor himself for penning her in.

Once there came to his mind the idea that love in want of an object is more of a goad than a career.

But, by God! she was a marvelous being! Well worth his excitement.

He grew very restless. The longer she continued to avoid him, the more he strained to see her. Between dinner time and 9:30 he made so many trips back and forth between club car and observation that most of the passengers knew his face far better than the conductor's. One woman who had made several passages abroad told her companion that the dark-haired good looking serious young man must think he was on shipboard. He was trying, it seemed, to get a bit of exercise before bed by taking several turns around the deck.

Near ten o'clock it grew chilly on the observation and Coville, lacking a top coat, was forced in. He felt ashamed to pass the porters again. However, he got up courage, gave up hope, and told himself that after a last smoke in the club car he would say good-by to his dream and climb into his berth.

But when the smoke was finished, he persuaded himself against all common sense—not to mention science—that he had a strong hunch that his lady, just then, was on the observation. This was, he knew, sheer superstition. What a ridiculous way for a young man of science to be acting! God help him should any of his patients see him now! For actually he was headed towards the observation!

He paused at his berth to get a coat and a cap which he pulled down over his face so as not to be recognizable. As he passed through the cars, brushing against berth-curtains, the lights were dim; and at both ends of the cars were signs cautioning "Silence." He had a guilty feeling as he walked through them. Had he not passed back and forth enough either to own them or owe ten times the regular fare?

Also, his heart felt as if it were pounding high in his chest. What if she should be there? "My God! After all this, I'd look at her speechless like a born idiot! And then—what wouldn't she do to me!"

The observation car was vacant, but as he entered it he thought he saw a form sitting on the platform. His heart stood still. Then, quaking, he moved forward cautiously to make sure.

It was! It was! Now what was he going to do? He felt like running in the opposite direction. If he went on the platform his action would be so obvious; and too, she could not fail to see that she had had him on the run all day. What a perfect chance for her to cut him dead and make him feel like all the fools in hell! Well, what had he come back for? To run? One opportunity already had been lost. Not this one!

He walked boldly towards the door, stepped out, saw her recognize him with a start, draw back, and then remain suspended, undecided whether to ignore him or immediately leave.

He surprised himself by smiling easily and quickly asking her in a casual but interested tone of voice:

"I saw you waving. I could not help noticing it. I'm interested. I wonder if you'd tell me—if you'd mind telling me why you do it? Of course I have no right . . . But just as a matter of interest."

She regarded him without a quiver, with no expression save something which suggested that she was weighing whether to leave him at once, or first to tell him he was completely out of place, and then leave.

There was, for Dr. Coville, a trace of humor in the situation. She seemed to be looking through every inch of him. At the back of his head he had to tell himself: "Now, my dear Doctor, you are getting some of your medicine. Impersonal analysis. Do you see how it feels? Poor patients!"

He was more than surprised to notice her turn away from him, relax her body, and gaze out into the night they were rushing through. And then she asked:

"Is it your habit to ask and answer questions while you balance on one foot and cling desperately to a hand-rail?" Her voice was chill, a bit sarcastic, aloof. She did not smile.

She added: "Besides, you must have observed—you are observant—that with the rattle and clatter of the wheels, too great a distance makes conversation a strain. Are you fond of strains?"

"By God!" he exclaimed to himself, "I've run across sophistication itself!" This, his mind said.

But his feelings, already over-wrought, received a jolt. In truth, he was standing there like a silly ass. He immediately sat down beside her.

His mind said: "One point for her! If she continues in this way, she'll have won the game before I get started. Women are getting too sharp and quick for us. It's in the atmosphere. Spirit of the age. Woman's day. Yes, there's truth in it. Better perk up!"

But he did not know just what to say. If she did, she didn't mention it. So, for a short while, they sat in tense silence.

He could not see her expression, but the clean-cut decisive lines of her chin were evident. It was growing cold on the platform. He buttoned his coat and thrust hands in pockets.

Had Dr. Coville waited and worried himself all day and half the night in order to sit like a mute at the side of his sphinx-like beloved? He had not.

However, with a slight turn of her face, it was she who spoke.

"You asked me a question. Do you remember what it was?"

"Certainly," he answered, a bit irritated. He leaned forward so as to see her better.

"Are you really interested?" she asked. "Or was it merely a way of starting conversation—a prelude to what good looking young men are usually interested in?"

"How old are you?" he blurted out.

"Are all your interests so personal?" she asked, with aloof disapproval.

"Damnit!" he said to himself. "Point two!"

"Perhaps, for a change," he answered, and smiled to give the impression that he was concealing something of interest from her.

"You are usually impersonal?" she asked, and herself smiled faintly. "I suppose you view life objectively for eight months of the year, and then, for the other four, you try to live what you have observed? You are seven-tenths rationalistic, three-tenths emotional, and experience conflict between the two because you cannot blend them?"

"There is some truth in that," he agreed, and felt a bit uncomfortable. This girl, whoever she was, was giving him ideas straight out of his own mind. It was a strange thing, but experiences like this often happened to him. He reminded himself that he frequently ran into circumstances which were exact externalizations of the phase he was passing through.

"Do you succeed in either the eight or the four? Are you ever purely rational, or purely emotional?"

"Well—" he began.

"What do you do?" She wanted to know, and turned her face full on him. It seemed chiseled from marble, too strong for his liking, but very beautiful. "You write? You are a young professor? You are a scientist? You have some career?"

"Yes," he answered.

She looked away from him and said: "Then I do not think you can understand me."

"Oh, come now," he replied, piqued by her dismissal. "Careers are not substitutes for all intelligence."

She flashed a smile at him for the first time.

"Are you trying to resurrect it, your intelligence—now—after its winter nap?"

They both laughed and became easier.

"You are a very brilliant young lady," he told her.

"Where are you going?" she asked, ignoring his last remark.

"First to New York. Wait around there—see a few friends—until the boat sails, and then I'm off for Europe. Spain. They are leading in neurology—Spain is. And then to Paris, Vienna—"

"What boat?" she asked.

"De Grasse."

"Yes, I know it," she said. "Very well." A strangely intriguing smile played on her lips. Her eyes seemed to be seeing a very desirable something that had transpired on the De Grasse.

As he suddenly saw the possibility Coville thought to himself: "My God! Wouldn't it be marvelous! A passage with her! Too good for words!"

"And you?" he asked, eagerly.

"Abroad," she replied, obviously refraining from giving more specific information.

"What boat?" he asked.

"Not the De Grasse."

"Why not?"

"Just so."

"But you know," pressed Coville, "I could change, or you could change. I have a good agent. It could be managed. Wouldn't it be great!"

"Perhaps for you," she replied, definitely leaving herself out of it. And then she added: "You assume too much. You are just like any other young man." With this, she turned in seeming disappointment from him.

He was stung by her tone. But what could he say?

At length, he remembered to suggest: "Perhaps you will tell me—answer my first question?"

"I will tell you, if you like. But I must first tell you that you annoyed me this afternoon. I did not like your looking at me. And I thought you were very insensitive to force me to keep in my compartment."

"Then you did!—" he began, very pleased that he had had that much effect on her.

"It is nothing you should feel proud of. You put me to inconvenience, and I fully intended to avoid you."

He could not help blurting out in challenge: "Then why did you come out here—now?"

She drew away from him.

"Be careful, or I'll leave you," she cautioned, and meant it.

Impulsively he placed his hand on her arm. A swift thrill passed through him at the touch. It was meant to restrain her. Also, it was meant as a love-contact. Then he quickly withdrew and flushed under her gaze of chill disapproval.

After a pause she asked: "Are you interested in what I was about to say?"

"Of course I am," he answered with heat.

"Well then, I wave because I like too. When you pass anyone—it makes no difference who he is, if he is human—when, under the right circumstances you pass anyone, when you meet, and will meet no more, when you both know that there is nothing in the ordinary sense to be either gained or lost—sometimes then, more often than at any other time, a perfectly exquisite feeling may be born, live its moment—" her eyes flashed and faded "—and I guess that's all." She herself seemed to live for a moment, and then retire into an inscrutable resignation.

This sense of her made Coville madly wish to take her in his arms and hold her. He felt she was very lonely, pleading with him, in spite of herself, to give her assurance and human warmth. And yet, she was unapproachable. She held herself so contained and aloof that he felt she was beyond the need of anyone. He wished to hold her; yet dared not. Torn between these feelings, Coville felt helpless.

Then came the decisive sense that her very exquisiteness shielded her from his touch. He contracted, drew away; and his mind attempted to meet the situation which his emotions could not.

To compensate for defeat, he was over-aggressive in asking her: "Do you mean you actually felt all you appeared to feel each time you waved? I don't see how it can mean that much to you. After all, a wave is a wave. What would happen if you gave all of yourself? It's out of proportion to feel so much, to express so much, in a gesture. Of course I know there are some gestures . . . But you can't and no one can make those kind a dozen times in an afternoon. You see what I mean?"

"Yes," she answered, "I do." A barely perceptible quiver of pain touched her lips and was gone. Then, with a trace of amusement she continued: "No, I did not. Perhaps I did not feel all."

"Then why—?"

"Perhaps I made them for you," she smiled.

"For me?" said the surprised doctor.

"Perhaps."

"How do you mean?"

"Showing you something you could not do."

"Don't be silly," he advised.

"As usual, you are the silly one," she replied. Her eyes were gazing pensively at dark space.

"Well," he said, "tell me what you mean. It all sounds very profound and mysterious."

She answered: "You—no, you cannot experience what I described for you a short while ago."

"How do you know I can't? Why can't I?" He frowned professionally and tried to hold her eyes.

"Let us say because you are burdened by a career."

"How do you know that?" he asked.

"Whoever has a career is likely to be burdened by it. I saw you coming on, rushing to make the train. You looked as if the three million people of Chicago had been chasing you for an entire year—and you just contrived to escape them ten minutes before train time." She had to laugh softly as she recalled the picture of the hurried harried young doctor.

"You have uncanny perceptions," he told her with a feeling of considerable discomfort.

"I don't think so. Just good eyes."

"Well, what you say is right in part. I admit it. In fact it is something I've thought about a good deal."

"You might well," she said. "Lost opportunities haunt you, and you are rushed on against your will by hopes scattered in dazzling clusters over the years. It has taken much study, preparation, practice, to make you so? Yes, and now your training will not permit you to act otherwise."

"I'll be damned if it won't!—pardon me," said Dr. Coville, "but you see, I have some feeling on this subject. I've just fought it out, in fact I had to fight it out with myself in order to take this trip abroad, I go abroad—"

"For neurology," she said. "More that has to do with your career."

"Yes," he admitted. "But if the truth be told, I simply threw it in as a sop to my professional conscience."

"You think you will be able to cast it aside, once you arrive in Europe? You believe your professional conscience will obediently go to sleep and give you free rein to experience all you wish, in Europe? Even if it did . . . Men of your type must always find and have something past or future to hitch themselves to. If it is not one thing, then it is another. I am serious when I say that I doubt that you have ever experienced in your life one pure moment."

"That's nonsense," he said, with heat. "Your ideas are all right—true enough. I tell you again that I've thought about this thing a good deal. But what you say, does not apply to me. What am I doing here? Doesn't my very presence here disprove your theory?"

"Would you give up your career?" She flashed one swift searching glance at him; but he, now concerned only with his ideas, neither saw it nor sensed her.

"No, of course not," he answered. "In order to experience moments, as you call them, we've got to eat and to be able to eat the bread and butter of a world that runs in time. Since the time-world is dominant, we must master it before we can live in more desirable worlds. Since they are here, and we are in them, we've got to be able to live in skyscrapers before we can be in cathedrals. We may not like this world, but we got to meet and master it before we can move on to the next."

"Again, dear Doctor, you are a futurist. Has it never occurred to you that you can sincerely strive to master both, now, at this present time? Have you never considered that both paths must be pursued at the same time, else you will progressively commit yourself only to one?"

"Yes, I have considered it," he said. "But what's to be done? One must have money."

"Suppose you had money enough?"

"But what's the good of supposing? I haven't got enough. I've got to make it. And that's that."

Then, as a very pertinent thought flashed in his mind, he suddenly turned full on her and said, in semi-severe tones:

"You are a fine one to be talking of living in and for the moment. You understand what I mean? All afternoon . . . Yes, where was the present moment then? Tucked away under the berth of your compartment. And what about now? You feel to me as if you were deliberately hiding yourself in a box of ten years ago, or closing yourself in a very exquisite urn from which you will emerge perhaps ten years hence. Why not permit yourself to live now? Now is the present," he said emphatically. "You and I *are.*" Then, with a sudden change he thrust at her: "No, you won't be."

He was venting the feelings generated and pent up during the afternoon and early evening. His expression showed that he considered himself quite right in the matter.

She did not flinch; but a wave of pain, very sensitive, passed across her face and was gone. Again there settled on her the look of resignation. Almost as if thinking to herself she said:

"Yes, men are clumsy. The art of life—I am sure that the art of living has always been with women. I am sure that if the truth were discovered we would learn that the only reason why men have become great artists in the eyes of the world was because they knew they were not artists naturally. They had to show what they could do. They have to make a display in order to reassure themselves." She turned her eyes on him, giving him a queer sinking sensation. "You, my good Doctor," her tone was cutting, "I suppose you are a doctor. Could you, can you live art? Would that satisfy you? Or would you have to show it—and spoil it?"

Without allowing him opportunity to reveal in voice the hurt he felt, she glanced at her watch and said: "It is very late. I am cold."

She arose, and forced him to rise also, though awkwardly.

The train sped through the black night. The platform seemed a reckless place. It was waving and wagging like the tail of a dog.

He tried to support her by the arm, but she withdrew.

"Good night," she said, and held out her hand.

He had to take it. He was confused, apologetic, hurt, longing to keep her with him. He was grateful. He presented to her the feelings of a very sincere human being. Also, he was much like a handsome boy, slightly pouting, very winning in a simple, direct, unconscious way.

A deep feeling came over him and his eyes tried to tell her what his lips could not. He held her hand and pressed it. He lifted it and held it near his heart.

She averted her head and released her hand from his.

And then, before he knew what was happening, she had turned impulsively, swiftly, given him the most exquisite kiss he had ever received in his life—and was already through the door, walking away from him with firm quick strides.

He had presence of mind enough not to try to overtake her.

Fifteen minutes later, as he switched out the light in his berth, his face was still radiant, radiantly amazed.

"By heaven!" he told himself. "I did taste that moment! If she isn't the marvel of this world!"

He was up bright and early the next morning, feeling he had already experienced a long and joyous vacation. The entire earth and mankind seemed in springtime. He told the porter he had slept excellently. In fact, he had slept very little, and didn't feel the need of another wink.

After shaving, he looked carefully at himself and was delighted to see that, if anything, he was more handsome than usual. There was a light in his eyes which, unfortunately, had not shone for some time. Without a doubt the world was at last again full to the brim with its essential something.

A hurried breakfast, and then he made a bee-line for the observation. The platform was a good old friend of his. He took the chair he had occupied the previous night, and waited eagerly, impatiently, for her to come out. She was missing the country through which the train was speeding.

It was lovely green hill-country, so different from the flat grey lands of the Middle West. The farm houses, the towns, everything looked as though it had been standing there mellowing for years. He did not know whether the state were Maryland or West Virginia. He thought it was one of these. And then Coville saw the soft high forms of mountain ranges, perhaps the Blue Ridge, perhaps the Alleghenies. Something of the poet awoke in him; and he recognized that these forms were feminine. Yes, and the great Rockies and Sierras were masculine. And the great plains of the Middle West were neutral. Not in years had he experienced beauty so pure and deep. He felt eager and able to give her an entire scale of subtle tender feelings.

Why didn't she come out?

Each time the door opened he looked around, expectantly.

The train thundered through Harper's Ferry. He could see the yellow waters of the Shenandoah join with the Potomac. They were speeding down the Potomac River valley. In little over an hour the train would be in Washington.

A disturbing notion came to him. "What if she gets off at Washington? She didn't say she was going through to New York. My God! Or it might be Baltimore, or Philadelphia! I've got to see her at once!"

He scrambled to his feet, dashed in the door, passed through one car, and then, having reached the swaying vestibule of the second car, he came to a dead stop. How was he going to locate her? He knew neither her car nor her compartment. His one plan appeared to be this: he would have to go methodically from car to car, find the porter of each, describe his lady, and ask if such a person were in any of his compartments. But, on second thought, he saw that this plan was absurd, out of the question. It would involve an unwanted publicity. Then what? There seemed nothing else to be done: he would have to make the best of it and take chances of running into her. Perhaps, if the truth were known, she was sleeping late, having been kept awake half the night by dreams of him, as he had been kept awake by thoughts of her. So, giving a nervous sigh, he trudged forward and finally reached the club car.

When the train pulled into the station at Washington, Coville jumped up with a start and did the only thing he could think of doing. He left the train and posted himself where he could see everyone passing, getting off at Washington. She did not pass. He was sure of it. When, in due time, the train started again, he jumped on and began, it seemed, again taking exercise back and forth between the club and observation cars.

At Baltimore he repeated the strategy of posting himself where he could see all who got off. At Philadelphia, the same. And then he could no longer suppress the sinking feeling that his lady was again deliberately avoiding him and had no intention of ever seeing him.

His emotions swayed and tossed between a blue depression and an harried over-wrought state. By God! He must see her! By God! He never would!

Not long after leaving Philadelphia he allowed himself the one distraction the train afforded: he ate lunch. But he barely touched the meal. His appetite was gone, and there was risk that he get nervous indigestion.

When once again in the club car, a train official came up and explained to him that motor coaches, making connections with different parts of New York, would be awaiting the train's arrival at the Jersey City Station. A sufficiently distracted Dr. Coville decided to take the 23rd Street coach, and was given the proper ticket. He put it in his pocket and thought no more of it.

No sight, no sign of her all morning.

When, after a time, he looked at his watch and saw that according to schedule they would be in Jersey City in thirty minutes, a wild idea caught his mind and urged him to go the length of the train, knocking at and opening each compartment door. Feeling a strong impulse to do so, he severely caught hold of himself and asked if he were going crazy.

In due course, the train pulled into the station at Jersey City and came to a stop. Coville suddenly became frantic. He dashed the entire length of the train, running into passengers who already were getting off. Then, in sharp reaction, a sort of stupor came over him. Somehow or other he soon found himself with coat over arm, descending the steps, tipping the porter.

The large motor coaches were lined up, waiting, nearby. He mechanically showed his ticket and was directed to the coach which headed the line. After looking as best he could at the occupants of the motors to the rear of him, he allowed himself, under compulsion of what everyone else was doing, to be forced to enter his own.

Once in his seat, he began craning his neck in an effort to locate her. And then there flashed upon him what a fool he was. She would have to get off here. This was the last stop: she would have to show herself. Why hadn't he waited for her outside near the train, even if it took ten hours, even if he missed all the coaches and lost all the baggage in the world?

The driver entered, closed the door, and started off.

As his coach sped towards the ferry, Coville caught a glimpse of his lady getting in what appeared to be the last coach of the line. His feelings gave a jerk and his mind raced to find some way of meeting with her. In the midst of this psychic uproar, he had one lucid moment. He told himself:

"I've spent all day spoiling the moment of joy she gave me last night! My three million patients are still chasing me! Well, hell! What does she expect of a man?"

He returned to scheming how to locate her. She would have to cross the Hudson on one of the ferries. So much was certain. Which one? He determined at all costs to find out the minute the thing he was in stopped and permitted him to get out.

There was a slight delay because of traffic. Soon, however, his coach entered the 23rd Street ferry and drew up to the front. Dr. Coville almost plunged at the door; but had to wait until the guard opened it. Then, looking as if he were bent on one of the most serious of surgical cases, he dashed through the boat, aiming to leave it and search the others. As he neared the stern, an attendant yelled at him and told him in effect that if he wanted to cross with his baggage he better stay on. Coville was shocked to a halt. He glanced wildly about, but remained suspended, undecided. The whistle blew, bells rang in the engine-room, and the gates were lowered. Before he could bring himself to act, the ferry started chugging. A gap of water appeared and gradually widened between it and the dock. Coville was caught on.

Further down, one of the other ferries also blew its whistle and started chugging.

For a short while, Coville stood staring in a sort of blank agony at the receding pier. He seemed asking, mutely, that the indifferent weather-beaten form reveal and surrender to him his beloved.

And then, neither thinking nor feeling, he stumbled towards the bow and leaned against the rail. The great New York skyline across the river held no interest, no promise. With feeling gone, all else was empty. New York was just another collection of stupid skyscrapers. His eyes stared down at the choppy glistening waters. His body slouched, and was limp, almost caved in.

The other ferry, about four widths to the side of him, was also pulling out. Mechanically, he raised his eyes towards it. They chanced upon a form which caused his heart to give a great leap and pound furiously. By God! It was! His lady! Standing near the rail with gaze direct on him!

Of a sudden his body stood upright as a great surge of joy swept through him and lifted his arm in a gesture of salute and cheer. She seemed more stunning than ever he had pictured her. A gorgeous brightness filled the world. With a beautiful free wave she returned his gesture; and then, in a twinkling, she faced about and was gone.

"Gone!" he cried. A hopeless tragic expression gripped his face and displaced the joy which had marked it only a moment before.

Immediately he fell to berating himself.

"Gone, by God! To disappear and be lost forever in the world's people. What chance of ever seeing, finding her again? Who says the world is a small place? And she was, was she not, a radiant agent of the world I wish to live in? Ass that I am! I don't even know her name. Or where she lives, or where she is going." Then, bitterly—"I'll bet anything she asked me what boat I was sailing on to make sure of avoiding me. What is the matter with her anyway? What's wrong? A neurosis somewhere. I could fix it in a jiffy if she'd give me half a chance. Oh, well, Docter Meron Coville, my dear young man, she was too much for you. Better pursue your blasted career!"

Then of a sudden he came up with a start:

"My god! She was right! All morning what did I do? What now? I spoil—have spoiled—that one last sweet glorious sight of her! 'Tis so. There is an enormous difference between the strictly professional and the strictly personal. Skilful Dr. Coville is a very clumsy young man."

[1928–1929]

Man's Home Companion
An a-drama in one scene

The scene; a model modern interior.

Time; towards 7 P.M. any workday of the week any week of any future year, or, perhaps, this year.

The Characters: Bert Diggs, the husband.
                        Lucille, the wife.
                        Argive, the technochaser, as the maid.
                        An aniphograph of Lucille.

First note. A technochaser (pronounced tech-no-chaser) is a greatly improved and subtilized bi-sexual robot, able both to speak and to respond to the spoken word. In this a-drama it will assume a female role, that, namely, of the maid, and so we will call her her. Her name is Argive, pronounced with a long i. She is not an ordinary cumbrous over-complicated robot resembling a clodhopper suit of mail. She is slim, elongated, streamlined so to speak, made of bright shining metal, semi-transparent, but ten times as strong as steel—a dazzling spectacle, wonderfully and, somehow, sinisterly fashioned. Into her construction has gone not the slightest effort to imitate the human figure. What human resemblances there are are strictly functional. If, for example, her limbs are somewhat like human limbs, this is because the inventor, after long experiments, convinced himself that for a thing of this kind he could not improve upon Nature's choice of means of locomotion. Her head is elongated, that is, somewhat oval egg-shaped. It is entirely without sutures and has only three apertures: one, a lip-like opening inlaid with a bright brassy metal which serves as a mouth; and two others, gill-like openings, two slits on each side of the head. Underneath one of these is concealed the ingenious mechanism for recording and registering sounds, including the sounds of the human voice. Under the other is the mechanism for doing the same thing as regards radio-transmitted power and control. She has no neck at all. Her elongated burnished head rests on bearings directly connected with the body. Her chest is narrow, and also elongated. But instead of tapering down, as the ideal human figure does, it sort of streamlines out into what we humans beings would call a jolly round belly. In this belly are the main works, delicate and ingenious beyond words. Her limbs are elongated and slim, amazingly beautiful forms reminiscent of those aimed for by sculptors of the abstract who desire to model perfect proto-types of fishes, birds, and so on. And her feet—perhaps it is these that cause Argive to seem sinister. They are queerly shaped, equipped with projection-springs, by means of which the technochaser can spring into the air with the agility of a cat, pad-like shock-absorbers for landing, and claws that can be bared or drawn in. Her hands are similar to her feet, padded and clawed. Besides all of this, she has a faculty for taking on the moods and tempers of the people surrounding her, together with the corresponding facial expressions—in so far as her metal-egglike head permits.

Second note. An aniphograph (pronounced an-e-pho-graph), as the name suggests, is an animated photograph, in other words a talking picture. In appearance it looks like an ordinary photo. In reality it is one of the most amazing of modern inventions. By a special process the picture is taken by a very special camera. To make it respond, all one has to do is to call the person's name while at the same time syringing it with a highly concentrated plasmic fluid. Once this is done you can talk with the picture as if the person himself or herself were present with you. Obviously it is an excellent companion of one's lonely hours.

The husband, in smoking-jacket, is seated before a hearth electrically lighted to appear like burning logs. He is reading the evening newspaper, a bulky sheet of fifty pages. At his elbows are a dozen or more weekly and monthly magazines. Now and again, with an anxious frown, he peers at the clock and then at the door, evidently restive about his wife who has not yet come home from her affairs.

The technochaser, with a piece of stylized metal-sheeting slanted across her middle to suggest a maid's apron, prepares dinner in an adjacent laboratory in test-tubes over a series of electric flames.

The dining-room table is a high metal stand with a bright washable top, around which are grouped three high stools similar to those at bars and quick lunch counters.

The maid sets the table, though there are no knives or forks or spoons or napkins. As she passes to and fro she glances with pity at the poor husband as if understanding and sympathizing with his plight.

Presently foot-steps are heard. The husband casts his paper aside, springs up, and makes a dash for the door.

Wife enters. He takes her in his arms and tries to kiss her. The maid looks on and sadly wags her head. The wife withdraws and wipes the kiss from her mouth, as if kisses were archaic.

Wife (breezily) : Hello, darling. Wish you wouldn't touch me with those . . . oh, dear, what are they called? Oh, yes . . . lips. Am I late again?

Husband (joy at seeing her getting the upper hand of his peevishness): I'm sorry. Forget sometimes, and lapse back into historical habits. Yes, darling, you are. Half an hour late tonight, but husband is so happy to see his darling that nothing else matters now. I do hope, though, darling, you won't have to go out again tonight.

Wife (still breezing, tossing her wraps on a lounge, throwing him honied looks in-between times): I'm afraid I must. Don't scold now. Don't mind. I'll be back before dawn. No more late hours for me. (comes towards him, takes his hands in hers) Don't look so woebegone, darling, I didn't want to go for anything. I told them I simply had to have one night a month at home with my husband. But you see, darling, tonight the board's auxiliary meets, and you know that awful Mrs. Boseevius. She's an ugly Caesar. If I'm not there . . . well, you know what she does, and I simply refuse to allow anyone to install showerbaths in our airships. Can you fancy such a thing? Why, it only takes two hours from New York to Chicago and here this Boseevious person complains that unless we install showers at once our rival companies will steal our passengers. Imagine anything so silly!

The maid (entering and casting a pitying glance at the husband): Dinner is served.

Husband, wife, and maid clamber upon the high stools and begin drinking from test-tubes as the wife continues to tell about absurd Mrs. Boseevius and her ridiculous proposals.

Wife (exclaiming): I didn't know I had such an appetite! My, what delicious steak! These carrots! (to maid) A fine meal you are giving us tonight, Argive. Thank you. But why are you looking so sad? Has someone of your family died? Oh, dear, I hope not. Deaths are such inconvenient things. I should think Nature or Science could find some more expeditious way, a more [subtle?] way, to dispose of us.

Wife finishes dinner, springs from the table, gets her wraps, and pauses at the door for the usual tweak from her husband. Husband strolls over and sort of beaks her as if begrudging the waste of his perfectly good emotions on his plainly otherwise-occupied wife.

Husband: Success, darling. Don't be late. I'll try to keep awake for you.

Wife: I shan't, darling. If I find I simply must be out after two o'clock I'll give you a ring.

Off she goes and the door slams.

The maid looks sorrowingly at the husband and goes about her work of clearing the table and cleaning the laboratory.

The husband, after shifting about aimlessly and forlornly, slumps into his chair, takes a tiny drop of quintessence of tobacco, picks up his paper and begins absently scanning the pages, already thrice scanned before this.

The maid finishes her work, gets a hamper full of his socks that need darning, comes over and takes a chair near his, and begins mending the socks. Ever [sic] so often she casts furtive sorrowing glances at the lonely man.

In time the husband throws down the paper, stands up, stretches, yawns, looks at the clock, glances about, sees the aniphograph and his face lights up. He goes to the aniphograph with a smile as to an old friend, treats it in the prescribed manner, places it on a table near him between himself and the technochaser-maid, and again takes his chair.

Husband (to the aniphograph): Well, darling, what will it be tonight? A show? I hear there's a peach at the Palace. No? No show tonight?

The aniphograph of his wife shakes her head.

Husband (a bit provoked): Why, darling, what's the matter? Nothing seems to please you. Nothing I suggest. How about the radio and a good jazz band? You won't have to move or feel or think to hear that.

Both the aniphograph and the technochaser smile and nod their heads. The husband, less grumpy, turns on the radio and into the room comes [sic] the strains of a seductive jazz-melody.

Husband (bright all at once): Now I want to dance!

Aniphograph (also brightly): So do I! (wistfully) Wish I could. Someday they'll make me full length.

The technochaser: I'll dance!

Husband: Bravo! Righto, Argive, old girl! Let's clear the floor!

So the husband and the maid dance and whirl until the husband, but not the maid, is dog-tired.

Husband (stopping, mopping his brow): Whew! I've had enough. Let's call it a night. Thanks, Argive, a good work-out. Thanks a lot, old girl.

He turns off the radio. Both sit down, she meekly as she resumes mending the socks. The husband tries to carry on conversation with the aniphograph. It peters out. So he turns off the aniphograph. He yawns, looks at the clock. Just then it strikes midnight. The husband takes more drops of tobacco. A vigil begins. At one o'clock he can stand no more. Up he gets.

Husband (to the maid): And so to bed. Can't help it. (yawns and stretches) Argive, you've been a good girl. Thanks a lot for everything. Goodnight.

The maid (putting up the mending): Thank you, sir. With practice every night I'll soon know how to dance without disappointing you, sir.

After casting another pitying look at him she quietly leaves the room.

Husband (preparing for bed): No telling what time that darling of mine will get in. Said she'd phone if she'd be out after two. Bet she rings.

He puts out all the lights except the one over the door, then crawls into a sleeping contraption, itself resembling a test-tube, of which there are two, twin-bed effect. Soon he is snoring.

Times passes. The clock strikes two. At exactly one minute after two the phone bell rings. But the entire household including the husband, fast asleep, does not hear it. It continues jangling.

[1933]

Lump

Johnathan [sic] Curtis was a tall semi-distinguished fellow with a stoop, gradually using up the vitality of his one-time athletic body. A serious person in his early forties, accustomed to position and influence, he could nevertheless, at moments, forget his vanity and egotism and laugh at himself. This laugh was his one bid to being democratic.

Curtis was used to having people look up to him. Often he dominated them, sometimes genially, sometimes with arrogance. He was pretty well determined that no one should ever dominate him.

He had never been seriously ill. Save for the loss of several teeth, his body still retained all the members it had been born with. But back in him somewhere, the strange fellow had a premonition that fate was leading him straight into a hospital. Perhaps he was under the belief that we bring upon ourselves the thing we fear. he did fear, not disease, but hospitals and clinics. He feared them peculiarly.

Not at all when, in the company of friends who were physicians, he strolled down sterilized corridors, seeing through open doors the patients in beds. No, at such times he was at ease, almost at home, talking with doctors and perhaps being taken for a doctor himself.

But let him identify with the patients, let him see himself stretched out in white, and he was immediately involved in a superstitious dread. The hospital became a graveyard, the nurses gravestones, the surgeons ghosts, himself down in the ground entombed alive. This very circumstance might have given him a clue to the explanation of his strange fear—if he had been looking for clues. But Curtis was content to tell himself that each man, even the most intelligent, has a crack in his reason somewhere about something. This superstition was his crack—and he let it go at that.

Nor could he by any force of reason reason it away. True, in a sick world clinics and hospitals were good and necessary institutions. Very true. But reason itself could not fill the crack in his reason. His dread continued. That is, when he thought of it, or pictured himself as a patient, or saw ambulances, or watched wretched humans trudging into clinics at the appointed hour.

For the first forty years of his life he was spared the actual experience. Then things began happening.

In the post-boom years he lost money, was much reduced, and faced the prospect of being compelled to become democratic after all. This economic attack on his sense of security was less painful than the attack on his sense of specialness. It was one on him; and Curtis had a chance to laugh at himself.

In these same years he was plunged into psychological strains and stresses which began to tell on his physical health. Or so it seemed. His old standby, his hitherto reliable body, was failing him. Eyes went bad. He had to wear glasses. His stomach got out of order, and he began to read ads of remedies for stomach disorders. Pains, or curious ominous pressures which caused pain, annoyed his heart. Now and again he'd gravely wonder if in truth he did have heart-trouble.

Common sense said he ought to go to a doctor and be looked over. He put it off with the thought that he could not spare the money just then. Besides, had he not been healthy all his life? This was merely a phase which would soon pass. There could be nothing radically wrong with him. Nevertheless he felt weighted and oppressed, under a cloud, unable to enjoy the present because of an ever increasing sense that he was a man doomed in the near future to a fatal malady. His friends noted the change and often remarked that he was not himself. Curtis kept his fears secret and simply said he was very tired and ought to take a rest.

Then, quite by accident—or was it accident?—he ran across notices about cancer. The movement to spread cancer-information to the general public reached him. In magazines, in newspapers he read items concerning this dreaded disease, at first without applying anything to himself. It had never occurred to him, even as a remote possibility, that he might one day fall a victim. His ancestry was of the best, with no fatal disease of any kind in the records. He had always taken exceptionally good care of himself. Cancer? Nonsense.

One evening, however, to his vast surprise, he read that there was such a thing as mouth cancer. This was entirely new. A fairly fine student of literature and philosophy, Curtis was not at all informed about organic pathology. Mouth cancer! It was not only new but, for some reason, alarming—perhaps only because he had had a very hard day which had put his nerves on edge. But this much he had to grant in all soberness, namely, that his mouth was the only part of his body that had ever given him trouble—his teeth, that is. Then and there he told himself that if cancer were to strike him it would strike him in his mouth.

The news item spoke of lumps. Any lump in the mouth was to be examined and held suspect. It might be innocent. On the other hand it might prove a source of trouble. A lump! He'd never thought of such a thing.

It was then that semi-distinguished Johnathan Curtis vaguely recalled seeing, or perhaps feeling with his tongue, a lump in his own mouth.

How long it had been there he wasn't at all sure. Indeed he wasn't sure it was there. No dilly-dallying, he'd investigate at once.

Walking briskly to the bathroom he felt pleased with himself because he was showing, if only to himself, that he could make a decision and act upon it, if the occasion demanded. This was one thing, a possibly important thing, which he would not be in the dark about.

Before the mirror he saw his face wearing a very grave and somewhat worried look. He hesitated, and was all for using Christian Science. Finally he had to force himself to open his mouth, pull the cheek back, and look. There, sure enough, *was* a lump. Something hit the pit of his stomach quite unpleasantly, and again he had to compel himself to look. The lump was a curious, rather soft, almost transparent affair on the right side opposite a vacant place left by an extracted tooth. Small, harmless looking—but, a *lump*.

Curtis felt marked, struck, and wronged. What had he done to deserve a lump? His imagination began picturing pains and horrors. His life was done. Then he got angry against whatever had played him such a trick. He, Johnathan Curtis, with a lump, perhaps a fatal cancer-lump, in his mouth. He used a mouth-wash and tried to wash it out. When he realized how silly he was he clamped his jaw shut and strode off to more befitting occupations.

During the days that followed he went about his affairs as usual, saying nothing about it to anyone, often forgetting the lump. But a pall was upon him, a depression and foreboding which he could not shake free of; and when in his rooms alone of evenings he'd suddenly remember the specific cause of it all, and run his tongue over the lump to see if it had changed any. Or he'd go to the mirror and look. An increase of size would have plunged him into panic. Even though he saw no growth, even though the thing gave him no trouble, he kept picturing himself becoming an inmate of a dreaded hospital and going under a dreaded knife.

And he read all he could about cancer in lay books, thus hoping to learn enough to make his own diagnosis and prescribe his own cure, all with nobody knowing of it.

After quite a bit of reading certain facts stood out. One of them was this. Cancer, it was said, was often caused by irritation. It did not take much reflection to convince Curtis that his own pet might well have started in just this way. Opposite the lump was the vacant place where the tooth had been. Extracting it, years ago, the dentist had broken it. A snag was left in. This snag pushed to the surface; and Curtis had let several years pass before having it removed. Yes, true enough, the irritation caused by rubbing against this snag could have produced the lump. This was not encouraging; and he would have become quite distressed if he had not reasoned thus: the snag was removed at least three years ago; if the snag caused it, the lump has been in my mouth at least three years, and even now it gives me no trouble and is still innocent looking; in fine, it is not very active and possibly, therefore, not at all malignant. Could he have trusted his lay reasoning about this little thing which had become such a big thing in his life, he would have dismissed the lump with the joking remark that he had a pet in his mouth which he was quite willing to feed and care for for the rest of his days.

Curtis also learned that cancer was most likely to occur in people over forty. This was not so good. However, it was also said and emphasized that, if caught in time, the disease was curable. Immediate attention to any lumps or persistent sores was advised. Go to your dentist, go to your physician at once, it was urged. He told himself he should go. Besides, several of his teeth were in need of treatment. He could kill both birds with the one stone. But decisive Curtis put it off; meanwhile taking even better care of himself to build up his resistance; meanwhile, too, keeping strict track of the changes, if any, that happened to his pet.

One day Tom Cummings, a physician friend of his, paid him a visit. Here was opportunity coming to his door. Tom was a brilliant young city doctor connected with a large hospital, with one of the best clinics in the country. All Curtis would have had to do was to say, casually, "By the way, Tom, I'd like to ask you something, or, rather, show you something," and the matter would have moved smoothly and quickly. For even if Tom himself did not know, he would know exactly where to send him, properly introduced. But no, Curtis held his tongue—especially when Tom began telling him of a mutual friend of theirs, a man also just over forty, who, on chancing to look into his mouth one day, had discovered something which greatly upset him. Here and there in his mouth was the tissue—Tom used the technical term for it—under which the cancer germs are often found. This friend, Max by name, had immediately taken himself to the clinic and had had his mouth cauterized. Cauterization, said Tom, was the treatment, not at all painful, a sure cure for cancer in its incipient stages.

Curtis visualized himself going to the clinic and having his own mouth, or, rather, lump, cauterized. The crack in his reason widened frightfully and let all manner of superstitions escape. Fearing he'd give himself away, he managed to ask further questions which were over-determined to be detached. He said nothing about his own personal lump, but he did mentally resolve that if time passed and his pet bothered him he would seek Tom, tell him about it, and get introduced to the same clinic. After all, he was an intelligent man living in an intelligent age, and it would be criminal of him to run the risk of having a serious disease merely because he shrank from having a little lump taken from his mouth.

Several weeks later Curtis was called out of town. He stayed away two months, working at a high pitch of nervous tension which, somehow, caused the lump to make itself felt for the first time. At night when he was very tired he'd feel little burning pains, like stitches, in the region of his pet. No doubt of it, the lump had grown, not much but some. Surely he ought to have it looked at. By now he knew its symptoms, the way it would be soft and hardly noticeable after a good night's rest, how it would be hard and prominent after the strain of the day—and he could intelligently talk to a doctor about it. But he put off going because he was away from home. As soon as he returned he'd go to his dentist and have his teeth fixed, and then, by the way, bring out, "Oh, Doc, I almost forgot something. Take a look at this little fellow, will you?"

Which was just what he did. Back home again he felt energized, for some queer reason. He felt active and purposive, as if he ought to and would, right then, take himself in hand. No more dilly-dallying. No longer a prey to waywardness and superstitious dread. This tiny thing, he now admitted, had gotten a hold on him and weighed him awfully. It was in the back of his mind all the time. Something in him had even accepted the fact that he did have cancer and was doomed to drag himself through life until he died a horrible death.

His dentist looked at the lump. "Don't know," he said, rather gravely. "If I were you I'd see a doctor. These things are nothing if they are treated at once."

Curtis was surprised at himself because he was impressed but not alarmed by the dentist's grave tone. Apparently he was not the kind of man to be frightened when it came right down to it. His fear was of fancyings, not of facts.

This dentist was the first person to whom Curtis had, so to speak, confessed. The thing was out. The dentist's assistant had overheard. The thing was socialized. Now it was public knowledge that Johnathan Curtis had a lump. And right there in the chair he was released. He wanted to speak, to overflow, to tell the dentist all about it, its probable origin, its symptoms—but, the next patient was waiting to come in. "Thanks, Doc," he said, and went out.

That night in the seclusion of his bachelor quarters he picked up a newspaper and almost the first thing to catch his eye was a report of a dentists' convention with an item on cancer which read:

The cancer organism is a gangster cell. It is lawless but it can be controlled. Cancer of the mouth, which comprises 4 per cent of the 125,000 annual fatal cases, can easily be taken care of by surgery, radium or surgical diathermy.

Close observation of every mouth sore is all that is required to reduce mouth cancer to the vanishing point. Persons over forty are urged to take particularly close care of mouth sores, taking their case to a physician if lesions do not disappear in two to three weeks.

The very next day Curtis gathered his forces, got in touch with Tom, and introduced the matter without delay, priding himself not a little that his fear and trembling were indulged in remote from the line of action; once he actually got to the line he showed sufficient courage.

Tom washed his hands and had a look. "Not serious," he pronounced.

"Didn't think it was," Curtis smiled reassuringly. And it was true. All along he'd had three attitudes. One attitude said it was nothing. A deeper belief said it was very serious. A still deeper voice had told him, as it now appeared, the truth.

Tom continued, "It's not in my line, however. Can't be sure. Better go to the clinic and let them look you over."

Which was just what Curtis, after all these months, now at last wanted to do. Procrastination was paining him more than the lump. Ignorance was weighing upon him more than his fear. Yes, hospital or no hospital, ghosts or no ghosts, he wanted action, something definite at once.

Said Tom, "It is slight in itself, but it is a cause of irritation. You can't tell what may develop. The lining of the mouth should be smooth. I'll introduce you to Dr. Bradford. An excellent man, one of the best in the country."

"The one who did the job for Max?"

Tom nodded. "They'll probably cauterize it with an electric needle. Give you novocaine. It won't hurt. For a while your mouth will be sensitive. Better have it done. In the clinic it will be cheaper than if you go elsewhere. Besides, as I say, you can't find a better man than Bradford. He's known in Europe too."

Tom went on to say that though he'd introduce him, Curtis would have to be admitted to the hospital in the regular way.

"Of course," and Curtis wanted it done that very afternoon.

Said Tom, smiling, "Be at my office in the building about 10:30 tomorrow."

That night Curtis was by turns deeply relieved and calm because he had committed himself and things were under way—and, on the other hand, ever [sic] so often he'd be seized by ghastly visions of this electric needle which he had never seen but which he could picture burning a horrible hole in his cheek, himself as helpless a figure in a nightmare.

The next morning was a bleak day in early March, with a raw chill that got under his skin and seemed to shrivel him. However, as he walked towards the hospital he laughed at himself and said, "Today's the day.

Never in a hospital. Never in a clinic. Sir Johnathan, your fate has caught up with you. No use fancying in advance and worrying therefore. You'll go through the mill. You'll see what that damn needle will do to you. The next time you walk down this street you'll know it all, and perhaps your pet of six months standing will have been parted from you. I hope to God."

In one of the corridors he ran into Tom's secretary, who knew him. She showed him into Tom's office, chatted a while, said Dr. Cummings was in another part of the building but she'd get in touch with him.

Curtis sat in the private office, with the door leading into the hall open. So here he was, in one of the cells of the labyrinthine institution, waiting his turn like any other common man. No, not quite this last—not yet. He was Dr. Cummings' friend, sitting in his friend's office, even if he did have a lump in his mouth. Tom, of course, once the routine of admission was over, would personally escort him directly to Dr. Bradford; and Dr. Bradford, after making the diagnosis, would himself give treatment at once. Curtis had a twinge of pity for the poor beggars who came in off the street and had to go through the red tape and take what they got.

There on Tom's desk were books he recognized. An ash tray. He lit a cigarette and was somewhat conscious that in some strange way he was anesthetizing himself. Now that he was on the spot, gone were all his dreads and silliness about clinics, graveyards, gravestones and ghosts. True, the electric needle was somewhat ominous, still, but he had no trouble keeping his mind off it. So at ease was he that he felt something must have happened to him, that strange restrictions in him had been broken down. Just what they were he was not sure; but he made the passing observation that he'd probably had a lump in his psyche far larger and far more harmful than the lump in his mouth—and he laughed at himself.

Someone had stopped at the door. It was another doctor whom he knew. They chatted a while.

Then Tom came in, dressed in his white coat, brisk and professional, fresh from his morning rounds.

"All right, John," said Tom. "Better leave your coat here, and come with me. I'll introduce you to the admission clerk and then I'll be back in a short while."

Down a long corridor they went, Curtis and his friend Dr. Thomas Cummings of the hospital staff. The corridor didn't suggest a hospital at all. None of the odors, none of the looks. It was more like a university building or a club. However, it was very long and from it one could judge the huge size of the institution. Curtis sensed the machine-nature of it but did not mind. He was not a patient yet. Besides, because of his connections the machine would grind quickly with the desired special care for him. In an hour at the most he'd be finished and out.

In what looked like a waiting-room Tom introduced Curtis to a girl who sat behind a desk. Several anonymous members of mankind were about, waiting for something or someone. Curtis barely noticed them. The girl nodded and smiled. Tom said something, winked at his friend, and strode off. Curtis, thus suddenly, was on his own. He didn't like the feeling of it; but, after all, he *was* an adult; after all, too, he had been on his own before in far more taxing situations than this.

The girl handed him a blank form and asked him to fill it out. He did so and returned it. She glanced at the information, gave him other papers, and told him where to find the next station.

As he went out he looked around for Tom. Saw no Tom. As he walked away he ran into patients, nurses, doctors, none of whom knew who he was or cared who he was.

At this second station another smiling girl took the papers from him, put a card on her typewriter and began typing in. Curtis looked at her, all the while feeling the machine getting a stronger hold on him.

"Your full name, please."

Curtis gave it, with resistance.

"Where do you live?"

Curtis told her, with mounting irritation and protest.

"How many are dependent upon you?"

"Either none or very many." He smiled at this, and so did she.

"Any insurance?"

"Once a month, unfortunately."

They were on better terms.

On the form she had seen he was, among other things, a writer. So when another girl came by and left a printed paper on her desk she told Curtis that this was the magazine gotten out by people in the hospital but she guessed he wouldn't be interested in it, not in writing for it anyway. He let it rest at that.

She gathered the forms together, handed them to him with a smile, and directed him to the next station, the desk at which he would pay the fee.

Still no Tom.

Behind a high stand he found another girl, but she was not smiling. She seemed embattled and distinctly hostile. The stand itself, an impregnable wooden affair, looked like a small fortress. On it was a cash-register. With a frown the girl looked down and reached for the papers.

"How much?" he asked.

"Four dollars, please."

It was a very low fee and he was quite prepared to pay it double or more, but because he disliked her and felt rubbed the wrong way he retorted, "I thought it was three."

Her eyes flashed. "No, four."

The register rang and she gave him a receipt.

"Up those stairs," she directed, "and straight down the hall until you come to the door marked Laboratory. They will tell you where to go from there."

Curtis was going to do as he was told when the word laboratory suddenly hit him. "Laboratory," he said, as if it were preposterous. He eyed the embattled girl and she eyed him. "Why laboratory? I understood I was to see Dr. Bradford. My friend Dr. Cummings is coming back to take me up."

The girl stiffened with resentment. He felt quilty, realizing that by mentioning his connection he had waved the red flag of Privilege in this democratic public institution. He'd have to stop that. No more of it. If he were going to accept their services he'd have to accept their ways too.

"You must go to the Laboratory first," she said firmly. "Dr. Cummings can do nothing for you. You are not in his clinic." And her contemptuous tone seemed to add, "You're a nice baby to need your big brother."

Curtis laughed at himself, raised his arm in military salute, wheeled about and began striding for the stairs. Into his mind came the old tune, "You're in the army now." Indeed he was, and a private at that, and as a private he'd obey orders.

This bit of comedy helped him to adjust. Helped him to step outside the role of the semi-distinguished Johnathan Curtis and accept his lot as one of the common people going through an expert mill to get a job well-done. Even as he went up the stairs his mind told him all of this. It told him, too, that the girl had been right. He had been a baby. A nice baby leaning on his big brother Tom.

A sudden thought struck him. Tom, the rascal, had of course known. Tom had never intended to return. Tom was deliberately letting him go through the machine alone for the removal of something more than the lump in his mouth.

He was laughing at himself and not following directions. Somewhere he must have made a wrong turn. From a room whose door was ajar he heard a nurse call out and halt him. Having seen the papers in his hand she had known he was off the track.

"Wide awake, these people," was his muttered comment.

After turning about and walking a way he saw the door bearing in black letters the word Laboratory. He opened it and went in. There, against one wall, was a high narrow hospital bed. A bed! He was, then, actually in a hospital! As a patient! No doubt of it. This was a business-room. By the opposite wall was a table with bottles and paraphernalia. The entrance of a nurse gave him no time for further observation.

This girl was smiling, with rosy cheeks, a springy step, and a general air of competency and excellent health. She must, he thought, like her job and get well paid. No ghost or gravestone, this; but a very living creature. Fresh as an idealized milk-maid. That was it. A milk-maid come to birth in a big city clinic.

But she too meant business. Said the nurse, "We'd like a sample of your urine, please. Use that bottle and when you are through, rap on the door." Out she went into an adjoining room which Curtis judged was the working part of the laboratory where the tests were made.

He smiled to himself. "So, they're going to find out about things. Thorough, these people."

When he rapped on the door the same nurse came in, with her same bright smile and blooming cheeks. Out went the bottle. He wondered if she had seen the drops he had inadvertently let fall on the floor. On her next return she said pleasantly but briefly, "Roll up your left sleeve, please."

Curtis frowned and fixed her with a look. "Just a minute. What's this for? Blood?"

"Yes."

He kept looking. "Is it necessary? You know, there's nothing seriously wrong with me. Just a little something in my mouth. I expected to see Dr. Bradford."

"We'd like to have it, but if the patient strongly objects we do not insist."

She too was looking at him, and he wondered if she, like the girl at the desk, was thinking he was a nice baby.

Said Curtis to himself, "Damn these women. To hell with this place. But—on the other hand, why not? Didn't I agree that I was in for it? Then the whole hog. Besides, it won't be a bad thing to have a check on my blood. And all for four dollars."

However, sound though these ideas were, he hesitated a moment longer because he'd never liked the notion of having a needle run into his vein and blood drawn. Besides, how could he be sure that she was competent?

Curtis smiled to the girl, laughed at himself, took off his coat, and rolled up his sleeve. The nurse looked at the veining of the inside elbow, a quick professional glance. "The other, please." Curtis did as he was told and rolled up the right. The girl made a quick comparison and decided upon the one from which she would draw blood.

"Lie upon that table, please."

Curtis obeyed. While a second girl tied a hose into a very deft knot about his arm, he couldn't resist asking aloud if this was the place where Mr. Max Elting had come for treatment about six months ago. He also mentioned Dr. Cummings.

"Mr. Elting was here. You know him? And Dr. Cummings too?"

Curtis granted he did; and felt all right upon the bed.

"Clench your fist and hold it that way until I tell you not to."

Curtis obeyed.

"Now look towards the wall and don't look this way."

He knew the nurse was kneeling near his out-stretched downward-pointing arm, with needle and bottle ready. Soon he knew the needle was in. Soon it was over. A piece of gauze dipped in antiseptic was pressed against the spot. The tourniquet was removed. He was asked to bend his arm up from the elbow. Shortly he was told he could get up.

"It's over?"

She nodded. "Do you feel anything?"

"A little queer at the elbow."

"Not dizzy?"

"No," he laughed.

She kept her eye on the spot. "Bend your arm again. I want to be sure it was stopped." When he had done so she added, "That's all right. That's all. Now you go down the hall, turn to your left, walk way through until you come to the corridor which parallels this, and you'll find the dermatology clinic just opposite this room on the other side."

"Then do I see the doctor?"

"Then you see the doctor."

He put on his coat, took up his card, and said good-by.

As he made his way to the next station he chuckled. "Wonder what they think? Syphilis, gonorrhea? Maybe it would make their job easier if I told them I've never even had the claps. Might not believe me, of course. They certainly do a thorough job here. And all for a lump. But wait! Not one of them yet knows what in hell I came for. As for Tom, he's missing a sight. Not everyone has a chance to see special Mr. Johnathan Curtis treated like an ordinary Bill Jones."

It was quite a walk. As he neared and designated place he could see signs reading Dermatology and Dentistry. At the proper desk he handed over his card. Another smiling and quite pretty nurse with dark hair asked him to be seated until his turn came, when she would call.

Quite a number of people were waiting on the benches, common members of mankind with something the matter with them. Curtis seated himself among them, knowing that they knew that he too was in trouble—and nothing more. It was like being a name—less than a name—among other names in a phone book.

Near the entrance to the dermatology rooms he saw a number of young people standing about, talking, all dressed in the official white coats; but not until later did he have reason to know that they were senior medical students sent to the clinic to get practical observation-work under Dr. Bradford.

When the pretty nurse called his name he followed her into a room with a curtain across the door end.

"Undress, please, and lie on the table. The doctor will soon be in." She gave him a sheet and a white jacket, drew the curtain, and went out.

Curtis knew he was in for a physical. Well, again, good. He'd been wanting one all these months. It too was to be thrown in, all for four dollars. As he undressed he wondered if the doctor she had mentioned would be Bradford. He also wondered about her. Not only her good looks but some fine thing inside of her had caught his eye.

Soon after he had stretched himself upon the bed a youngish man with grey eyes, surely not Bradford, came in. Curtis greeted him, as one personality [to] another. The young doctor barely nodded; and Curtis knew that the man regarded himself only as a physician, and that he regarded him only as a body, one of the thousands of bodies that came to the clinic.

Maintaining his noncommittal impersonality, the young doctor went to work at once with stethoscope, blood-pressure taking, percussion, testing of reflexes. His hands were deft, his face expressionless. He said nothing. With each new test Curtis felt more than ever that he was only a body.

Then the man went to a desk, asked questions, wrote down the answers. Curtis wanted to know the results of the urine and blood tests. The doctor said they'd tell him later. In no way could Curtis get a personal wedge in. Moreover, all of this had happened and he was still in the dark as regards his lump. Nor did the clinic know why he had come. If this went on much longer . . .

The young doctor came to the bedside. "What is the matter with you?"

At last! At last he could speak and tell! Curtis blinked, started to speak, and all at once confusion caught him. Now he felt guilty of having put them to a lot of trouble over nothing. His small innocent lump! He sat upright and idiotically pointed to his mouth.

The young doctor had no time to lose. Nor was he interested in his patient's sudden emotional state. Using a flat mouth-stick he examined the mouth and found the lump. He said nothing, but what he saw did not impress him as serious. Curtis, watching him narrowly, was sure of this.

Just then Tom came in. Tom, all smiles. "So here you are!"

Curtis almost leapt from the table to shake his hand, the hand of his friend Tom, Dr. Thomas Cummings of the hospital staff.

Said Tom to the young doctor, "Dr. Masters, this is my friend Johnathan Curtis. Do the best you can for him. Are you afraid he will live?"

Masters smiled for the first time. Curtis glowed. Dr. Masters admitted he was afraid that Mr. Curtis would live.

"Just dropped in," said Tom. "Must be off."

Masters went as far as the door with Tom; and Curtis was sure he heard Masters say, "Nothing much at all. In good shape." Then why didn't the young sphinx say that to him? Why keep him in the dark? For all he actually knew to the contrary, his lump might still be a cancer lump. Was this a rack—or what?

Masters returned, resumed the examination, finished it, and told Curtis simply to rest there and take it easy. Out he went.

Left alone, Curtis found himself all worked up. Worked up, it seemed to him, out of all proportion to what had happened—though enough had happened, or failed to happen, God knows. What was it about? Now his internal upheaval concerned him far more than the lump in his mouth— so much so that he delved into himself and almost forgot he was sitting unclad on a table in a grey-walled cell of a clinic.

His ego was suffering, his pride, his vanity, his desire for special attention. Obviously and evidently. But this did not explain why he felt that some profound change was taking place. Nor could he explain it. After a time he gave up the attempt, stretched out on the bed, and again became aware of where he was.

He could hear people passing along the hallway. The white curtain hid them from view. Once the pretty nurse came in. Curtis exchanged smiles, said something, and a bond sprang up between them. At least he felt it did. His first human contact in that institution. If there was going to be any cutting and cauterizing he wanted Dr. Bradford to do it, and this nurse whose name (he didn't quite know how he had learned it) was Miss Reynolds, to help him. Curtis even played with the idea that with Miss Reynolds on hand he'd be willing to go through most anything.

From the adjoining room, for a brief time, he heard the voice of a doctor talking in a quiet firm tone to a woman patient, assuring her that nothing serious was the matter. Was it the truth, or was it one of the white lies which doctors sometimes tell to keep serious issues from the patient's knowledge? What of his own pet lump? He was not worrying about it, yet, damnit, not yet was he absolutely clear of doubt. How much longer was this sort of thing to go on? And what was coming next? Why not get into his clothes and leave the esoteric place?

Just then he chanced to remember the observation he'd made while sitting in the private office waiting for Tom to appear, namely, that he'd probably had a lump in his psyche far larger and far more harmful than the lump in his mouth. This time the idea struck him with such force that he sat bolt upright in amazement. So this was it! Here, by god, was the clue to what had been happening to him!

Perceptions flooded him; and he saw, or thought he saw, it all.

His dread of knives and surgeons and hospitals—a mask of another fear. No, by god, he did not really fear them. What he did fear, what he did resist with every atom in him was the surrendering of himself to any person in a vital situation. Johnathon Curtis, the dominant. No one should ever dominate him. But in the patient-surgeon relationship—ah, god. A symbol of submission in its most acute form—the patient passive, paralyzed, at his worst, and utterly at the surgeon's mercy; the surgeon active, dominant, at his best, doing with the patient according to his will. So this was it! And what had happened?

Curtis was not given time to answer.

Into the room came a mature looking doctor, followed by a number of medical students, one of them a girl. The shock was so great that to Curtis it seemed that all the students rushed up to him with wild enthusiasm, mouths agape, eyes popping, eager to gobble up his defenseless naked-ness. The most he could do was to draw the sheet over his privates.

He wanted to drive them out. To tell the doctor this was an outrage. To let the whole world know that Johnathan Curtis was not and would never be a specimen "of what happens to people's dermatology." Not for the sake of science. Not for the sake of anything. And then, for the most important time of his life, Curtis laughed at himself.

Of course, this *was* a clinic. The fee was low; and somehow the institu-tion had to get a return. So be it, then. He was in for it—so the whole hog. Let the eager youngsters pounce. Someday they'd take pride in telling everybody that once upon a time they beheld the naked torso, even the bare privates, or a great man. Let science in general and dermatology in particular be benefited. If this was his contribution, he'd make it like a soldier.

His sight was still doing strange things to him, however. Somebody, he was not sure who, introduced him to Dr. Bradford. He shook hands. Before him he saw a quiet self-confident man with level grey eyes. He saw, but more dimly, the students. He saw Miss Reynolds in the back-ground. He believed that Dr. Masters was there.

Without more ado, Bradford proceeded. First he called the students' attention to certain markings on the skin of the body of Johnathan Curtis. The students drew closer to look. Bradford then asked Curtis questions about them. What, Curtis asked himself, had these marks to do with the lump in his mouth? But he answered as best he could. There was some discussion. Verily the clinic was getting its money worth. There was no doubt in his mind that he was.

Then Bradford asked to see his mouth. Curtis opened. Bradford looked at the lump. The students looked at the lump. Bradford explained that it was what was called a cyst.

Ah! At last Curtis had the real name for it. Not a cancer, not a tumor, not an ulcer, but a *cyst*!

Bradford went on to say that the cyst was formed owing to a small gland in the mouth which, having filled up, had failed to discharge.

"Nothing serious," he added. "I had one myself. It was cauterized and I've had no trouble since."

Whereon, he smiled to Curtis and began making his way out of the room, most of the students following. Before he reached the curtain, he paused to remark significantly, "We will give treatment."

It was a foolish thing to do, but Curtis could not help it. At the departing doctor he shouted, "I have a cyst in my psyche too."

Bradford turned a surprised face. "How's that?"

"Nothing," said Curtis, lowering his head.

Two students remained behind, still looking at Curtis, wondering, talking amongst themselves. Just then a belated newcomer appeared. The two told him about the cyst. Obviously he wanted to see with his own eyes. Curtis rewarded the new student's scientific curiosity by himself suggesting that he come over and have a look—which the student did.

Miss Reynolds, very active, very busy, still very pretty also, came in and told Curtis he might dress now and then come out, as the treatment would be given in another room.

He obeyed. So at last the real business was to be done. For the first time in his life he was to be cut, if only a little, by a surgeon's knife. He felt not much of anything, save a certain gratification that the thing was to be accomplished, and soon, now. He moved along realistically without alarm or fear; though he did wonder what the electric needle would look like; if he would feel anything; how his mouth would be after; and he did want Bradford to do the job and Miss Reynolds to help him. On this latter he was quite set.

Miss Reynolds met him in the hall and took him into another room with a curtain. There, first thing, he sought and found the needle. It appeared more like an iron. The nearest thing to it in his experience was a woman's hair-curling iron.

Miss Reynolds busied herself, preparing.

"Ah," said Curtis, "she *will* be the one to help!" A very great deal in life seemed suddenly to depend upon this.

She was eating a hurried mouthful of lunch. "We've had 43 cases already today."

"That many? All before lunch?"

"Some days we have as many as 70."

"Don't have much time to yourself, do you?"

She granted she didn't. And he—it was uncommonly nice just to chat with her.

She asked him to take off his coat and get upon the bed. When he had done so she put a white thing over his chest and remarked with a laugh that he had long legs, too long for the bed. Lying there he watched her move and caught her eyes and smiled. A really splendid person, this Miss Reynolds.

She saw Dr. Masters passing, and called, and said everything was ready. To Curtis she confided, "Have to catch them when we can. They're awfully busy too."

So. Masters and not Bradford was to cauterize. Ah, well, he accepted this also, and the acceptance was made easier by the fact that, in any case, Miss Reynolds with her sweet face and lovely dark eyes and rosy cheeks and black hair and deft hands would be there.

Then she left the room. He did not like this.

From an adjoining room another nurse came in, and began busying herself.

"Grief," cried he, "I must get rid of her."

She asked him, "Do you know what you are here for?"

Know? Of course he did, the ignoramus. What was she butting in for? "Certainly," said he. "They are going to cauterize a cyst." For a moment he permitted himself to feel a flush of boyish pride at his newly acquired precise scientific terminology. But only for a moment. He added distinctly, "I believe that Miss Reynolds is already scheduled to help Dr. Masters."

The new nurse made no reply. From somewhere she got a sheet and covered the entire length of his body. Damn her anyway, why did she have to put him under a ghost-sheet when Miss Reynolds had seen fit only to cover his chest? He was about to kick the thing off, to invent some potent way of supplanting the intruder, when, as unexpectedly as she had appeared, she disappeared through the same door.

Curtis breathed his relief. For a time he was left to himself. Not a thing in the world was troubling him, even though, any minute now, he would go under the knife. Nothing this day would trouble him if only Miss Reynolds would return. He was happy to confess that he had a feeling for her, a curiously deep feeling of their relationship which might be expressed thus: This nurse is a woman, and this woman knows how to care for me, to care for the needs of my body which I, a man, am likely to neglect. Just this, quite simply, quite sheerly, quite purely.

When Dr. Masters came in he saw a happy man. This man was happier still when he saw Miss Reynolds following.

Nothing much was said. She adjusted the light, then stood behind Curtis' head and, using sterilized gauze, held his mouth open. When Masters was about to inject the novocaine she whispered, "It may hurt a little." But it didn't, not as much as a dentist's hypodermic.

Curtis saw Masters take up a pair of small curved scissors. Into his mouth they went and he knew the cyst, his lump, his pet of six months standing had been cut out. The place was treated. Next Masters took hold of the iron, asking Miss Reynolds to get a firmer grip and open the mouth wider as the spot was awkward to reach.

Into his mouth went the iron. Masters said it would not hurt. It did not. Curtis could hear a faint sizzling every time the iron touched. Once while this was being done he thought of the possibility that Masters' hand might slip and the iron burn through his cheek. Inwardly he smiled. He too had learned that strange faith which patients have in those who operate upon them for their good. Really, the faith of a child.

Again the place was treated. Miss Reynolds let go her hold. The doctor turned away towards something else. She removed the sheet, remarking that somebody had certainly wanted him covered. Curtis sat up. His mouth, on that side, was numb. "That's all?"

"That's all." Masters added, "It will heal in two weeks, but will be a bit sore at first. Use a mouth wash twice a day."

"Nothing more?"

"Nothing more."

With a rush of feeling Curtis suddenly realized that the thing that had been troubling him was out, out successfully, everything neatly done and finished. In its way it was sort of miraculous—not at all, perhaps, to a member of the profession, but certainly to a laymen, a formerly fearsome layman at that.

"What shall I eat?"

Curtis had a faint notion that this question, patently childish, was a measure of the degree to which he had put himself in their hands, as a child would surrender to an adult—and that, having thus so completely submitted himself, he was still to some extent a child, not yet having recovered his own grown-up individuality.

Masters smiled and threw over his shoulder, "Whatever you want." He was going out.

Curtis sprang from the bed and ran up to shake hands. "Thanks, thanks, very much." He wanted to say more, to do something to show

how grateful he felt. This man had performed for him a real service. True, Masters had; but for Masters, apparently, it was all in a day's work. Not even by gratitude could Curtis wedge the human in. Masters nodded and smiled and walked off to his next case.

Dr. Bradford happened to be passing. Curtis shook his hand. "Glad to have met you," said Bradford, and walked on.

Johnathan Curtis ran back into the room where Miss Reynolds still was, to shake her hand. She seemed a little surprised, as if she had thought he had gone. Pleased, too. Again, perhaps even more, he wanted to say something. What could he? After all, it was a clinic, this was an operating room, she was a nurse, and she also had her next case, with no more time to give him.

"Thank you."

He saw her clearly. She was very beautiful. He flushed, almost stammered . . .

The next thing he knew he was striding down the hall, heart beating fast, all of him confused, all of him aglow.

As he passed the dermatology office an unknown nurse called after him, "Have you made your appointment for next time?"

He stopped dead, wheeled around. Miss Reynolds, going towards the office from the operating room had heard the question. Flashing him a last smile she answered for him. "Mr. Curtis is discharged," she said.

Curtis brought his hand to a salute, faced away, and marched off down the corridor.

[1936?]

The Spoken Word

The most simple, the most natural, use of words is the spoken word. For centuries man has been speaking. The oral tradition preceded the written tradition. Religious doctrines, ideas, opinions, as well as myths and tales, were passed from person to person through the spoken word. In the western world printing and the written word are only a few centuries old. But, as if in illustration of Emerson's law of compensation, the written word, having spread so widely in so short a time, is likely to supersede the spoken word. For the past thirty years we have heard complaints that the art of conversation is a dead art. The famous literary salons are not of this century but of previous ones, and should anyone voice his wish to have a place for the gathering of people who would engage in lively, intelligent conversation, we would look askance at that person as if he were proposing that which is both impossible and undesirable. Just as there are no Madame de Staels among us, so there are few Bernard Shaws. So much for conversation as an art.

But even conversation as a means of simple communication seems to be passing out. The old-fashioned gathering of people around a hearth after dinner, with talk that lasted far into the night, is not present in these modern days. And indeed, should most of us face the prospect of such an evening, we would face it with a groan. No, the fact is that we do not wish to talk with each other. And the fact is that we do not talk to each other. We have adopted many and various means of occupying our time. We have invented and now use, on an unprecedented scale, substitutes for speech. One of the most obvious of these substitutes for speech is the newspaper. If we are with another person and do not know what to say to him or her, or do not want the trouble of saying anything, we can hand him or her a newspaper. In this connection there is to be noted a striking difference between American railroads and cafes and European railroads and cafes. The American commuter train is relatively silent. But each person has his newspaper. The Europeans are trying hard to imitate us in this. But still there is to be noted in their trains the sound of voices in conversation more animated than the rustle of turning pages. A similar difference is to be noted in cafes. Magazines and books play a similar function. If you cannot or do not wish to discuss with a person the subject, say, of the controversy between the Humanists and the Anti-Humanists, you can at least suggest or give to him a pertinent book to read.

If one is apprehensive as to what to do with dinner guests, there are a number of solutions, any one of which will fill the gap of absent conversation. We will, of course, first give our guests cocktails, and if they have enough of these they cannot speak in any case. Then we can turn on the radio, or play bridge. Perhaps we will go to a theatre. Or, if there is too much conversation on the legitimate stage, we will switch them to a talkie or a "silent." Or, if these are too strenuous we will take them to a night-club, where jazz and bootleg both prevent and incapacitate speech. Having had a good evening with our friends, we will drive them home in a strangely silent motor car, and say, "Good night"!

I have been somewhat satirical in the above description, but I hope that the temper of its expression will not mislead the hearer as to the bearing this condition has on the serious matter of the creation of literature. For there is, in my opinion, an intimate connection between speech and writing. It is true that it does not always follow that because a man or a people speak well, he or they will write well. Indeed, as I pointed out at the beginning of this talk, many of the ancients, though gifted with the spoken word, wrote comparatively nothing. This, however, does not mean that they could not write. And it is also true that there are those who can write well but who speak poorly. Nevertheless, I do not think that a mute nation could possibly produce great literature. We are far from mute. And the condition is as yet not alarming. But I simply want to point out that, if we consciously or unconsciously minimize the value of the spoken word, if we become increasingly disinclined to use it, if we become increasingly inclined to use printing and other inventions as unwise substitutes for speech, we may find that this condition will seriously affect both the creation and appreciation of genuine literature. How can a person conditioned to speak hardly at all, conditioned to hear only the words and tones of the radio and the talkies, either produce or respond to the words and tones of a Goethe or a Blake?

[1930]

Winter Road

It was a cold blowy day. I had been pondering life and the ways of man, thinking particularly of that mysterious barrier which walls a man off from himself and from his fellow men. As I drove into town I approached a man walking along the state highway, going the other way. Cars passed him, in his direction. None stopped to give him a lift. The men seemed sealed in the cars. He hailed no one. He seemed sealed in himself.

He was dressed in brown, color faded like last year's crop-fields. Swinging a bundle by its string, he strode along with the gait of a man accustomed to following horses down furrows. As my car went by, I seemed to take him in at a glance—his brown blown hat, his worn brown overcoat, his large eyeglasses, his long nose, his life's tan still on his face, his jaw thrust into the wind. Perhaps it was this resolute jaw, alone on the road, that touched me. Perhaps it was something else—like meeting one's self.

I was filled with that man and felt I must do something about him.

I hurried through shopping, wondering where he had gotten to on that road I knew so well. Maybe someone had picked him up, stopped and asked him—and I would never see him again.

Finished with my last purchase I raced the car through town and out onto the highway. At a spot farther along than I had expected, I saw his back, plodding along, swinging his bundle, the wind sending cigarette smoke behind his head, as if his face might be on fire. Now I knew I had known with certainty that I would come across him again.

Cars passed him as before, they not stopping for him, he without even the idea of hailing them.

I drove up, prepared to stop. I caught sight of him side-face, and something in him—or was it in me?—impelled me to put my foot on the gas.

I drove on, uncomfortable that my foot had been stronger than my wish. Soon I came to the fork and the branch road which I'd usually take, returning home. I kept to the highway. At a farther cross-road I stopped the car, to wait until the man caught up to me, yet not quite knowing what to do when he did.

I took a dollar bill from my pants pocket and put it in my overcoat pocket, handy. To give him money—was this all? Was this the measure of my first impulse? I looked back along the road, to see him heave into sight. It was taking him a long time to cover the distance on foot.

I pretended to read a paper. I wondered what exactly I was going to say to him, and what he would say.

I looked back again, and, still not seeing him, wondered if perhaps someone had picked him up, and he had whizzed by me in a closed car. I turned my car around, resolved to stop the car should I see him still walking, stop it, jump out, give him the dollar, and drive on. Yet this wasn't at all what I had wanted to do when I first saw him walking, being picked up by no one, asking no one for a lift, that long cold road before him.

Again I saw him, striding along as first I had seen him. I succeeded in slowing the car just enough to attract his attention. A strange communication flashed between us—not recognition, an expectation of curious intensity, as if an inward hope, as ancient as the race, suddenly opened and as suddenly closed. But I drove on, because he seemed so resolute and going it alone that I recoiled from splitting his independence with a gift.

Yet what might it mean to him, that dollar bill, just it, and the way it would come? Besides, the urge was still in me. From behind it pressed against my navel.

I circled a by-way and reached the vantage point of a hill from which I could see him as he passed the cross-road. I wanted to come up behind him, making it appear that I had just chanced upon him, he and I both going the same way. As I sat there, waiting, on the lookout, all I had thought about life and the ways of man seemed to boil down and connect with this incident between myself and this man. There was a meaning which pressed to be lived, undiverted, between being and being—

I saw him, small, far down there, moving along the state highway still alone, following the ribbon of the road without knowing that into my mind came the thought that the color of his coat was the same as that of last summer's corn fields which flanked the highway to either side. But for knowing him, by previous close contact, to be a man, I might now have pictured him as an object, a bundle of corn-stalks moved by the wind; or, if man, then of no meaning to me.

I coasted down the hill, slipped onto the highway, and came up behind him. This time my body obeyed my wish. I stopped and asked if he would like a lift.

He ran up, thanked me, and got in. Looking at him direct, I saw his face was good, not as strong as I had supposed, older, but good, and resolved never to ask anyone for anything in the kind of life he was now forced to live, lest just this asking bind him and make him belong to a life that was not his.

"Where are you going?"

"Newark."

"That's about sixty miles away. Come far today?"

"From Lancaster."

We had passed my side-road by a number of miles, and soon I would have to invent a cross-road at which to stop and let him out, unless I intended driving him all the way to Newark.

"Will you have enough to eat, on your way?"

"Well . . . no. I guess that's the only trouble."

We came to a cross-road. I pulled to the side and stopped. I gave him the dollar bill. Something opened in him and I saw his light. He said he never begged. He said this wasn't his life, and he wasn't going to allow himself to get used to it.

"This will give me all I need to eat for those sixty miles to Newark," he said. The light never left him.

"My friend," I said, "there are more than sixty miles, to where you and I are going."

[2/26/37]

George Washington

When I was much younger, I began to wonder about George Washington. Whatever I heard concerning him was not entirely satisfying. He was honest. He was the Father of his Country—that is, our United States. He was a great statesman. He rode a horse. He chopped down a cherry tree, and admitted it. The symbol of him was a hatchet. There were many facts about him in books in school. He made Cornwallis surrender, or words to that effect. He was born a very long time ago, and had been dead a great while. His birthday was a holiday. His wife's name was Martha.

None of these things made much difference to me, as a boy, except the holiday. I liked that, every year. I got something out of it. As for honesty, that was just something that parents expected of their children. I saw very little simple honesty around me. As for what it might mean to be the Father of our Country, I could not see it at all. Washington was merely the first president of the United States, and somebody had to be first. As for statesmen, and what that might amount to, I saw plenty of statesmen. In fact, most of my early information about Washington came from the open mouths of politicians, and most of their bawling about him sounded insincere, not quite honest. We children were told to be like Washington, and tell the truth, and become great some day. I wondered why they didn't take their own big advice. Plainly they were not great men, and nobody considered them really honest. So I did not care for what the political wind-bags said about Washington.

Later on, I saw that this George Washington was an excuse for a bank to stay closed, or something to help the manufacturers of red paper hatchets for decorating at women's parties, so still I continued to feel no relation to this Father of the Country.

Still later, perhaps in my twenties, I happened to do a little more thinking about the matter. I saw that movie heroes were not like George Washington, and people imitated the movies. The men with the big money were not at all like Washington, and everybody was trying to pile up big money. In fact, I could not find anywhere, the least evidence that anybody had taken Washington seriously. He was a legend, like Santa Claus. I met people who openly studied and imitated Napoleon, and behaved like him, but nobody imitated Washington. He was just a man on paper. That is what he was to me, and to very many other young men—merely an unreal figure.

So it did not jar me at all when I learned on the best of authority that the hatchet and cherry tree story had no foundation in fact. The very story of his honesty was itself false—just somebody's imagination. For me, George Washington was dismissed.

But I happened to visit his home. That was something different. It was a real place, and a very beautiful place. Quite obviously, somebody had lived there, long ago—somebody with good taste—evidently a wealthy man who knew how to live as a man should, as any man might like to. The house on Mount Vernon was no legend, and the river was a true thing, and the view from the front porch was wonderful. I saw the rooms where this George Washington had lived and moved, and where be had died, and all the fine things he kept around in his sight. All through school, nobody had mentioned this. It became important to me, and started me thinking all over again.

In those surroundings, his white wig and long blue coats with brass buttons on them, were suitable and right indeed. I saw this old piano, and the old pages of music on it, and could readily understand how Washington and his guests had danced a light minuet on those old fine floors. But in my school days, Washington could only fight and pray and ride a horse and make somebody surrender. Now this was altogether different to me. And for the first time I got a faint notion of what it must have meant to George Washington to get up out of this beautiful place, and try to win a war in the woods.

From that time on, George Washington was a man to me. He had lived in a real place, and the place was still there. If he were still living, he certainly would not allow such mobs of tourists on his lawn or trooping through his parlor and his bedroom. Some of his black servants would appear and chase off the people who strew the place with candy boxes and sandwich papers.

Little by littel he began to grow, in my own mind, as a man. I came to appreciate what it meant, for instance, that he was a very expert surveyor—not just to set a fence for somebody's corn field, but to establish accurate boundaries for the States that were to be united. In another connection, I was surprised to learn that he was a very good miller, and that he understood exactly what good flour was, and how it must be made, and he made it in his own mill. Perhaps he never heard of a vitamin, but be knew about food and insisted upon having a right kind of flour. By this time, to me, he was quite a man.

More recently I had occasion to study into the early facts of our Nation—facts that never were clear to me in school days. I could at last see Washington as not only a man, but a most remarkable man.

Perhaps it was my own fault, or the fault of the old text books, but it seems a shame to me that I had to piece out for myself, through the years, how remarkable a man he was, and what he was actually like, and what he suffered, and what a sterling character he had. I feel cheated, somehow, that I could not have been given to understand all that in the first place. Because he really lived and breathed as we breathe, and met obstacles and faced terrible odds, and mastered them—a wonderfully strong character, a man to be copied, not in terms of paper hatchets and postage stamps, but in terms of actual daily life—such a man as our country greatly needs today.

He was no noisy politician. Simply by the strength of his character he was placed in the highest office. There was nobody else to do it as well as he, and he did it. He was no parade warrior, but under necessity be could fight, and he fought well. Four horses were shot from under him, one after another, and he went on because it was not in his make-up to turn back and quit. But he took no credit to himself for winning a war. He knew quite well, even without a radio or a newspaper that was less than three months old, that if the French had not taken their opportunity to pounce upon England just at that time, the outcome of the first American War might have been entirely different. But the great point is, that his own part would not have been different. No amount of "ifs" could change his character. Both as a general and as a president, he acted against his own personal inclination and tastes. He had nothing to gain. He had no ambition for fame. And he did not need to be told what to do. He could think, and he did his own thinking. He had feelings, and it is clear that his sense of duty often sustained his actions against his own private wishes. He was physically strong and fearless. He understood and enjoyed the best things in life; he faced and endured and came through the worst.

Afterwards it was easy for others to call him a man of great destiny. But at the time he was doing those things, he had no such applause. In fact, on all sides of him, he heard the most terrible criticism. Yet he did his work. First, and last, he had great character. And whenever he found it necessary, he developed rare ability to do what had to be done, as dictated by his own character.

It may be true, in one sense, that Washington had the kind of opportunity that comes but once. A new nation is not born every day. But any thoughtful person realizes that our nation today is loaded down with opportunities just waiting to be seized by the right young man who has enough capacity to think, to feel and to act, to see him through for the sake of his convictions.

In politics today, we need a George Washington, or somebody like him in character. But to compare our present-day orators with him is cruel sport. They are more like those who harshly criticized Washington in that past day. It may be that our present-day leaders also heard of Washington in their childhood, and dismissed him as a man on paper, to be used in speeches and in naming new streets or parks. And perhaps it is reasonable to assume that we might now have some genuine national leader, if our present crop of talkers had been somehow taught in their childhood that George Washington was actually a man.

However that may be, it seems quite certain that with our own national affairs as they are, and the four principal nations of Europe striving hard toward another big war, there will be plenty of opportunity from now on, for a new man like Washington to do equally important work in the world. If such a genuine leader arises, he may be a youth or a child right now, somewhere—perhaps one that we know. And also it is reasonable to conclude that this young person will have been taught, in some way or other, that the Father of our Country was a human being, and that his greatness lay in his character, such as even the poorest child may have and develop.

[11/8/32]

Atomic Energy

The very fact that it exists and is available to men, draws men's attention to it, whereas man's attention should be directed towards spiritual energy. More than any form of material energy has ever done, it catches the imagination, etc.

Since it is available to man, public officers such as David E. Lilienthal do right in trying to arouse the people's/public's concern about its use, into whose hands it may fall. He is discharging his duty to the public when he warns that atomic energy may [be] taken over completely by the military or fall into the hands of private profiteers. But all of this increases the call to attend to atomic energy, increasingly takes man's mind off of spiritual energy.

Its use in war would be instantly disastrous. Its use in peace would be as disastrous, but more gradually. Its peacetime use would increasingly divert men from the spiritual to the material. It would increasingly externalize and mechanize man. It would result in a human world increasingly organized apart from Nature, from man's real nature, and from God.

[1947?]

V

A Children's Story

Editor's Note

The typescript of "Monrovia" is undated. The story's lyricism and setting are reminiscent of the White Island section of "Winter on Earth," which appeared in *The Second American Caravan* in 1928. However, the setting also suggests the Pacific coast around Carmel, California, where Toomer lived with his new wife, the writer Margery Latimer, in 1932. That same year Margery died in childbirth, and it is tempting to read "Monrovia" with its narrative of overcoming sorrow caused by the death of a loved one as Toomer's working out his own loss through his writing. At any rate, speculation aside, "Monrovia" does contain a theme of recurring importance to Toomer: the development of an independent, whole, and creative personality that is a meaningful part of the community at large. Monrovia's story illustrates this.

While Toomer certainly did not generally write children's literature, he was interested in the importance of traditional legends and fables for psychic growth, and he felt that children who had not been exposed to such literature would grow up to be less than fully developed adults. With its fairy-tale quality, "Monrovia" may also reflect the influence on Toomer of his Uncle Bismarck, his mother's brother; when Toomer was a child, one of his favorite pastimes was to listen to Bismarck read him folk tales, fables, and myths.

In the fairly rough typescript of "Monrovia," Toomer consistently omitted the apostrophes in his contractions, as he did in *Cane,* but rarely afterwards.

Monrovia

The white does lay in the yellow-green grass, very still, dark eyes sad.

Monrovia was stretched out by the oldest, one arm round its neck, thick black hair pushed back from her forehead. Her gray eyes watched the beach down beyond the cliff.

"How purple the sand and how silver the little fish washed up by the sea," she was thinking. The magnolia blossoms in the trees above gleamed like star-beams. The water was green as jade. Monrovia watched the tiny red crabs that flecked the shore.

She felt the doe beside her move a little. It brushed her arm with its nose, breathing warm sweetness towards her. Over her head the leaves rustled. There was a hum of bees in the salty air. Her scarlet gown spread about her, the grass still cool underneath it.

Through the heat came a sound of bells—as if from under water. Monrovia held her breath. All morning she had been waiting. She felt the doe's heart, like her own, beat faster.

A sharper tinkle of bells. Along the beach below swift feet sliding. A sudden crash in the bushes. A louder chime. The does about Monrovia made an arrow flight, disappearing obliquely in the thick brush behind. Their eyes quickened but were still sad. Monrovia seemed about to follow when Asrael caught her. The silver bells on his coat clanged with the quick movement of his arms. He had one flash of darkening gray eyes before her face hid in his shoulder.

"You are as shy as your does, my sweet, only you cant run quite so fast," he laughed. "Were you going to leave me? Arent you used to me yet?" Her hair against his cheek smelt of fresh leaves. She was feeling her heart beat.

"Wont you look out?" he whispered. "See how green the sea is and how the sea gulls are crowding. Look, Monrovia!"

She turned in the curve of his arm towards the sea. It was sunny and seemed deeper. White foam capped the waves. Asrael watched the smooth curve of her cheek for an instant. When he reached down to her pomegranate mouth the sea blotted out. . . . .

Monrovia clung to him for a long moment and there was silence on the cliff except for the hum of bees and the swish of the wind in the branches.

When the sea and the bright gold air swung back once more into existence Asrael drew her round quickly towards the edge of the cliff.

"Where are you going?" her long eyes questioned. His hair seemed to her amber in the sunlight.

"Let us look once more at our island, Monrovia! It is only a little way and you can come back to your does. Come!"

Monrovia kept her eyes on his face as they went down the path to the shore. Her red gown swirled about her in the grass. More certain and even more dear Asrael seemed to her, so much so that it hurt her heart. They moved easily over the wet sand, she curled in his arm. Her dark head was snug against his shoulder. The noon sun dazzled them both as they went round the curve of the shore.

"Can you find it, Monrovia? That little black spot out there? When you see it closer you will know why I chose it. Such dark cool woods and such bright winged birds! The air is like white wine there and the noise of the sea is like a song. There are all the flowers and the fruits you could wish and nuts of every sort. And much long grass for your does. I have finished our tower, and it is firm and dry. Are you glad, Monrovia? Are you ready to go? Tomorrow I will come for you." She nodded shyly. "Brother Myon will meet us at the chapel down the beach. Tomorrow I will have everything ready. There is plenty of wood gathered and cut and today I take flour and woolens and linen. One trip more and everything is there. You are going to be safe and never lonely. I shall be there always. Are you glad, you little fearful doe?"

Monrovia's cloudy eyes and oblong mouth smiled at him from the safety of his arm.

They drifted back, dreaming, to her green shelter. The does sprang once more sidewise to the forest. The wind was blowing harder. It whipped her long yellow-red gown about him. He shielded her with his height. His hard brown cheek pressed against [her] cream one. They stood for a moment [in a] world alone.

The sea had become black emerald. There was almost a solid sheet of foam. Drops of cold spray blew up to them from the beach below. The dampness made the magnolias more [heavy?] sweet.

"How dark it is getting!" Monrovia murmured suddenly against his rough coat, "and how the wind crashes! I shall be afraid without you. Cant you stay with me today, Asrael? Just for a little while? I have only old Ismael to talk to, you know. He is good always. But it is so dreary. Couldnt you stay just for a little while?"

"I wish I could, my sweet! But I must hurry for tomorrow. One trip more and everything is done. Then I will come for you and I will never again leave you. My lovely little warm one! Look at me, Monrovia!"

She gave him a breathless glance. But the sea fascinated her. It was blackening. All bright gold was gone. The white gulls swooped up and down back and forth in wide circles. The waves pounded on the shore.

"Be careful, Asrael," she cried, her hands holding him. "Something is the matter! I am frightened of the sea today! Hear how relentlessly it sounds! There is a wild storm coming. Wait one day more, Asrael! Stay here with me! We can surely wait one day more! Tomorrow may be sunny and still. I cant bear to let you go! I feel only complete when I am with you."

His steady arms were comforting.

"Always afraid, my dearest dear," he laughed. "Will you never be used to the sea? There is nothing to worry about. My boat can ride any storm. And nothing can hurt me today. For tomorrow you are going with me! Have you told Ismael to bring your chests to the cliff? He and your does can come later. Dont be afraid, my sweet! Say good-by just once more!"

He reached again down to her oblong curved mouth and again sea and wind and sky were forgotten . . .

Monrovia watched him from the edge of the cliff go shouldering down the path easily. Her heart ached a little and her thick hair kept blinding her. He waved joyously from the sand. "Dont be afraid, my sweet. We will soon be together always!" came back to her dimly through the wind. And a sound of bells from under water. Asrael disappeared round the curve. The sea boomed.

The does had gathered again among the trees. They were nervous in the thrashing bushes. Monrovia moved towards them, her face was frightened but starry. She pressed her cheek for a moment against the fur of the nearest.

"Ismael will be waiting. We must go back quickly. How cold it is getting . . . Do you know that tomorrow we are leaving this cliff and going with Asrael? You and I and Ismael. I am going to be safe and never lonely. I will never be alone!" She felt again, very close, Asrael's certain strength. . . .

With one hand on a white doe's neck, Monrovia hurried back through the dusky forest. There were deep rumblings behind them. Even way back in the hollows where usually everything was silent, the pounding of the sea could be heard. Quick gold flashes in the green light made Monrovia shudder. The does ran faster and lower before the rain. Asrael's face and nearness stayed with Monrovia as she flew with them through the underbrush.

"Keep him very safe, O Lord!" she whispered breathlessly. The wind was tearing at her hair and her berry-red gown.

●

The morning world glistened. It was as shining and expectant as Monrovia, who sat on the leafy cliff among her white deer, with long eyes as black as the rain that had beaten down all night. The sea in front of her was sapphire. It was swishing softly onto the purple beach and tossing iridescent drops over the small red crabs.

She sat on a chest, in a silver gown—only her long sleeves scarlet—shy and proud, and still as her ivory white does. Her pomegranate mouth was curved with delight at the morning. The magnolia blossoms were pearl lanterns among the wet green of the branches, the sea was a turquoise, and the silver fish leaped and darted in gold sunlight. It was a world that might be hard to leave, she felt for a moment. But the thought of Asrael's face and Asrael's voice came in between.

Hours passed. The sun rose higher. The sea grew more smooth. And still no Ásrael. Where was [he]? Monrovia sat for the most part quietly, looking out towards the edge he would come over, but her silver gown grew very heavy and her feet, in their silver sandals, restless. She thought of Asrael, of the blazing autumns to come, of the long summers, of the thousands of breathless days together . . . Underneath her thoughts something else was mounting. . . .

Down the beach below heavy footsteps sliding. Someone was stumbling up the path. Branches snapped. Monrovia ran towards the edge. Her eyes were flower-black.

"Where is Asrael?" she cried. Ismael shook his head as she pulled at his arm. "Where is he, Ismael? Where is Asrael? . . . I have waited so long. Why doesnt he come, Ismael? Where have you been? You must find him for me! Brother Myon was to meet us in the chapel, you know. I will never have to wait again. I will never again be without him! Only this long morning, Ismael . . . Where is he? Why hasnt be come? I am afraid, Ismael! Find him for me, Ismael! Find him! Find him!"

Ismael looked at her. His rough head was shaking. His face was drawn. He patted her hands. What he said came slowly.

"Asrael is down there, my lady. Down on the beach below. I have found him, my mistress. You must go to him. It is hard to say—he can never come again to you. The sea took him last night—his boat and his chests and himself. Only his body is left, . . . only his body.

Monrovia thrust past him. Her long red sleeves and silver lengths were torn as she hurtled down the path.

Asrael lay on the sand near the water. His hair shone in the sun. His familiar dark face was white. He looked strong and peaceful as she flung herself down. But neither his strength nor peace were for her. Nor his ever ready arms. They lay heavily at his sides. They did not once reach up to her. She put her head in the curve of his shoulder. It was wet and cold. No arm went round her, no voice murmured, "Monrovia, my sweet," no heart thudded against hers. . . . .

"Asrael, Asrael!" she cried. "Dont leave me! My dear love! This is our morning, Asrael. Dont you remember? Asrael, Asrael, dont leave me! Asrael! I am nothing without you! I cannot stay without you! I cannot let you go!"

Asrael lay quiet. Everything was still. Monrovia heard finally her own voice shuttling through the stillness. Old Ismael stood on the cliff's edge looking down. The water went on lapping . . .

The oldest doe made a pillow for her when Ismael carried her up to the cliff. He laid her down very gently, his old hands trembling.

Near the tower on his waiting island, Ismael buried the dead Asrael.

Monrovia sat each day on the cliff. Day after day, week after week, looking out always towards the sea. She never saw it, with its always changing blues. She did not know or care if the wind blew or whether the day was warm or gray. She looked always out towards the island. And always slow crystal tears dropped down her face. Sometimes onto the heads of the does, while they licked her hands gently.

Her heart ached always. She felt torn in two. What she had used to love she could not endure. The blue-green skies, the bright gold air, the wind, the rain, the sea—these—everything—were only thick walls she could not break, between herself and Asrael. She could not reach him. Yet she must. She could not suffer so! She could not be so alone! He was going to be with her always. Now she was always alone. Hammering against walls she could not break. And part of herself was gone.

Down her cream-petalled face slow dripping tears ran. From her gray eyes, making her pomegranate mouth salty, onto her purple gown. Between the masses of her dark hair her face was still. But the tears fell always.

The white does would press closer as they chewed their cud, their fragrant breath blowing upon her, their gentle noses nudging. There was no comfort anywhere. Only sea and sky and unendurable endless days and nights.

Monrovia seldom spoke or thought. She ate and drank and clothed herself as Ismael urged. As he waited on her his dim eyes were red and his stiff hands tender. He coaxed her to notice her does and the sunlight. She wanted only to be on the cliff and to look at the sea. And these gave no help.

Villagers from round-about came to watch from the edge of the wood. The flow of crystal down her still face became a tale of the country round.

One day was strangely bright and warm. The air was heavy with sunlight, the sea again clear green. The bees' hum was golden as their honey. The magnolias were rich cream in the gleam of the day.

Monrovia sat on the cliff as always, clothed in dark violet, powdered with sunlight. The white deer lay in clumps in the grass. Down her face, this day as always, onto her always more transparent hands, shining tears rained. The sunlight touched even the tears now and again and turned their stream to topaz.

But Monrovia still did not see either the sea or the sunlight. She sat there like an image covered with a veil of tears. Her face was thinner. Her heart was dulling. But the world was still a wall between herself and Asrael.

Again this afternoon there were footsteps sliding on the beach. Branches crackled on the path. A stranger came over the cliff and sat in the grass beside Monrovia. She was leaning against a tree, her eyes towards the island.

She did not look at him. She hardly knew he was there. But his voice and his words troubled a little.

"Monrovia," he said. "I have heard of your sorrow and of your beautiful quiet tears. What are you doing, Monrovia? Can you not learn to be alone? Only he can be whole who can be complete alone. You must be whole, Monrovia. Only then will you be unafraid, only then will you be at peace. All else is useless. Suffering is a gift. But one must suffer with open heart and open eyes. Then the pain in your heart will help you to grow. Like the sun when it comes over the horizon and fills the sky. Open your heart, Monrovia. Suffer Asrael to leave you a little while. Look about you. He will come back to you. Do not resist the world of your pain. Use it for growing a great heart. Yours is too small, Monrovia—small as one of your tears. Suffer wholly, willingly, and you will grow and all about you will move. To move one must make use even of pain. Otherwise you cannot be as much as one of your white does. Are you listening, Monrovia? Try to remember. It is all one can do for you. The rest you must do yourself."

Monrovia did not look towards him. She did not know when he left. But she sat that night late in the thick warm darkness on the cliff, and heard the does breathing and saw dimly the stars between the trees. With the water lip-lapping on the beach the words kept coming back. They melted some ice in her. She watched the fireflies sparkle in the darkness. And suddenly she knew that she was grown and that she must so live.

Months passed and the days grew shorter.

Monrovia came still to the cliff, and tears still fell down her face. But not in so continuous a stream. Her eyes now saw the sea and her does and even Ismael.

Each day she changed. The villagers still came to the edge of the wood to watch. Each time they feared yet ached to come again. For they could see that Monrovia of the Crystal Tears was changing, in some curious, wondrous way. Each day her face became brighter and clearer, as she sat in a yellow gown on the bee-rimmed cliff. It was beginning, they could see, to shine dazzlingly, even through the falling tears.

Always more often could be heard the hum of her wheel through the hum of the bees.

As time went on she spun and wove for the whole countryside. What she made was cherished for generations after, for usefulness and loveliness.

The villagers came to know her and she them. She would leave her cliff and visit the country about. People of all kinds came from even far-off parts to see her. Almost always she found sorrow and gave gladness. Asreal always seemed more near.

As years went by her beauty startled and her radiance healed. Those she passed were moved to do great deeds. The country grew more dazzling and Monrovia more wise. Her face came to be like a star of early morning. Her peace was deeper than any she had dreamed of. The crystal tears were gone. Her heart was growing.

Presently she died, quietly, one morning.

The whole countryside mourned—with an open heart.

Facing Asrael on his island, they buried Monrovia, on her green cliff in a high crystal tomb that shone with such a splendor it became a beacon at night for ships far out at sea. People from all the world came to stand in its light. It stirred them strangely and made them more whole.

There on the cliff, by the purple sand, with the white does and the rustling trees and the yellow-green grass. Where, deep in her crystal tomb, Monrovia of the Great Heart lay shining with the radiance of a thousand stars.

[no date]

VI

The Land

Editor's Note

The striking descriptions of rural Georgia in *Cane* demonstrate Toomer's acute and sensitive awareness of the American land early in his career; his appreciation of the land brought forth some of his most lyrical writing. And Toomer, always searching below and beyond the surface for spiritual and intellectual meaning, was rarely content to describe merely what he saw with his eyes. Rather, he probed for the *significance* of what he was seeing. Wherever he stayed or visited, Toomer became deeply involved in the landscape around him.

"Highways Should Be Rightways" is a good example of such involvement. This typescript, by "N. J. Toomer," was probably written in 1939. At this time there was citizen outcry against a proposed rerouting of Highway 202 in Doylestown, Pennsylvania, where Toomer lived on a farm with his second wife, Marjorie Content. (His first wife, Margery Latimer, died giving birth to their daughter, Margery, in 1932.) In early January 1939, Toomer, signing his name N. J. Toomer, wrote a long letter to the president of the Doylestown Chamber of Commerce, detailing the agricultural, esthetic, and even commercial harm the rerouting would cause. Addtitionally, in 1939 he wrote a letter on this topic to the Doylestown *Daily Intelligencer,* which the same year he also privately printed as a pamphlet, *Roads, People, and Principles.* The article Toomer mentions in the introduction to "Highways Should Be Rightways" is most likely his *Daily Intelligencer* letter. The book by Sears discussed later was published in 1937.

"It Used To Be" comes from the third typescript of the collection "Essentials" (see Editor's Note to Part III). "Why These?" is from "The Wayward and the Seeking," an unpublished collection of poems Toomer compiled in 1947. "The Extremes Are Great" (my title) is from page 3 of "World America," an undated typescript.

The piece I have titled "New York" is a combination of part of an undated story or essay entitled "Break," which Toomer included in a proposed collection, "Lost and Dominant," of 1929, and the first two paragraphs of an undated draft typescript, "Notes for a Novel, Book I, New York," in which Toomer describes the setting for a proposed novel and then outlines the personality of the central character, who experiences a "psychic breakdown. Leaves New York for a mountain country. Sensitized by convalescence. Touches self, momentarily. Need to retain self in a more complex setting. Desires to test. Again New York. Again shredded. Forces converge and drive the character down South: Washington, first, Georgia." I have indicated the excerpt from "Notes for a Novel" with italics. The description of the Catskills, which comes from "Break," suggests that the piece may have been written around 1923, when Toomer spent August and September in Ellenville, New York, where he occasionally retreated for peace of mind.

"The Briliant Brotherhood: New York City during the Mystical Experience of 1926" (my title) is an excerpt from "The Brilliand Brotherhood," Chpater XX in Part II of "From Exile into Being" (see Editor's Note to Part II of the present collection).

From 1936 until he entered a nursing home around 1965, Toomer made his home in Doylestown. "Doylestown" (my title) is made up of excerpts of an unfinished novel, "The Angel Begori or Exile's Bridge," begun in 1940, shortly after Tomer returned from a five-month trip to India. The narrator of this novel, Phil Gosh, is planning a trip to India with Begori, who is actually an angel with the power to bring harmony to human beings. They plan to go to India to study the "psycho-religious techniques" practiced by the Indians. The novel breaks off while the characters are sailing to Europe on the Queen Mary. Gosh leaves for India from Doylestown, and it is in the early pages of the book that Toomer writes the pastoral descriptions I have put together. For ease of reading, I have added a few transitional words, in brackets.

"The Presence of a Field" comes from an undated, handwritten rough draft. The manuscript has two versions of its page 8, one incomplete. I have used the complete page except for a few words and phrases I judged more effective in the incomplete page. For similar reasons, I have also chosen a few of Toomer's interlinear additions when it is clear that he was still unsure of which version he preferred.

The statement on "The South" is my amalgam of "The South in Literature," a 1923 essay, and the "Notes for a Novel" that I used for part of "New York" earlier in this chapter. The purpose of "The South in Literature" was, Toomer wrote by way of introduction, "to present two books: *Holiday,* by Waldo Frank, and *Cane,* by Jean Toomer, a brief survey of which will convince the reader, that, through them, the South is an important, though it may not yet be an equivalent contributor to the general ferment now evident in American letters." Toomer was planning to submit the essay under an assumed name; however, it was not published.

"Night" (my title) comes from a very rough, penciled, undated draft of what seem to be jottings about a lynching. The page on which these notes are written is among other penciled fragments on the same type of paper, one page of which is dated October 1951. The line breaks for "Night" are of my devising. I have chosen Toomer's "ain't," written over "I'm not," in the first line.

Toomer first went to Chicago in 1916, where he was a student at the American College of Physical Training. Subsequently, from November 1926 to 1931, he made his home base there, establishing and leading Gurdjieff study groups. "Chicago" is an undated typescript draft probably written while he was living in Chicago in the late 1920s.

Toomer's initial visit to New Mexico occurred in 1925; he returned a number of times during the next twenty-two years. Perhaps of all the places that Toomer lived in and visited, New Mexico around Taos and Santa Fe was the most spiritually stimulating to him. He found it a land of overwhelming beauty containing a cultural and ethnic mix that fascinated him.

Most of "To the Land of The People" (my title) is taken from an undated typescript draft of Chapter VII of the autobiography "Incredible Journey," which Toomer was working on in the 1940s. The nattative appears to be a somewhat fictionalized account of Toomer's trip with his first wife, Margery Latimer ("Marian"), in November 1931, shortly after their marriage in Portage, Wisconsin. ("Marian" is the name Toomer uses for Margery in his unpublished novel "Caromb.") To my excerpts from this account, I have added at the end a paragaph of reminiscence from Phil Gosh, the narrator of "The Angel Begori."

"Rainbow" is an untitled, undated typescript from the group of short pieces Toomer called "Sequences" (see Editor's Note for Part IV).

"The Dust of Abiquiu" is my title for a selection of excerpts from the first twenty-three pages of an undated, handwritten notebook of rough, sometimes sketchy musings, impressions, and descriptions of New Mexico. With interlineations, I have chosen the word or phrase I think best for the context. I have also coventionalized some of the capitalization and punctuation. Because of the rough nature of the manuscript, I have rearranged and cut some of the parts in order to make the selection more coherent and unified. Although the notebook is undated, the references to the atom bomb suggest that it was written during Toomer's last visit to New Mexico, in 1947.

"Taos Night" is my title for the opening page and a half of stage directions for "A Drama of the Southwest," an unfinished play of 1935.

In December 1939, Toomer returned to the United States from India by way of the Pacific. He then drove east to Doylestown, making a quick stop in Santa Fe. "New Mexico After India" was probably written shortly after this, some time in 1940.

"Part of the Universe" is another untitled, undated typescript draft from Toomer's "Sequences." The draft is quite rough, with a number of handwritten additions and interlineations, some of which I have included when they seemed apt. This essay must have been composed after 1945 since it was written "in the shadow of the bomb." "Santa Fe Sequence" (Toomer's title) is from an undated, handwritten draft, again from the "Sequences" and written under the bomb's shadow.

In 1932, shortly after their marriage, Toomer and Margery Latimer lived in Carmel, California. It was in Carmel that the newlyweds suffered the most from the publicity in the press about their so-called mixed marriage. The 1932 autobiographical novel "Caromb," dedicated "to my wife," is set in Carmel (Caromb) and tells of John and Marian's attempts to make themselves a home there, both psychologically and physically, although they do not feel welcome. The novel becomes a long Gurdjief-fian discourse on the importance and development of personal and social harmony for John and Marian. In my selection of excerpts from the third draft of the 260-page typescript, I have slightly rearranged the original chronology of some parts to give a narrative flow to the descriptive passages I have chosen from the original typescript. My selection begins with the first two paragraphs of the novel.

"America's Proposed Riviera: A Chicagoan's Impressions of Los Angeles" constitutes most of a fairly rough typescript draft of a section of Chapter VII of "Incredible Journey." There are a number of duplicates, rough and partial drafts, and handwritten insertions in the original type-script pages. I have chosen the most coherent sequence and done one sequential rearrangement. Although Toomer worked on "Incredible Journey" from 1941 to 1948, "America's Proposed Riviera," which is undated, may have been written early in 1932 when he and Margery Latimer visited Pasadena on their way to Carmel from Santa Fe. His comment on the Olympic Games, which were held in Los Angeles in 1932, strengthens this possibility.

Introduction

Highways Should Be Rightways

In justice to the highway department and as further information for all concerned I feel it would be well to mention certain developments that have occurred since I wrote the first article on the highway problem.

Several members of the Philadelphia office of the highway department have been to see me. After getting a rough idea of the damage that would be done to my property were the latest proposed re-routing of U.S. 202 to go through, the highway men explained the plan for realigning 202 from Montgomeryville to New Hope, and gave reasons for their present preference for the line from Doylestown to Lahaska that has aroused such protest. They believed this highway would be the righway—and, I am bound to admit, they had some grounds for so believing. I then gave my reasons for objecting not only to this line but to the general all too prevalent practice of engineering—and living, too—without due regard for all the vital factors of the situation. I believe[d] and still believe this highway would be the wrongway—and, I think they are bound to admit that I have grounds for so believing.

It was educational, this meeting. We agreed in principle that highways should be rightways. The question was and is: What makes a highway a rightway? When is a highway a wrongway, when is it a rightway? What chief factors should be considered? I am frank to say that the men brought to my attention certain factors which they, as engineers, had considered, which I, as a student of man's relation to himself and to Nature, had not considered. I am sure that they in turn frankly say that I called their attention to factors which they had not seen. As the talk developed it became clear to me that the problem is more complex and is more interwoven with the general conditions of modern living than even

I had suspected. I wondered and still wonder, among other things, if the engineers of the highway department ever get the opportunity to lay the routes and to build the roads that they, as engineers, think best.

As the men were leaving I gave them a book to read. It is by Paul B. Sears. It is called *This Is Our World*. This is the book that a year ago opened my eyes as to what we do to the earth and indeed to our entire world when we go ahead with our partial knowledge and our powerful machines and radically disturb the balance that Nature had patiently established during countless centuries. This is the book that made me realize, as never before and in a new way, the following truth. We did not make the Earth. Therefore we had best be careful how we re-make it, lest we wreck it and destroy ourselves.

I suggested to the engineers that after reading the book they reconsider the proposed highway in the light of the new knowledge gained from this source, and from what I had pointed out. I asked that they bear in mind these three sets of vital factors: (1) the actual nature of this land, (2) the needs of the people as human beings, and (3) of course, their own plans and problems as engineers and as members of the highway department. I suggested that in this way, and in this way alone, could the proper steps be taken to make sure that this highway would be the rightway, not the wrongway.

Needless to say, I hoped they would do this, now and in the future, not only as regards this relatively short stretch of road but also as regards all the roads to be re-aligned or newly made in 'Pennsylvania. I asked this, not for my sake alone, but also for their sakes, for the sake of all of us who live upon this earth, who will suffer the same consequences if we violate Nature and will enjoy the same benefits if we cooperate with her.

Those with a realistic sense of how things are done in the practical world may ask if I really expect the highway men to give weight to a book. I certainly do. They gave weight to books during their college days. Thus they learned how to build roads. Are they not students still? They, as do all of us, know very well that they have not learned it all. By this book they will be helped to build better roads, rightways. A good physician, out of interest in his work and a sense of responsibility to his patients, reads the latest books that have a vital bearing on his profession so as to keep up to date and improve his skill. Highway engineers are professional men. They too have interest in their work. They too have responsibility to the public. So they too will give weight to books that have vital bearing on their profession so as to keep up to date and to improve their skill.

In *This Is Our World* they will find needed knowledge that they were not taught in their engineering courses at college. This knowledge is one of the most recent and important contributions of modern science. The highway men cannot afford to do without it. Nor can the general public. None of us learned it during our school days. The knowledge was not available then. It is available now in this short, clear, simply written book. All of us need to learn it now, if we would continue to live upon this earth. Some men, some time, will be compelled to learn and apply it, compelled by fear of calamity if not by the desire to improve things. Why not these men now? Why not all of us now? Why put off to some future time, a time that may be too late, what can and should be accomplished today? It is wise to defer evil. It is stupid to defer good.

Is a knowledge of cooking necessary to us? Is a knowledge of agriculture? Just as necessary is the knowledge of Nature, of our place in Nature, of what we do to Nature, as revealed by this new science in which Dr. Sears is a leading worker. Without it, the day may come when nothing will grow for us to cook. Dr. Sears lets us see Nature as she really is, as she has worked and is still working on this very earth of ours. He shows us the communities of life, how they came to be, what our relation is or at any rate would be to the rest of Nature. He makes us realize that men, because our power is greater than our understanding, have become a source of danger, indeed the greatest source of danger, both to ourselves and to Nature herself. Now that we have science, technology, and machines, and so often misuse them, the danger is critical. Our very survival is at stake. The Frankenstein monster is seen to be no myth. It is seen as an all too real fact. Each of us, we realize, has something of a Frankenstein in him, and out of us have sprung those tools of progress which in unwise hands are becoming the weapons of our destruction.

Nature, we must come to realize, is an interrelated community of living forms, each with its function, each dependent upon all others. She is extraordinarily well organized for her purposes. Disarrange one department and you disarrange all others. Upset one, and you destroy the harmony of all. Nature is better organized than are man's governments, businesses, and industries. A business man knows what happens to his organization when any single department is upset. We know what happens to us when any single bodily organ gets out of order. It is the same with Nature as a whole. It is not otherwise.

A farmer knows that if he wears a wagon road in the middle of a field, even this simple road is going to affect the field in many ways, including the water content. Some of the water that otherwise would have been held in the ground, now runs off down the hardened tracks, and is lost to this field, and may get into another field where it is not wanted. From this one change many other changes inevitably follow. Consider, then, what a modern highway may do to the land through which it passes. If a highway is a wrongway, it will damage Nature and, in the long run, damage every man. Only if it is a rightway, all factors considered, will it benefit all men and do no harm to Nature.

Our ancestors, you see, lacked the machines and the knowledge with which to radically change Nature. Moreover, they travelled horse and buggy. Out of necessity they went the routes laid out by Nature, usually following the contours of the land. There were positive reasons, too, why they let Nature be. It is evident, for example, that the people who lived before us in Bucks County loved this region and understood what to do so as to adapt the country to their needs without throwing things out of balance.

In consequence, they handed on to us of the present generation a land fertile for farming, good for living, and lovely to behold.

But we of today? I will not say we have less love. Certain it is, however, that we have much more power to change Nature for the better or for the worse. We can use our knowledge and put our machines to work and in a few months plow through hills, fill up marshlands, cut down woods, rip through fields and lay a road that may, on the one hand, be a marvel of construction and a boon to everyone; or may, on the other hand, be the initial step in the deterioration of an entire community.

What will we, who rule and run the world today, pass on to the coming generations? What we do today will decide whether we pass on to our children a land good to live in or a land despoiled and unfit for any living creature.

Therefore our very power should give us cause to pause. Never before has it been so urgently necessary that we look before we leap. No men of any age have so needed to stop and think, to stop in order to be able to think. Our greatest need is to think humanly, to think according to reason and the abiding values, to think less of present gains, to think more of the broad issues that determine the common well-being of the human race through the years.

It stands to reason that when we follow Nature's lines we proceed in accord with her; that, on the other hand, when we go counter to her lines we invite trouble. When I say lines I do not mean only the evident shapes, the ups and downs and curves. I also mean, indeed I chiefly mean the deeper lines upon which the entire balance of any given region is founded. If, then, we accord with this harmony, all is in accord, Nature with us, we with Nature. If, on the contrary, we upset or violate this balance, all is in discord, we with Nature, Nature with us, and we will necessarily be discordant within ourselves and with each other.

The same is true if we proceed in accord with the lines of our own natures, our own reason and values. Then we shall be in concord. But if we violate these lines, then and there begins the dis-ease of the soul and body that is ravaging the modern nations like a plague.

Apply the above principles to the highway problem and we have, I think, the basis for avoiding the construction of wrongways, the basis for the construction of rightways. Highways, as with all the other ways of our life, should be rightways. However, neither I nor anyone expect [sic] the men of the highway department to forthwith produce perfect rightways. No, this is a thing to be worked towards. But I and everyone does [sic] expect of the men of that department [that they] give to us what they themselves would want of us should they have occasion to need our services as physicians, dentists, educators, business men, etc. This is, that, in cooperation with us, they work to the best of their ability to avoid the wrongway, to select the rightway. Having met some of them, I believe they will.

[1939?]

It Used To Be

It used to be a rest, this quiet land,
A place of rolling hills unto my home,
Where I, too high suspended from the earth,
Might gladly go and fold myself in sun
And meadows, stars, white snow, yielding
To benefit by grace of natual force—
I felt I floated on the sacred river.

I used to have a building well in view,
It had verticals for space and air
And horizontals for the earth and future;
But more than this I will not mention here.
Enough to tell that to this quiet land
The sub-dividers came; soon after them
Racket and the wreckers who scrapped
            my building too.

[1930]

Why These?

The ants that build, the slugs that sleep,
Why these out of the deep, and bugs?
The men who breed and kill and breed
To kill again, the seed, the seeds
Recurring with the seasons, for these
Millions can there be as many reasons?
The earth, and rocks splitting into
Pebbles, the seas and biped docks,
Finance, factories, bulls and bears
And you and I and all our wears [sic]—
    Why all this stuff? For God
    Was not the sky enough?

[1947]

The Extremes Are Great

* * * In New York I feel depression most. New York is the most depressed city in America. And, it is the most electrically active. America is this way. In any place where you find one thing extreme, you will find its opposite extreme. We are a country of extremes, a juxtaposition of intense opposites. In Chicago I feel something sinister most. Chicago is the most sinister city in America. And, it is the most reassuring, the most friendly, with most good-will. Along the Pacific coast I feel lack of purpose most. Yet, something quite new is happening in it, especially in Los Angeles. In the South I feel hate. Yet right there I also feel the most love.

The extremes are great, and we must find a force strong enough to reconcile them, to combine them in a significant unity. * * *

[no date]

The Northeast

New York

Some miles northwest of New York, perhaps a hundred and fifty as the crow flies, there is a valley flanked by the southern spur-ends of the Catskill mountains. The valley is well watered. In summer, the natural grass and agricultural growths spread out in rich green waves and solid ractangles. Looked down upon from the mountain top, when the sun is shining, this carpet of the valley is amazingly fresh and brilliant. Towns, valley villages, irregular in form, houses for people and barns for cattle, belonging there, are clustered and scattered over the verdant lawn. The house[s] are white; some dulled to grey and greyish brown by long weathering. Most of them, built years ago, were built to stay and be homes. They are honest. The barns are red. The old red barns, among the finest forms of the American landscape.

Peace, an active repose rests on this valley, wells up from it as dawn and twilight rise upward from horizons. When bands of cloud hang over it or drift slowly like great airships, the scene is magical. Particularly is it so if looked down upon from a mountain top when the sun rises and strikes these clouds, causing them to lift, turning them to mist and iridescence.

I once fed a horse named Harry at sunrise.

One of the towns of this valley is Ellenville. Good people, friends of mine, live there. There are other spots of America where good people, friends of mine, dwell. They live linked within me. Men and women who have never seen each other, and perhaps never will, exist within my spirit side by side, forming the single form of the best I have received and can give. * * *

Southeast of Ellenville, a distance which thought can travel in an instant, lies New York, our centre of culture.

How New York got built, no one knows. Yes, one is acquainted with a small fraction of the factors and the forces which are supposed to have led to its founding and subsequent huge growth.

We have divided the supposed things which make men move, into, for us, convenient categories. We hape that these divisions, together with what content we are able to give them, will enable us somewhat to understand the human world. We, who live today, have a history of New York.

History is one of our means of approach. But in truth there is no history. There are only certain kinds of activity which now living men engage in. One form of this activity is called historical because it is supposed to deal with what our ancestors are supposed to have done. Did they do as we now suppose? Did they do only what we say they did? Who living can place his finger on their mainsprings? Why did anyone come to the place now called New York? (Or into the world?) From where did they come? Out of what mystery which, if we wish for our convenience, we can reduce and call someplace in Europe? Why did they settle just here? Why have they come and come in increasing numbers and multiplied so rapidly and so much that we who now exist in New York count ourselves and tell each other we total over five million?

I personally have never counted the population of New York. I have kept no record of the number I have seen.

Yes, history is good. It is good because a few good men sincerely exercise their minds historically and give us the by-products of their efforts to understand something of the nature of human existence. History, together with the arts and sciences, is one of the spans of that great bridge which we, the best of us, build, to stand on, to have our being in, between one unknown and another unknown.

It does not give us the means, though it may contribute to the means, of profoundly knowing why and how New York, or any city, got built.

From one point of view, New York is no more than the name just written. It is the name we give the place we live in. It is the minimum reality contained in a word.

If New York is more than this, if it is something in itself, an entity, a being, much as I am or you are, though on a larger scale, then it may be that only New York itself can write and understand its history. Biographies are failures. There is enough happening in any one person in five minutes of his day to occupy a biographer an entire lifetime. One would have to exist longer than Methuselah to describe and understand what happens one noon hour in New York.

In ordinary states of consciousness it is as difficult an undertaking to write autobiography. But at least in this, one is dealing with what he can directly observe.

Perhaps New York, if it is a being, will someday awake to superior consciousness, write its own history, and let us, the cells and organs composing it, see the truth of its life. Perhaps you or I may be among the cells engaged in this activity. Perhaps then we will know how New York came about and grew to be this huge assemblage of human beings and their outgrowths.

The history of an individual, is it known? Who, after effort, honestly thinks he can write an accurate complete self-history? How then to know the history of a great city?

How to know the mechanics of the present? How are all these diverse millions with their multiform activities co-ordinated so as to exist in equilibrium in so huge a single form?

Here it is. Without dispute it is the centre of America, and, if it had to, as Chicago seems to have to, it could claim itself the greatest city of the world.

New York a city of brilliant, rampant surfaces. Surfaces of art, music, literature; surfaces of philosophy, of economic thought and social attitudes. Mostly European derived, and Europe-tending.

Below these surfaces brief fleeting glimpses of a scattered humanity. Immigrants, first and second generation Americans, old colonial stock.

Also, New York is a dead city. A vast pile of giant tombstones. Someone has called it the catacomb of America.

In the place we live, we die.

New York is unreal. A simple tree is more real than it.

It is the fantasy of a mechanical God.

New York is a monster furiously disemboweled by men like maggots.

Had religion given rise to it, what would we sincerely think of this religion? * * *

[no dates]

The Brilliant Brotherhood:
New York City During the Mystical Experience of 1926

* * * I was prompted to go out onto the streets of the city.

Grass in the yard, tree, flower bed, iron fence, concrete of the pavement, steel of the street-car rails, street cars, trucks, bricks and stones of buildings, people, every one, every thing—in the Universe, part of the Universe, in God, part of God.

There was a radiant interweaving of things with things, life with life, beings with beings.

Walking westward towards the Hudson River I came to the end of 23rd Street, and boarded a ferry. The boat moved out across the river, with sun upon it. Fresh waters mingled with sea waters. Water, ferries, tugs, ships, sea gulls, fish, floating debris, men, women, children, boatmen, pilots, shoe shiners, on the Earth, of the Earth, in the Universe, of the Universe, in Life and of Life.

After landing on the Jersey side I made my way up a hill and stood on a palisade. Below me was the river-life. Across the water was Manhattan. Its tall buildings were rods and masses that caught the sun. Buildings, boats, and water seemed bathed in a vital sparkle that issued from them and blended with the brilliant shower of sunlight from above.

I felt unbounded joy, and it seemed to me that my realization of the mysterious flame was being enhanced because my body was in a position to contribute its impressions of the world to my total experience.

No words can describe my sense of sheer aliveness, my feeling of the wonder of existence, that I as a being was privileged to be a conscious part of this reality. Here it was, there it was, within, without, everywhere—the secret but now manifest fraternity of all that exists, the brilliant brotherhood of things and beings.

After a time I re-crossed the river and went on foot down the west-side river front of Manhattan in the direction of the Battery. I saw beings on the streets, beings called longshoremen, ship stewards, ships officers. I saw men entering and leaving eating places and bars. Each and all were in membership with one another, and I with them: all belonged.

Walking around the Battery I came upon beings called bums, and some called cops. There were those called street walkers, and business men, Americans, foreigners, Jews, Christians, blacks, whites. And with them all, without exception, it was the same, the same radiant weaving of being into being, of beings into God.

I rode a street car up Broadway. Beings were packed close around me. I could smell their body-odors, hear their bodies breathing. It was the same in the car as on the palisade, as in my room.

During the course of this day and the next I visisted Fourteenth Street, Fifth Avenue, Central Park, Riverside Drive, Harlem, the East Side, Chinatown. I met some of my particular friends. To one I expressed in words something of what I was experiencing. And wherever I went, whomever I saw, it was the same. Nothing broke down, or could break down, the wonderful reality.

The radiant weaving was not be be stopped by human barriers. The seamless fabric was not to be ripped by man's violence. The light was not to be darkened or dimmed an iota by the blindness of people. The sacred root was not to be in the least violated by the profanity of uprooted minds and ugly emotions.

I saw what was going on in the false psyches of people. But I was not in that, nor were the beings of human beings in it. I also saw what is going on in God's terms. I was in this, and so were the beings of human beings. Brothers—whoever you are.

There is Fraternity, not many fraternities but one. It is secret only to those who have not entered it. It is hidden only to those who have not found it. In this one fraternity all belong: men and animals, plants, metals, the Earth and its waters, rain and ice, the Sun, the matters and the forces of the mysterious God who created this Universe and its beings.

[1937–1946]

Doylestown

[During the afternoon] * * * I strolled out onto the lawn and stood there looking around. It was good country, this country, good to look at, good to live in. I'd wager that you could bring a man here from anywhere on earth, bring him blindfold[ed] and with cotton in his ears so that he wouldn't be influenced by names and labels, and stand him where I was standing and take the blinder off, and he'd look as I was looking and he'd know as I was knowing that the people around here cared for the earth, were decent towards each other, and had reason to feel that there is something in life more important than financial status, more worthwhile than fighting your fellowmen and conquering them.

There was peace in this scene, a sort of lush serenity that comes to some countrysides when plowing is over, when growing things stand in the fields, when harvest time has not yet come. The wheat grows and ripens, the corn stands up and unfolds, but they mature quietly. The leaves on the trees are still, except when they gently rise and fall to a breeze that only they can feel.

Now there was brilliance too for sunlight seemed to be everywhere. One might think of the light as issuing from a huge sun in the heavens, but what one saw was light coming from the ground, sparkling from the leaves, shining from white houses and stone barns, flooding from a sky that seemed as golden as it was blue. Glory was out this afternoon.

I took it all in, serenely fascinated by a view that I had seen countless times before. The full fields made me feel that they were just as they ought to be, productive, and getting ready to yield earth's supplies for human living. The gentle slope of the ground towards the millstream imparted a quiet activity to what otherwise might have seemed static. I thought of that stream in the old days when it turned the wheels that ground the grain for the entire locality. It was a small stream, really, but surprisingly vigorous and utterly dependable. It ran now, I felt sure, just as it had done a hundred years ago for the millers, a thousand years ago for the Indians. There it was, flowing along where the two slopes met in the hollow. Times had changed. There it was, but it had no human work to do. And now as always it was slowly carrying the minerals of these lands to larger waterways and thence to the ocean.

This last thought started me thinking of what one finds out about this scene, as about all the countrysides of America, when one probes beneath the surface and looks with a critical eye at what man is doing to Nature, at what man is doing to man. Just then I heard a tractor start up, and my thoughts along these lines were further stimulated.

Then I stopped these thoughts, just closed them out of mind. They were worth thinking. Indeed it was very necessary that they be thought, and thought out, and put in action intelligently, by some of us. Else the countryside, even as a scene lovely to the eye, would break down and become among the innumerable regions of the earth, once fertile, which men can no longer inhabit. But thoughts such as these were not for now. I wanted to retain my mood of flowing serenity. These were my last days here—and, who knew, what some of my friends said might be true, perhaps I'd never return. Isn't it better to say goodbye with love, even with sadness, than with criticism?

Between a northern pine and a sycamore maple, trees that must have stood there when the first house was built on this land, a hammock swung. I went to the hammock and stretched out. My eyes looked up into the overhanging foliage of the maple, very green and full and rich this year. Through one opening I could see the blue sky. Through another the sun came, transfiguring several leaves into luminous light green pendants, and streaking across part of my face. After a while I shifted position and as I did so I caught sight of something sailing high in the air, far off the earth, a small dark object quite prominent against the immense blue. At first I thought it was a plane, but I heard no motors. It was a buzzard, I decided. Flying high, flying, flying, a buzzard flying. From where? Where to? Why? Looking for food. All of that sailing, that amazing flying that floated, floating on outspread wings, was a means to food that would be found somewhere on the surface of earth, down on my level. Fly to eat. Eat to fly. What did he, that buzzard, that very buzzard, what did he make of it all, I wondered.

Once again the tree claimed my attention. I remembered how several winters ago in January a false Spring had come, and trees all around had put forth buds. This tree budded more than the others, because it had been artificially fed the autumn before. I feared for it. The false Spring had ended and again there were snow, ice, and zero weather. The tree seemed to suffer, as if it had been tricked and betrayed. It seemed to shrink, as if it had been blighted. When true Spring came I watched the tree as if it were a friend whose life I was unsure of. A few branches put forth puny leaves that stayed all summer but never prospered. Other branches remained bare and dry. Life was still in it, and this ecouraged me; but would the life ebb or flow during the coming critical year? For myself as for the tree there was nothing to do but wait and see. More than once I went to the tree and placed my hand on the sturdy trunk, wishing and strangely feeling that life-force was being transfused from me to it.

When Spring came again I was thankful and happy to see buds form on most of the branches. From the buds came full green leaves, and there was no further doubt that life and the tree had overcome the blight. The few limbs that were dead beyond hope were now evident, and we cut them off. The tree, ever since, has been alive and dormant with the seasons.

I found myself saying, saying and feeling, goodbye to the tree. It particularly I had singled out. The house and fields were in my heart too, as were the entire countryside and the community; but I addressed the tree alone and wished it well until my return. * * *

[For supper] we had edible pold [sic] peas, beets, potatoes, salad, all fresh from the kitchen garden, the vegetables cooked in as little water as possible and served each in its own juice with butter liberally added. We had bread, honest bread, not blasphemed wheat. It was made of flour of the whole grain, stone ground by the Great Valley Mill, and home made. We had Valley Forge beer, cold, so that the bottles sweated in the warm air. We had fresh fruit for dessert. * * *

[After supper] we faced the same view that had appeared so serene and lovely to me that afternoon. Its quality had somewhat changed with the light, as a thing changes that is about to pass from memory. There was still enough light for us to discern the far fringes of woods, the corn in the field across the road, the walnut trees that bordered the road on this side, the willow midway down the lawn, and of course the nearby plot with the croquet wickets showing white against the green grass. A few late robins moved over the lawn in their characteristic way, running, stopping and throwing their breast out or standing with head to one side and close to the ground, listening for sounds from the earth that you or I would not hear. A few early fireflies glowed and went out, suggesting beacons strewn at random along a coast that no ship ever passed. Six barn swallows, the last birds in the air, gyrated overhead. Cool breeze there was not, but the quiet of Nature at twilight gave some measure of quiet to us who contemplated her, and for a brief time at least those who suffered from the heat respite. * * *

The next morning as I was putting bags in the car, Ramsey, our farmer, came up. I could tell by his lively gait and the sparkle in his eyes that he brought good news. If it had been bad news, such as the death of a pig whom he had come to feel as part of his farm family, he would have been bent over like a man of sorrow. It was good news. The wheat, one of the best crops ever, was ready to cut. This was Ramsey's way of saying goodbye, to tell me of the wheat, the oats, the corn, the hay, potatoes, the horses, cows, and hogs, all doing fine. * * *

[Before his departure Phil Gosh writes to Ramsey:]

The sacred grains are ripe. Sun is in them, all necessary chemicals, and life itself. Wheat is ready once again to leave the fields and pack the barn, safe from further vagaries of climate. The fields, friends to grain and man ⸱like, have done their work, and now man's work begins again.

Reaping will be done, and binding. The tawny bundles will be stacked. Men, pitch forks, and a rack wagon, and the wagon will be loaded many hauls. It will be hard fast work if a storm is coming. You who labor will swing into the rhythms of it, elation in your hearts, power in bodies to work on even if body becomes weary. This is the harvest. It will mean to you what it has meant to those of our kind throughout the ages who realize that harvest decides survival. It will mean to you an unnamed triumph.

You will not sing, you wil not dance, you will not celebrate or give thanks in any outward way; but you will be touched none the less by the Power that created man and wheat and gave them to each other so that both might fulfill the purposes implicit in all that grows and ripens.

Be blessed, men and fields and the grain thereon.

[1940]

The Presence of a Field

Up back of our barn there is a seven acre field that curves and dips in about every way a field can. Before men came along and marked off divisions, it was an undifferentiated part of one of the several low hills of this rolling country. Now it has boundaries: a fence-row, a dirt road, a woods, a cluster of human buildings. The fence-row of trees, sumac, and brush is the legal line of demarcation between mine and his; the field on the other side is my neighbor's. Neither mice, dogs, pigeons nor hawks know the difference.

The records are incomplete. They do not list the names of all the men who have held title to this plot of ground, saying what manner of men they were, of what flavor. Some were farmers; some were millers; some probably of other trades or professions. The first white man to settle here was undoubtedly an English Friend, one of the people called Quakers. Whoever he was, whatever else he did, I like to think of him as a man of prayer. I like to think that as he worked the land, our earthly ground, he blessed it, and was himself blessed by the Divine Ground. I like to think that as the sunlight showed him what to put his hands to, the Light Within showed him what to put his heart to. And perhaps he learned, partly from within himself, partly from the Indians, the beauty of living in harmony with Nature, overcoming temptation to set himself up as a conqueror.

William Penn first came to the New World in 1682. In 1683 he made the "Great Treaty" with the Indians. As long as he lived there was peace between the in-coming white men and the established red men, in these parts. By 1700—nine years after the death of George Fox, nine years after the death of Brother Lawrence—Philadelphia was a seedling town, and people were pushing inland, some settling around here. For about 250 years this field had been cultivated. If Indians farmed it before white men came, there is no telling how long it has been producing for human use. The field itself may remember; but it cannot speak the language of men. It cannot tell of the hands that have scooped up its soil to feel the quality of it. It cannot speak of those whom it has housed: the worms, the mice, the woodchucks, the rabbits, the skunks. It cannot sing of the seeds and plants it has supported as they grew towards the sun.

Looking up from the house, that fence-row is the high horizon. In summer, all the trees look alike. In winter, you know one of them is dead.

There it rises, silhouetted against the sky, thrusting up from the ground like a wrist and hand that has been blasted, charred black, its fingers broken and immobilized in perpetual rigidity. Sometimes a hawk will perch on one of the stumps, or a crow. Other birds shun it. The reason why its condition is not seen in summertime is because poison ivy has grown all over it, and from a distance the ivy leaves look like the tree's own. You think it is in full foliage. It could be cut down; but there it stands year after year, perhaps as a reminder of the mortality that underlies the living flesh.

A living tree is a wonderful thing. How adequate it is in its order of life. It does what it is designed to do. It fulfills its function in Nature's scheme. A tree's is a balanced life; and as it grows, each part grows in harmony with the whole. It is up-reaching, as a man should be. It is out-spreading, as a man should be. Its roots are secure, its limbs extending, its crown lofty. It harms nothing. True, if trees are over-crowded, a condition of scarcity exists realtive to those trees; and they, becoming almost man-like, enter into competition with each other, and some are stunted, and some die off. But no malice is in it, no greed, no fear. Trees seek the sun; they seek the rain; they love the earth, give themselves to all who need them, and unfold towards heaven. A tree is a splendid example for man. A man can have no better ideal than to aspire to become, in his order of life, as adequate as a tree is [in] its order. No better ideal but a higher one, and for this reason among others: mortality does underlie the living flesh, but in man, underlying mortality, there is an immortal seed.

The crown of the field, though not high as elevations go, is the highest point of our land. Go up there, and it is surprising what a sense of height and breadth you get. It is as if, by making this moderate ascent, you had left behind the little things of life and come upon the great ones. It is as if you had emerged from the narrow life of self into a larger life and being. Walk up there, turn around, and to your eyes you are in a different world, an open world. You look over the roof of the barn. You look down upon the house, which seems incredibly small, and down upon the pointed stone building that used to be a mill. You catch a glimpse of the stream at the bottom of the slope, a stream with water as clear as spring water except when heavy rains wash top-soil into it. Your eyes travel up the slope on the other side, up and up until they reach the fringe of trees on top. You look far away, over the trees, over the hills.

Once after a heavy fall of snow I trudged up there. The grey snow clouds were scattering, showing patches of bright blue sky, letting the sun shaft through, then hiding it again. Every time the sun shone, the light on the white snow was so brilliant that I blinked. When I reached the top a large cloud segment was drifting in front of the sun. I looked around.

The whole material world was a pure grey-white, perfectly still, immaterially alive. The covering of snow, unmarked as yet by rabbit tracks, bearing no human marks at all except my own, accentuated the sheerly lovely curves and forms of the landscape. Of a sudden the sun broke through full force. Flooding down, it was reflected by the snow with such intensity that I was momentarily blinded. I knew I was in a flood of light, and for a moment that was all I knew.

Saul of Tarsus, on the road to Damascus, was temporarily blinded physically, spiritually transformed, by a swift invasion of the Light of the World. Dante, on the other hand, would seem to have had every faculty gloriously enhanced by the unveiled presence of the Eternal Beam. I have had no great experience of the spiritual light. I have yet to be blinded by it, or transformed. But I can testify that it is real. There is a power that manifests to us as light. It is potent. It can work wonders in the life of anyone so graced. It can elevate, as no ascent of a hill or a mountain, or of the air, can ever do. It can awaken and unify. It illumines a world that the sun need not shine on. The early Friend who first settled on this slope probably knew by experience more than I about the Inner Light, or, as he would have referred to it, the light of Christ.

From the field I look down on the handsome stone building that used to be a mill. Men made a water wheel. Large it was, well-fashioned, well-knit, made of wood with [cogs?] of iron. It is still in place, still sturdy, but stationary now. Men fashioned the stones to grind the grain. Those stones are still around. The current of the stream was not powerful enough to turn the wheel. Out in the woods men built a reservoir of stones and earth, turning the stream into it, piling the water up. They built a mill-race from the reservoir to the mill. They opened the gates, and down the mill-race the water rushed, and underground through a culvert splash onto the wheel. The wheel turned. The stones ground grain for man and beast.

On the old plaster there is a marking, 1779. It was Ely's mill. It was Carvor's mill. It was the mill of forgotten men. For many years it was a busy place, a cheery, thriving place, in its way a community center. Processions of people came in daily with their wheat, corn, and other grain. Processions of people went out with their flour and meal. Those were the days before General Mills, factory bakeries, store bread. People were more independent then, and, at the same time, more knit to one another. They were more independent of centralized agencies, more dependent upon their neighbors. This community was more organic then in every respect. The world of the Quakers was larger and more potent hereabouts.

I do not say that was the Golden Age, even that those were the good old days. (I am not nostalgic for them.) But I know that something vital to human life has since been lost, and I am not sure that the gains compensate for the loss, or that we of today are essentially better off. The stream of life, moving from those days to this, is not a single current but several. One current, represented by advances in medical science and in methods of education, is indeed one of progress. But another, represented by the [comparatively?] increased mechanization of collective living and the atomization of individuals, is a deterioration. To be blind to such distinctions, to hail all modern tendencies as if they comprised a single surging movement upwards towards the heights, is one of the follies that may cost modern man his civilization, and his life.

Wheat from this field used to go down to that mill, there to be processed by the tools and methods of men, and water-power. The flour, stone-ground, retained the full substance of the wheat. Some of the flour was brought into the house and made into bread. When the bread was baking, the whole house came alive with the odor of it. If it were summer and the windows open, the good and wonderful odor filled the space around. Whoever whiffed it, his face lit up and his mouth watered. The bread, when done, was fit to play its part in the ancient sacrament of people gathering around a table to break bread together. I know how it must have been because we too bake bread that is worth breaking. Bread worth breaking. Through such bread the flavor of the earth enters into man; and man, by the very chemicals in his body, is related to the soil; and I am related to this field.

It used to be a relatively simple process. Wheat was grown in this and neighboring fields. The grain was short-hauled to a local mill, and there in a leisurely manner water ground by buhrstones. All of the vital elements were retained, the wheat germ, the bran, the middlings, as well as what we nowadays call flour. The whole wheat flour was short-hauled to local homes, made into bread, put into ovens and then put into man. From field to mill to oven to man.

Now, of course, we have made vast improvements on that simple old-fashioned process. Wheat is still grown on this and neighboring fields. But local mills, for the most part, have disappeared, given way to larger and, we are told, more efficient factory-mills. The grain, such of it as is to [be] used for flour, is long-hauled to a factory-mill. There a rapid and rather disastrous fate awaits it. The full-bodied grain is systematically and scientifically reduced to a devitalized powder. It is run between steel rollers which generate heat which promptly destroys some of the vital elements. Then the hapless wheat is taken hold of and, as it were, shaken down. The wheat germ is taken out. The bran is taken out, as are the middlings. Ah, but we get "pure white flour," refined flour fit for refined men. But most men do not get at it yet; they must wait.

This pure white flour, in other words this blasphemed wheat, is long-hauled to factory-bakeries, and there subjected to a chain of events remarkable for their number and intricacy. Do you know how many distinct processes are involved in modern mechanized bread-making? Ten or more. Do you know how many specialists, each working on a part of the mass-production of bread, give their skill and labor to it? There are upwards of five classes of such specialists. Some mix, others divide, others scale, others slice, others wrap. Can you imagine how many different types of machines are used? Upwards of ten. There are blending machines, mixers, and of course a fermentation room. There are dividing machines, rollers, molding machines, greasers, electric ovens, slicing machines, wrappers, heating units, cooking units. And the end-product—that which, wrapped, sealed, spick and span, tastes like nothing much at all. Wonderful, just wonderful.

But not yet do you get it. The loaves are long-hauled to grocery stores or to you, if you patronized a bread delivery route. If not, you must walk or jump in a car, dash to the nearest source of supply, and dash back home. And only then at last do you have it, the Wonder Loaf, the sanitary impoverished modern commercial version of the Staff of Life.

But don't feel too bad. Your sacrifice of full flavor, full body, full nourishment contributes to the public good. You are doing your part to keep the wheels of industry turning, to promote full employment. You are investing in the Great American Concern—Free Enterprise. Your purchase of store bread helps keep the grocer in business, helps employ the people he employs. The grocer, by his orders, helps keep the factory-bakery in business, helps employ all the people the bakery employs. So you, through your grocer, are helping to do all that. Nor does your service to the general public stop there. The factory-bakery is a purchaser of blending machines and many others, as we have seen. Its purchases help keep in business the factories that manufacture these machines, help employ all the people those factories employ. And of course the factory-bakery buys from the mills, large and small, and thus helps keep mill production running and people employed in those mills. The mills, in turn, are big customers of the factory-farms. And so on, and so on. In short you, my dear sir or madam, by ingesting and suffering factory-bread, really turn out to be, thereby, an important cog in the big machine of Big Business. Your personal sacrifice is a public boon. Nor is it entirely sacrifice. Your own employment may very well depend upon it. For, if many are employed, you are the more likely to be employed. If many are unemployed, you are the more likely to be unemployed. By eating bread factory-made of devitalized flour you may be helping to employ yourself, support your family, send your children to school, etc., etc. It is certain that you are helping goodness knows how many people make money—some of them big money. The more profits there are, the more money is made, the larger swells the national income. The larger the national income swells, the better everyone feels, or are [sic] supposed to feel. Surely this large happy feeling comes or will come to you—and it has or will offset any poor, unhappy feeling you may have on account of depletion and malnutrition due to the absence from bread of minerals and vitamins essential to human health and vigor. Besides, if you are ailing because of an inadequate diet, can't you go to the drugstore and buy, at a substantial price, the very vital elements that should be in, but have [been] taken out, of the Wonder Loaves? Thus you help keep the retail druggist in business, and the retail druggist the wholesale druggist the firms that manufacture liquids, capsules, and tablets containing minerals and vitamins. So be of good cheer, Mr. Modern Man, you may doubt that God is in His heaven, but you cannot doubt that all's right with the world, especially the Modern World, especially Modern America and its unrivaled standard of living.

[no date]

The South

The South

Within the last decade, American letters have been vitalized by the maturation of a sectional art. New England, through the personalities of Robert Frost and Edwin Arlington [Robinson], and the Middle West, articulate in Sherwood Anderson, Theodore Dreiser, Carl Sandburg, and Edgar Lee Masters, have each contributed notably to the general leavening. This fact already belongs to the literary history of America. It is natural therefore that cultural minds should turn expectantly towards the South. That they should feel certain that here too a splendid birth was imminent. For surely no other section is so rich in the crude materials and experiences, prerequisite to art. The South has a peasantry, rooted in its soil, such as neither the North nor West possess[es]. Therefore it has a basic adjustment to its physical environment (in sharp contrast to the restless mal-adjustment of the northern pioneer) the expression of which the general cultural body stands in sore need of. And, rising from its agricultural communities there spreads a southern life of rich complexity. Factories, Main Streets, and survivals of the old plantations roughly chart these degrees. It has the stark theme of the white and black races. But above all, the South is a land of the gret passions: hate, fear, cruelty, courage, love, and aspiration. And it possesses a tradition of leisure by means of which these attributes might find their way into a significant culture. * * *

Up till now, all writers concerned with the American scene, its historical setting and the general forces that now influence or direct it, have omitted the peasant-adjustment rhythm of the Southern Negro. The non-pioneer rhythm of the South. They have all isolated for consideration the extraverted, restless, urging, forward-pushing rhythm of the pioneer. At most, the South had been a rather exotic and unrelated fragment. * * *

I do not mean that the South has no pioneer rhythm. It has, it always has had. But it also has this large, thick block of settled life. And no one has taken it into consideration. Needless to say, I am not including it for this reason. I am including it, starting from it, because this element is one of the fundamental aspects of American life, to me, because a part of my own nature has its roots in it. And I feel and know that I am not unique in this.

[1923 and no date]

Night

"I ain't looking beyond myself tonight, sister."
mob up
dusty corn field
flares
white-hooded rider
and a white-hooded horse
robes and hoods
black robes with white sashes
long white capes with red [linings?]
bright the tow-soaked cross
"everybody gets on their knees [agonizing?] before Jesus
    Christ"
nigras
burr-headed nigra
mongrelization
red-clay roads
raw hillsides

[1951?]

Chicago

Chicago

In Chicago things stand out. A curious very vivid grey-white light seems to illumine and reveal each form and feature. Nothing can hide. Few things can be hidden. All of Chicago is exposed. Its buildings—the Palmolive, the Tribune Tower, the Wrigley Building—stand out. In a corresponding way its life—the underworld and gangland, politics, civic institutions, social groups, society—stand out. For some extremely interesting reasons Chicago, more than any other city I know, is glaringly evident. This is why it has impressed itself upon its residents and upon its neighbors, near and far, as no other modern city has.

Its geography has something to do with it. The flat openness of the prairies over-rides the outskirts and sweeps full through the entire city. The snug North Shore suburbs cannot keep the prairie out. The western suburbs, and Chicago's fringe of ragged houses, cannot keep the prairie out. South Chicago and the human settlements to the south cannot keep the prairie out. The men of Chicago, as it were, built a wall around their city, staking off from the vast lands a human-sized plot of ground. Growing Chicago spreads ever farther north, west and south. Each year it conquers and seems to convert more and more of the surrounding flat lands. But the vast openness of the prairies over-sweeps the walls, inundates the growth, washes the city, and joins hands with the spread of Lake Michigan. One feels the prairie in the Loop, in Michigan Boulevard, in all streets and parks, and even in the houses. For all of its hugeness, its skyscrapers, congestion, and parking problems, Chicago is still a part of the prairies, and almost as open. The men of Chicago had no choice but to have it thus. I think they wanted to have it thus.

Lake Michigan, washing the miles of Chicago's eastern length, is flat, and, like all large water-areas, it is utterly exposed. There is nothing to keep the vast exposedness of the lake out of Chicago. There are no human structures to break the lake—no network of piers, wharfs, docks. There are not many crafts, and but comparatively little shipping that a Chicago resident sees. Emerge from a side-street, motor along the long outer drives, and the empty open almost ocean-like sheet of water is full on you. If it were briny, I am sure one would smell it for miles inland. There is nothing to stop it. Every now and again it gets angry and demonstrates this fact by rising and dashing over the low concrete walls and inundating park and drives. The men of Chicago could have it otherwise. They could, so to speak, push the lake out of sight. They seem not to want to. They want its exposure. They feel that as it is it has an expressive relationship to their city.

Not long ago I was walking with a friend along the lake front, down the cement promenade which follows the water from Lincoln Park southward, and curves at the Drake Hotel. It was night. To the east was the glossy dark expanse of the lake. To the west, almost at arm's reach, was the long line of expensive skyscraper-apartment buildings. They looked like huge rectangles of lighted stone. They were standing sheer, exposed, and, it seemed, so near to the lake that a high wind might dash spray in their windows. Between them and ourselves, however, was a strip of park and Lake Shore Drive coursing with flashing motor-cars. My gaze followed the sheer flanks, bent at The Drake, and wandered out to the tip of the drive. In the night sky directly above The Drake a bright moon shone, casting a grey-white light like a rim on the roofs of the buildings, a silver sheen on the water near Oak Street Beach.

In times past this scene had evoked in me a sense of geometric beauty, a peculiar beauty, something uniquely of Chicago. But this night I felt it to be angular and almost unbearably exposed. And cold. It had to do only with steel and stones, a dead moon. It was, I felt, inhuman. I wanted something softer, more rounded, colorful. I wanted flesh and blood. I wanted human voices, human emotions. I could not help but picture to myself ways in which the setting could be improved. I thought of a French village. I thought of how the French would use a lake front. To my friend I said, "Wouldn't it be fine if there were tables all along here, and bright canopies, and buzzing waiters, and warm drinks, and people sitting about, talking, laughing? Over there we'd see so and so. At another table we'd run across others. This could be a marvelous place. Wouldn't you like it so? (It would be humanized.) Now it is as chill and dark and isolate and uninhabited as a steel girder." But my companion was far more true to Chicago than I. "No," she answered, "I like it just as it is. I wouldn't change it. This belongs here. Tables and color do not. I like them too. But I like them in France. I like this in Chicago. There is only one thing I'd change. I'd make the lake water salty. How I'd love to smell brine! If it were briny, I'd say it was perfect."

[no date]

New Mexico

To the Land of The People

For the first time in five years I would not spend the winter in Chicago. We—Marian and I—were off for the Southwest and the Pacific coast. I would miss the round of the Chicago season's activities—the carrying on of my own work, the doings of my friends, play openings, dance recitals, Berta Ochsner, Ruth Page, new artists, parties, and all the rest. I would miss winter in Chicago—Michigan Avenue bright and white and blowy in a blizzard. That was a thing not to be missed. A Chicago blizzard was an event in America. Michigan Avenue piled white was a vivid American scene. I would escape being stopped on the street and begged for money. Business conditions, I was told, were not as bad in the Southwest and far West. We had personal reasons for this trip, and I wanted to see the Pacific coast and thus complete my picture of America. New England, New York, the eastern seaboard, the south, the middle west, the southwest—these sections I knew. But for years California and the Pacific coast had been a blank in my map, a vacant spot in my vision of the country.

The train cut a straight diagonal through Kansas, a Kansas with sky overcast, rainy, chill, and bleak. It was like a mood, a sombre mood full of dark things. Dark telegraph poles, black leafless trees, dark pools, dark far stretches of flatland, dark squat houses, dark clouds. Save at the stations there seemed to be no men. The land seemed tenantless and desolate. It was like passing through one of one's own internal moods.

That night we crossed the state line into New Mexico. When the shade was raised we looked out upon a Southwest dawn. The sky, washed with gold, was an amazing bright blue. We felt a stimulating dry cold coming in the windows. "Look," I exclaimed, "a mesa!" Its stark majestic shape was like the body of an enormous living thing, struck there, turned into stone as it gazed across the sweep of desert and desert hills. Hill after hill swept by, all reddish-brown, barren, severe, and yet electric with the thing that is New Mexico. "This is it," said Marian.

At Lamy we took the bus to Santa Fe. "Oh, I like it," said Marian, "I've always wanted to live here." "Yes," I said, "so have I. Forms like these, these mountains, these hills, that mesa we saw, should help man to live. I wonder where they get their food-stuffs." "Nothing grows here?" "It does not look like it." The bus-driver was tall and western with a wide-brimmed hat. A woman in the service of the Indian Detour sat in the seat in front of us.

Though I had seen it before, Santa Fe, by this road's approach, surprised me. From a distance, save for the dome of the capital, its houses seemed but scattered bits of mud thrown in a basin by a boy. On either side were long ranges of high mountains. Down in the valley was this casual accumulation of the small things men build. "There it is," I said.

Our room in the La Fonda looked out on a street which bordered on the public square. It was Sunday. Dark-skinned men were loitering on the corner. "Indians or Mexicans?" asked Marian. "Mexicans," I said, and added, "Mexican-Americans." Do the Indians come in here?" she wondered, "Will we see them about the town? Or do they stay out in their pueblos?" "We will see some of them."

As we passed through the lobby to the dining-room, we saw Indians sitting about, sitting in a long row near the desk. They wore much jewelry, heavy silver and turquois. "Why are they here? Why are they sitting like that? They look fat and greasy. They look fat and greasy in Wisconsin. I thought the pueblo Indians were different. I've always heard they were." "I can't tell you. I've seen fine-looking poised handsome men in the pueblos. Perhaps these are on show. Perhaps they are here to sell things." "I don't like to look at them." * * *

The Way of Beauty of the Navajos. I remembered reading something of this Way in a novel of Navajo life by Oliver La Farge. I thought of those people, *The* People as they called and felt themselves, spreading over their vast land in the Southwest, to them a land with sacred places, to us a land with places of beauty and majesty. Centuries ago, presumably this Way and its religion had come into being by a marriage of the soul of those people with their earth and with their gods. At any rate the Navajos of today still have a Way, have a religion, and, according to those who know them, have a soul.

[1941–1948 and 1940]

Rainbow

A rainbow is over the town. Two rainbows are over the town, both more perfect bows than people had ever seen before. Behind and above the bows were the great dark clouds, now moving eastward, that had drenched us with rain. Below the bows were the hills, until just recently as dark as the clouds. Against that darkness the light and colors of the rainbows shone, like the hues of the soul against the darkness of the world. They arced above the town like a promise.

In places where the earth seems small, you can't see where a rainbow begins or where it ends. You see the arc, but not where it touches the ground. Here I could see both beginning and end, and I wanted to stand where a rainbow begins. To the south it comes down, touching the earth in a fold of the distant hills. That was too far away to go. To the north, it seemed to arise just where the pueblo was, three miles out of town. So I got in my car and drove out.

[1947?]

The Dust of Abiquiu

Men still hoe their vegetable gardens. Is not this a reassuring fact? I see two men now at work on a garden already overrun with weeds, only the sweet corn rising up to view. But there the patch is, and there the men. One of them wears a blue shirt and a straw hat with a black band. He is white skinned and on the stout side. The other has on a faded brown shirt and an old grey felt hat. He is dark skinned and lean. Both ply their hoes in a leisurely manner, and now and again stop work and come together, resting on their hoes, to have a talk. They do not talk about hating men, fighting, or making a million dollars. I am sure of that. They talk about simple things connected with their simple life. To one side of their patch is a lumberyard, with planks piled in the blazing sun and a buzz saw going. Behind them is a clump of trees dominated by tall Lombardy poplars. Behind the trees is the mountain, its folds and flanks in shifting light and shadow cast by shifting clouds. The mountain is one of many that form a variated [sic] rim around this high valley.

The Kansas bird—the lark.

The friendly tamarisks that become your companions in the desert. The fatal strip—Los Alamos.

In Llano Camado there is an earth colored church. Its front door is freshly painted blue and white, as is the bell tower, and on top of the tower is a white cross. I have heard that bell ring. I have heard the church bells ring in Ranchos, on the other loma, the sounds carrying from ridge to ridge high over the valley for miles around. Is there anyone who does not hear the bells? And I have heard bells in Taos and Santa Fe. Why do they ring? Is not the call from earth to heaven inaudible? Does God's voice sound like a bell?

Someone made a small forest grow in a land of sagebrush. I am told it was a retired forest ranger who brought aspens down from the mountains, and planted tall poplars and a few cottonwoods. Now there is a woods with trees so numerous you cannot see the end of them. The forest floor is grass covered and splotched with sunlight and shadows. It is very still in there; and looking in I have seen some strange things. First I saw the fawn colored cow, then the russet cow with the white markings. Slowly they appeared from the depths of the woods, following their noses as they cropped the grass. As they moved, they moved into a patch of sunlight and then into a patch of shadow. In the sunlight I saw them; in the shadow they disappeared. They were creatures alternately visible and invisible. They were like mysterious beings with the power to appear and disappear at will. They were like men living in two worlds, the seen and the unseen.

And once I saw a bent old man emerge from the depth of the woods. He came as silently as the cows, materializing out of nowhere. Bent he was, but as he came forward he bent way down to the earth and then straightened up as much as he could. On he came, bending and straightening up. When he bent down, if he was in a splotch of sunlight, an instrument momentarily flashed. The tool looked like an asparagus knife. He thrust it in the earth, cut something up, took it in his free hand and tossed it away. Slowly he went around the floor of the forest that I could see, bending down, straightening up. After a time he disappeared into the depths from which he had emerged. This goes on. Cars whizz along the highway that passes the woods on one side. Trucks snort and roar without mufflers. The sounds seem not to penetrate the forest. The motion of the highway is quickly absorbed by the stillness of the woods, small thin trunks of saplings, larger ones of full-grown aspens.

A hawk on a cross.

●

The dust of Abiquiu. It is powdered fine, dry adobe from the earth, crumbled earthern walls, grass and sagebrush dried and pulverized, cattle dung, human sweat, human blood. It coated my shoes with a fine tenacious powder. This was overlain by the dust of Española and Taos. I do not say that the dust of Abiquiu is different from dust elsewhere, though it is ancient. I am not going to write much of dust. But—

Abiquiu (pronounced Abique) is the name of a village in New Mexico. Formerly it was a Tewa pueblo; they tell me that some Indian families still live in houses set up against the hill.

In what shall we place our faith? I'll put mine in the dust of Abiquiu. It has no malice, no greed. It is not fearful. Sometimes it blows into your face, but you can turn your back. Sometimes the wind lifts it in a whirl skyward—Godward, some would say, but I think God is right here as well as up there. But the dust too is right here, and more tangible than God. Dust (the trucks of Taos) gets on my shoes and in my nostrils. God may be in my heart and in the hearts of men, but He has not made Himself felt for a long time. Nor is there any present sign that He is going to make Himself felt before atomic bombs pulverize us.

It is not much to see, Abiquiu. You leave the highway, go up a hill, pass a few adobe houses, a pig pen, a large barn-like general store, and go down on the other side. There are some three hundred people, but you see few of them, a Catholic church, a Penitente morada, a handful of houses. Not much meets the eye as you pass through. Why have I chosen the dust of Abiquiu as a symbol of something? I cannot tell you. The fact is the symbol chose me. I was there on that hill, and afterwards the words "the dust of Abiquiu" came into my mind, and I liked the words, the sound of them, the as yet unfathomed intangible meaning, and they kept repeating themselves. The dust of Abiquiu. The dust of Abiquiu.

But what does not meet the eye in Abiquiu? They tell me that Abiquiu, small as it is, is a stronghold of the Penitentes. They are called Los Hermanos Penitentes—the Penitent Brothers. I know little about them except that some of their numbers are called Hermanos de luz—brothers of light. They tell me too that along this valley of the Chama River, above which Abiquiu is perched, countless migrations of peoples have passed, far back into antiquity—people on the move to find a better place, (to improve their lot), people seeking what people have always sought. Perhaps they have left their imprint on the dust of Abiquiu, their hope and fear, courage and despair, cruelty, suffering, and the wonder of first love. Up and down the Chama they passed, stopping perhaps on the easily accessible promontory now called Abiquiu. (And there, today, a house is

being built.) * * * [There are] mesas in massed terraces behind Abiquiu. A solid mesa makes the Chama turn at Abiquiu. * * *

Abiquiu—behind it—here the mesas come down, mass upon mass, terrace upon terrace. The vast earth is piled up behind it. Here the Chama,
meeting a force too great for it, is turned in its course, but not deflected
from its aim to reach the Rio Grande. The huge buttress-like mesa,
though more powerful than the river, cannot move. There it obstructs.
Never anywhere else will it obstruct. The river yields but out wits it.

In front [of Aiquiu], cliffs, mountains, badlands, red earth, white earth,
lava-rocks—once settled by Spanish captives ransomed from the Co-
manches and Apaches; in the mid 18th century, a stop on the Spanish
trail from Santa Fe to Los Angeles.

Here Antonio José Martínez was born in 1793. A remarkable man.
Because of him a line through the air, a silvery cord, connects Abiquiu
and Taos. * * *

The two mountain ranges face each other across the river, across the
valley. To the east is the Sangre de Cristo, to the west the Jemez. How far
it is between them I do not know. Sometimes it seems that a mightly leap
would swing you through the air from the one to the other. Sometimes it
seems that you would trudge on for days, through a sculptured land that
defies description, before reaching the other side. If you are in the middle, which way do you go? If you are in between two worlds, which way?

In between the ranges flows the Rio Grande; and wherever a river
flows, unless it is through a gorge or canyon, you will see green. Badlands
and deserts may be all around, but along the river are trees and grass;
and where you see green you will find men. There men have their small
but potent stake in the vast life of the earth.

The region I am particularly thinking of is called Española Valley.

Sangre de Cristo—Blood of Christ, love of Christ, light of Christ. Over
there, Los Alamos—the zenith of material force in man's hand. In between, the life of ordinary men. And—the Indians. Their dance a prayer.

The Indian who could not be taught to play chess because he cooperated with his "opponent's" moves; could not compete. * * *

But what can be seen from Abiquiu! The fields. A man came. He saw
the fields and got an idea. He would get the Indians to sell him the fields,
then get the Indians to work for him. Thus it ever was with men who have
visions of establishing earthly kingdoms on this earth, themselves the
gods. He finally got the fields, but he never could get the Indians to work
for him. Southern planters without Negro slaves. Factory owners without
wage slaves. Now the fields are worse than useless. Untended for years
they grow grass that is harmful to cattle. They look fine, green and
plentiful, but they are poison.

And back from Abiquiu, across the mesas and the mountains, is Los Alamos. Some twenty-five miles due south, as a plane flies, over mesas and mountains, is the Hill.

"The mountain will smoke, great winds will come up, the world will be destroyed by fire." So say the old men of the pueblo, some of whom may have true vision and the gift of prophecy. Do we not hear the same prediction in different terms from scientists who know the fearful potency of the atom bomb?

What I do not know is—Do the elders of Taos vision the coming destruction as the end of man, or the matrix of a new birth? Will resurrection follow this death?—and, if so, who will be resurrected? White men? Red men? Black men? An entirely new race?

The Indians have developed, as far as their religious experiences and views are concerned, an effective non-violent resistance. It is a wall of silence which cannot be penetrated by outsiders. It just stops you, without hurting you, without making you angry or arousing the desire to force through it.

It protects them from disrupting outer influences. But it closes them within it.

What we need is not the mingling of bodies in copulation but the meeting of hearts, the unification in spirit.

The race between education and catastrophe will be lost by education. We have put off educating ourselves in the basis [sic] matter for 1900 years. How can that neglect be remedied in five years? * * *

I expect that before I finish writing this book something will happen in the world, something momentous. Either we shall be transformed, lifted above these little selves into larger beings, raised above these problems into a unity with all creation; or the third World War will begin. Either men and women with Christ-like qualities will appear in every country, or the atom bombs will begin to fall. If the first happens, I shall stop writing voluntarily (having something of more importance to do). If the second happens, I shall of course stop writing involuntarily, and stop breathing too.

I know by experience that human beings can be transformed—not simply improved but changed in the root, radically altered into new beings. We know by experience that atom bombs can fall. I grant it is more probable that we shall have a third World War than that there shall be a Christ in every country. Yet new men and new women are *as possible* as war. I will hold to the faith that we will be reborn until I see destruction sweep the earth and I am knocked to smithereens.

●

The dust of Taos blows from the north.
The dust of Domingo blows from the west.
The dust of Abiquiu swirls. * * *

Where hummingbirds perch on clothes lines and telephone wires   a
clump of tall hollyhocks   glittering green, a sheen of crimson. * * *

In a conspicuous place near the plaza of Taos the U.S. Army has put
up one of its come-on posters. It reads:

What Do You Want Out of Life?
Adventure — Travel — Education
Good Pay — Promotion — Security

There is a good career for you in the army ground forces.

And on the other side:

First Class Soldier and Citizen

A large red arrow catches your attention, as it is intended to do.
Perched on top of a one story building it points down at three red gas-
oline pumps. The building is in two parts, one a service station, the other
a cafe. You read the words painted in large red letters. Red Arrow Cafe.
Fresh Trout. Choice Steaks. Chicken Dinners. You Catch Em, We Cook
Em. Taos Vic. There it stands, the Red Arrow Cafe, one of the places on
the highway to Taos.

Take your eyes off it and look westward. A vast world opens up. You
see a stretch of cultivated fields, a horse or two grazing, with occasional
adobe houses under clumps of cottomwood trees. Beyond the fields runs
a long tan colored llano or flat topped hill not as high as a mesa. It is
barren except for spots of small piñons and cedars. It was on that llano
that I saw a hawk on a cross. Beyond the llano rises the mountain of the
three ears. Tres Orejas. A vast desolation sweeps westward to the shad-
owy forms of the mountains that form part of the Continental Divide.
Over there is Tierra Amarilla. South of Tierra Amarilla is the phantom
cone of Pedernal, and Abiquiu. There, over there, is the far rim of the
world.

Is God present in that sometimes radiant but often somber expanse of
land and sky? I have seen the sun set over there, forks of yellow-white
light spurting upwards as if the Sun God were there and this was his
hand, and an arching crimson-golden radiance flowing over the mountains and the valleys. I have seen blue-black storms over there, the light-

ning splitting through the clouds and the rain streaming to earth in black pillars, several cloud-bursts occurring at the same time. But I have not seen God. It is said that He is everywhere. Is He in that sunset? He is in that storm? He is in those mountains? He is in that vast desolation, and in the Rio Grande Gorge, and in the sage brush? Is He in that hawk and in the desert flowers, in the snakes and spiders and grasshoppers, in the horses and cattle and trees, and in the men who live in those adobe houses? Is He in the dust of Abiquiu? And if He is in them, what does His presence mean to them? What does his presence *do* for them? He might as well not be present in them if His presence does nothing for them. Is He active or passive most of the time in so far as you and I and all created things are concerned? Well, never mind. Just the other day, over that way, I saw the love-flight of two yellow butterflies.

The cook of the Red Arrow Cafe is an Indian from the pueblo named Pete. God, is a mite of your reality in Pete? How do I find it? How does Pete find it? Is a mite of Pete's reality in you? How does Pete realize it? Pete was in the war, but not by choice. You see how definite I can be about a thing like this. There is no question about it. I know. Pete knows. His wife and all the people of the pueblo and many of the people of Taos know. Pete was in the war, the war was in him. Pete now is out of the war, but the war is not yet out of him—nor will it be while he lives on earth. They drafted him, as they did other men of the pueblo, and many men of Taos County and all the counties of the United States. They? The government. The State. In the name of the People the State took the people and sent them to war. This was not the first time that the Indians have felt the heavy hand of the U.S. government; but this time it was different. This time the Indians were drawn, as millions of men everywhere have been and are being drawn, into one of the problems—some would say the outstanding problem—of our time: the relation of man to the State. The Indians, you know, are wards of the government; they are not citizens. How could the government draft them? As one person said—The government can do anything.

They made Pete cut his hair, sent him to several camps, and then to the Pacific. It seems that all of the Indians were sent to the Pacific. That was the right thing to do, I heard a white man say, and he added—The Indians were savage enough to fight the Japs. Pete was on what he calls a fighting hospital ship. He does not want to talk about his war-experiences, yet he does. Moreover it was a white-man's war, so it is something he can talk about to people who are not the pueblo—other people, I shall call them. Quite a lot came out the first evening we sat with Pete, his wife and two children on the second story porch of their house in the pueblo. Pete's ship was hit by two suicide planes. There was a terrific explosion. Many men were killed instantly, others blown into the water. Pete was not clear about it, but he must have had time to grab a life-jacket and a waterproof flashlight. It was the flashlight that led to his rescue by planes. It was night, and he had been many hours in the ocean when they spotted him. He showed us the flashlight. He still had it, though now he let the children play with it. It had saved his life. And now Pete is back home. From war to cooking. He gets up at five o'clock, walks three miles from the pueblo to the Red Arrow Cafe, cooks until three or four in the afternoon, and walks three miles back to the pueblo. * * *

A haphazard half-moon tumbled up over the rim of the mountain— but it straightened itself out as it travelled the sky. * * *

The tawny hide of the mountains showing between dark green spots of piñon and cedar. * * *

Space, which itself is soundless, absorbs sounds. It is in space, not in time, that one can obey the commandment, "Be still, and know that I am God."* Here I want to be still and silent. The silence of the Indians. * * *

Do not drive up from Santa Cruz. You will miss what I want you to see. Your back will be to it. Take another way up to Truchas. Take the road out of Ranchos de Taos to Talpa and up [U.S.?] hill to Rio Pueblo. (Remember that the elevation of Ranchos de Taos is some 7000 feet.) As you go up and up, there are opening[s] in the mountains, and you can look back and down and see, way down there, a patch of Taos Valley. From Rio Pueblo you drive on through hills and high valleys and mountain passes—Vadito, Peñasco, Chamizal, Trampas, Ojo Sarco. Part of the way from Trampas to Truchas is pure forest, thick with big timber, the northern end of Santa Fe National Forest. Here and there the trees give way and you can catch a glimpse of tawny Truchas Peak, the highest peak in high New Mexico. How high are you? I do not know. Perhaps somewhere between nine and ten thousand feet. Even so, Truchas Peak seems almost as high above you, and as inaccessible, as it does from Española Valley.

I am giving you words, hurrying you along because I want you to see something stupendous. But the words have a taste and a sound. Say them as the Spanish say them. Vadeeto, Penyasco, Chameesal, Oho Sarco. Each represents a mountain place where men have precarious hold on life. Each is placed where it is because Nature, there, had made a

*[From the Old Testament, Psalms 46.10.—Ed.]

meadow, a stretch of grassland, a plot of barely arable earth and men, by working it, can make a hard living. Every time you come upon one of these meadows in the mountains you are surprised; and surprised too, to see shiny tin roofs atop adobe dwellings that in other respects are built much as houses in the region were built three [hundred?] years ago. One of these villages has a reputation for knifings and murders. That is now. In the old days, when each village was an organic group-life, each village a cooperative community, to kill your neighbor was to kill your helper.

Vadito, Peñasco, Chamizal, Trampas. Ojo Sarco are remote from the national Congress and even from the state Legislature. The President of the United States does not know of Chamizal, or of Trampas with its mission church built so solidly from the earth that it would seem that not even an atom bomb could dissolve it. They seem to have believed, in those days, that the worship of God must have strong, solid, earthly foundations. Nor does Chamizal know of the President of the United States, nor of the United Nations Organization, nor of the stark alternative of modern times—One World Or None.

Once I had a picnic lunch with friends in the pine forest between Ojo Sarco and Truchas. Then we moved on. I remember catching a glimpse of Truchas in the distance, the road winding and going up and down towards it. I remember on entering the village there was a large dark wooden cross planted on the roadside. The land barren and utterly brilliant. No soft colors were anywhere, no shadows. From a vast blue sky the sun beat down upon this immensity of earth. All was radiant, all was dazzling, all was elemental. The very earth and rocks seemed to emit a golden light, a light more ancient than the light of life—a desert-light. Far down in the center, in the very bottom of this crater, was a tiny green spot, no larger than a dime. That was the fertile valley. That was where men lived.

I had a sense that what I was seeing was so immense that the state of Pennsylvania could be dropped in, and you would see it only as a small rectangle on the floor of the crater. The entire North American Continent could be dropped in, and still the cauldron would be far from filled to its rim. I had a sense that I was seeing the created Earth as God may have seen it relatively soon after He stopped work.

[1947?]

Taos Night

Night-black, night of the New Mexican Southwest, a luminous black sky, and the stars seem close to earth. Into this sky of quiet ecstasy the form of a mountain lifts. The mountain, vast itself, lifts into the greater immensity of the universe as manifest at this view-point. The surrounding hills repose beneath the intensity of stars.

The line of the slope is broken by a gap—a canyon to the country north.

This side of the mountain, fitted into its slope, are the two terraced forms of Taos pueblo, one on each side of the creek that comes down from Blue Lake.

On a high terrace of each pueblo building is the figure of an Indian, robed in white, face to the hills.

No lights show from the houses. No figures cross the plaza. No dogs bark. The only sounds are those made by the creek as it runs its course from Taos mountain to the Rio Grande.

The night, the mountain, the pueblo, the silent men—all seem simply to have come into being . . . being by birth . . . created but not labored—the night from all preceding nights, the mountain from the ample earth, the pueblo from all dwellings back to the cliffs, the men from all the people of their race.

It is quiet. In this silence, repose and intensity co-exist.

Then comes a call, human, but like a high bark.

Several robed figures emerge from the houses, pass across the plaza, and exchange greetings—"Hé-ah-ho." The voices are those of men.

The men gather at a bridge over the stream.

Pause. Silence.

Then suddenly a Taos song. Another song and another.

Then silence again . . . and life becomes existence again . . . and existence, focused for a time in a group of singing men, expands to the mountain and the close stars.

[1935]

New Mexico After India

In times past, I had always come to New Mexico from the eastern states of America. I had greeted Raton Pass and the land extending southwestward beyond, having in the background of my mind the low soft country of the eastern seaboard, the prairies of the middle west, commerce, industry, and of course the man-made canyons of New York. New Mexico had always looked grand, open, sunlit, a summit of ancient earth and historic peoples.

This time I came upon New Mexico from India and the Far East. Not directly to be sure, for I motored across California, Nevada, Utah and a part of Colorado; but still, India and the East remained uppermost in the part of my mind that makes comparisons. I was seeing everything against a background built up of experiences in India, Ceylon, Hong Kong, Shanghai, and Japan. I crossed the state-line, this time, up above Shiprock. New Mexico looked just as grand, and more than ever I felt it was a country in which I belonged.

In India I had seen hills that looked so tired, sunbaked, and ancient that I felt they ought to be covered by deep sea water so as to become cool, rested and renewed. By contrast, the hills of New Mexico looked recently formed, unspent, active, still able to profit by meeting with the sun, winds, rain, and man. Over there I had seen villages that looked as ancient as the hills, and that had in fact endured with but little change for centuries. By contrast, even the pueblos seemed to have a touch of the modern world, the Mexican villages seemed to be growing and changing as young things grow, Taos and Santa Fe seemed to be altering under the same impulse that created Chicago in some fifty years.

How we change, here in America! At any rate, how we change our environment. How quickly we rise. May it not be that we will as quickly fall.

The East has endurance. The West has sudden bursts of speed. Taos is speeding up. Santa Fe is speeding up. Even in the little villages between San Ildefonso and Highway 64 I noted many more buildings than before, and other signs of increasing activity. Over there, they still use bullock carts as their ancestors did five thousand years ago. Over here it is the motor-car. Compared to New York the Southwest may seem slow and unchanging. Compared to the interior of India, the Southwest is in rapid change. The Southwest is young, with a long future ahead of it— provided, of course, that its very activity does not run it into accidents similar to those now being suffered by the nations of Europe.

To endure is safe. To speed up is dangerous, unless those at the controls are wide awake and masters of the forces they evoke. I will not say we need fewer mechanical engineers. I am sure we need more and wiser engineers of human beings.

India revealed to me a bewildering number of different peoples speaking different languages belonging to more different castes and sub-castes than I can name. I had the impression that her people were entangled in a social complexity which no one could unravel, that they were held prisoners in an intricate maze of age-old customs and beliefs from which no one, not even a government composed of men like Gandhi, could free them. By comparison, how simple and free is the situation in America and the Southwest. We can thank our stars—if not ourselves—that we are not yet bogged down in a similar labyrinth.

Actually, of course, the situation here is not so simple, neither is it free. We have our own complexities, taboos, classes if not castes, racial prejudices, and knotty problems. By these we hold ourselves down far more than we have any real cause for doing. By these we fret ourselves and antagonize each other and impede the proper flowing of those forces that would work for unification among the American people. But all you have to do is to look at [a] man here and notice how he carries himself, how he behaves towards others, and you know that this man, even though he is placed among the lowest of our society, has had a measure of democratic opportunity that is denied to millions of human beings in Eastern countries.

Comparatively, men here stand on their own feet. The Indian is upstanding. The Mexican is upstanding. The Negro is upstanding. The white is upstanding. Let each continue to upstand, and at the same time bend towards the other on the basis of a common humanity, and we would become one people in spirit and fundamental aim. This is one possibility. The other possibility is that separatism here will increase rather [than] diminish. In this case, we can look to India today to see what we will become in the course of the next several hundred years—if we endure that long.

One of the very useful books that a traveler in India buys at the outset is Murray's Guide. Inserted in page 18 of this book is a map of the city of Bombay. On this map you will see the section of the city that fronts on the so-called Back Bay. Looking at this section you will discover seven squares marked off, adjacent yet separated. The squares are labelled as follows: Catholic Gymkhana, Y.M.C.A. Gymkhana, Grant Medical College Gymkhana, Wilson College Gymkhana, Hindu Gymkhana, Islam Gymkhana, Parsi Gymkhana. So it is in the actual city. Each group has its recreational house and grounds. Each group is jammed against its neighbor. Each group remains utterly separate from the others. Each is open to its own kind. Each is closed tight against all others. And they are, the seven of them, side by side! Nowhere else have I ever seen a more graphic example of the separatism that rules living men.

Now right behind these examples of living men separated from each other, there are three cemeteries, also adjacent, also separated, quite exclusive: an Old English Cemetery, a Muhammadan Burying Ground, a Hindu Burning Place. And so we have it—in death as in life, men divided.

There was one event in this my recent visit to New Mexico that was quite ironic and not without a general significance. I had made the trip to India with my wife and child. We had gone through disease ridden India, and not one of us had had a day of sickness. Malaria, cholera, dysentery, and minor ills had been avoided. Safe home at last, we came to Taos and Santa Fe, healthy places in a comparatively healthy country, and my wife got the flu. India has its malaria. America has its influenza. Malaria has undermined the health and vitality of countless numbers of India's people. Influenza, it seems to me, is becoming as much of a menace to us as are tropical diseases to the inhabitants of tropical countries. It is all very well to call influenza a "bug," but we might do well to realize that not the climate alone but also our way of living has a great deal to do with the fact that we are susceptible to it and are becoming more so.

In Ceylon I had visited Buddhist temples, some quite beautiful, and Buddhist sermon-houses that have simple dignity. In India I beheld samples of the extraordinary architecture of the Dravidians, the Hindu, and the Moghuls. In Santa Fe I went to the House of Navajo Religion built by the combined efforts of Navajos, Mary Wheelright, the Hendersons and others. Inside that house as I stood still, my eyes on the reproductions of the sand paintings, something spoke to me in a language akin to that which my own spirit might use were it equally skilled in symbolic expression. As I write these lines that House vividly comes back to me and I feel glad to know that in New Mexico there is a building that lives for the spirit of man, a microcosm created and maintained by Americans cooperating upon the high plane of symbolic meaning and religion.

One place gives you what others can't. You give to one place what you cannot give to others. I have never tried to put in words the unique gift of New Mexico to me. It is enough that I feel it, that I know it, that I recognize it without need of words. Something of New Mexico came to me for the first time fifteen years ago. It was a penetration deep under the skin. Ever since there has existed a special polarization between this human being and the people and earth of the Southwest.

Do all you can, it is sufficiently difficult to become a citizen of the world. You may overcome prejudices and move towards universality; but preferences linger, and preferences tend to localize you. Even though you bring yourself to meet all men as friends, you find yourself preferring to meet some men. Even though you acknowledge the human family as one family, you continue liking some people better than others. Even though you break away from the weights that would hold you narrow and static in one place, and move out as a man upon the earth, not all places are equally acceptable, and it usually happens that one part of the world retains its hold upon your heart as home.

[1940?]

Part of the Universe

Look at the sky and what do you see? A sticky sky, a drippy sky that is not worth looking at? A low ceiling of dull clouds that increases your sense of being hemmed in and depressed? A grey or yellow watery light? Haze, and through the haze a greyish watery blue? Soggy nondescript clouds earth-pressing, their edges blurring into the ever present haze? Blotches and shadows that drift about to no purpose? That is the way the sky appears in low humid country where excessive moisture combines with the fumes of man's cities and factories to smear the heavens and stifle the inward flame.

Here in this dry highland the sky burns with brightness. It is pure blue and vast, incredibly high, incredibly near, illimitable. It is a fit medium to receive the undiluted sun. There is immense sky here. One can understand why people, not knowing the kingdom of heaven to be within, believed heaven to be up there. The clouds pile up and rise. Clouds sheer white, shining, vital grey, intense blue-black. Some form and reform before your eyes in magical mutations. The amazing shapes stand out so sharply that it is as if God had drawn lines of light around each one. Here the clouds have missions.

Look intently. Concentrate your being sky-gazing. Let the glory of things seen suggest the glory of things unseen. From contemplating this vast blue radiance slip into a sense of the vast invisible. Think of God's Being as this great. Think of his Light as this powerful and blazing, his Love as this golden and warm. Think of his abundance—and your scarcity.

Something becomes possible. Something becomes probable. It is possible to believe, as did Bartolomé de Las Casas, that God is a flame burning towards man, and man in the very core of his being is a flame burning towards God. (This was discovered in the sixteenth century by an uncommon Spanish priest who underwent transformation, who rose up into a being above himself and came upon a vision of what human life in the New World should be, but who never journeyed far enough to see this particular sky and earth. It was discovered by him through new birth.

And we, here, may believe that his discovery is true of you and me and our relation to the universal Being, may we not?)

Look at the land and what do you see? Hills that block the view? Monotonous flatlands unmarked except by wire fences and telegraph poles? Swamps, mires, bogs? Sooty buildings? The rubble of bombed cities? Modern wars are fought on and over lowlands close to sea-level. A really "first-class" war never has been waged on highlands six to seven thousand feet elevation.

Ruins are around here in this flaming earth, the ruins of ancient cliff dwellings, of great community houses built of stone upon high plateau and mesa tops, the ruins of more recent pueblos and single adobe dwellings; but these have been worn down by the weather, even as mountains are worn down, not blasted by man.

The earth is as big and open as the sky, and more variated [sic]. Mountains, mesas, buttes, broad plateau; bold bastons, tawny cliffs; gaps, canyons, arroyos; red earth, yellow earth, white earth, black and brown slabs of rock; every color the eyes of man can see; sagebrush plains sloping up to ancient sands. Above the sands the scrub cedars and piñons begin. Above the scrubs are sturdy growths. Above the full piñons the heavy timber begins and goes up and over the mountains. This prodigious wealth is not scattered about helterskelter. The whole, and every bit of it is designed. Who designed it? Heat and cold, the winds, the rain, invisible hands.

Though filled with every conceivable shape and form, this world is orderly overall and laid out with respect to the four directions. (Its length is north and south, its width east and west.) Since it is a world, not the world, it has boundaries, noble boundaries. To the east, running north-south from Santa Fe beyond Taos into Colorado, is a grandly fashioned mountain range, the Sangre de Cristo. To the west, anchored on top of a mammoth plateau known as Pajarito, rises an almost parallel range, the Jemez. This western range, to the eye, is the more dramatic and spectacular. It mounts as it moves northward. In the region behind Española it piles up in a massively towering blue mass and, to the eyes, comes to an abrupt and mighty end. Here is a gap; and through this gap, winding down from the northwest, the river Chama comes in. North of the gap, continuing the western boundary, is not a mountain but a mesa. The Black Mesa continues north out of sight. Whenever the mountains stop rising, wherever there is a dip of the crest, a deep gap, a canyon or a valley between hills, the sky fills in. The earth is the shore, the sky is the sea. The sky fills in as if it were a weightless cerulean sea teeming with sparkling life.

This world is unified, an integrated whole, a glorious world, a cradle of greatness, a furnace of light. For human purposes, at any [rate] for my purposes, it will have to be delimited. It begins, we shall say, with Santa Fe and ends with Taos. If you are a Taoseño you may insist, without opposition from me, that it begins with Taos and ends with Santa Fe. In any case, the hills of Santa Fe are the southern end, the valley and mountains of Taos are the northern. The hills of Santa Fe, the red hills, the warm hills. The valley of Taos, child of the mountain.

And the clouds. Over the mountains, over the high ridges the clouds gather, hang, hover. The clouds hold junta over the mountains. There they meet, around the high humped backbones, clouds like pennants, streamer-clouds. There they rest, the grey-white caps, the clouds in strata. There they gang, the blue-black [hoods?] [heads?] thunder-bearing. Sometimes, behind and above the highest peaks, will be seen a titanic cumulus piling up, its multiforms rounded like celestial cotton bolls, all of it a dazzling white, the whole creation slowly soaring into the heavens.

Between the Sangre de Cristo and Jemez ranges, in the region of Española, is a huge structural trough known as Española Valley, through which the Rio Grande flows. This valley, from Pojoaque or the pueblo of San Ildefonso on the south to the village of Velarde on the north, is some twenty miles long. From the foothills of the Sangre to the foothills of the Jemez—the [torso?], perhaps the heart of the Rio Grande world—it is, at the widest, some thirty to forty miles across. An ample place. It is in fact a tremendous place of ancient forms and elemental forces. Anything can happen here. Most things do happen here. The pulse of man is heightened to the pulse of earth. The pulse of earth beats time with the rhythm of the universe. Most parts of the earth are of the earth. This part is (manifestly) part of the universe. If you are rightly stationed you can oversee the entire area. You can take it all in in one great apprehending glance.

At night, when men are not looking, the mountains stir and move towards one another. As living forces the two ranges interlock in creative tension, the valley receiving the charges and discharges. The forces rhythmically circulate east-west from crest to crest, over the valley, under the valley, through the valley. They penetrate the life of man at every point. The forces rhythmically flow north-south, over and through the elevated earth, down and around and under, coming back through the mountain-roots.

Many a time I have driven a car, with the top down, a short distance up the road to Santa Cruz and turned north and out onto the sagebrush flatlands that slope towards the hills, the ancient sands, the sculptured badlands—and parked there, facing westward. I used to make a practice of it every afternoon when the hills began to cast shadows. It was the way I worshiped then, earth-contemplating, sky-contemplating, prayer-gazing, opening to this large splendour, trying to feel my connectedness with all that is.

The town of Española is elevation 5590 feet. At just about level the Rio Grande flows, coming down by the Black Mesa some five miles west of my parking place. I am a hundred or so feet higher. Behind me rises the Sangre de Cristo, up, up to the mountain village of Truchas, up, up where no roads go to bald Truchas Peak, the highest point in high New Mexico, elevation 13,306 feet. I am backed up. I am backed mightily by the mountains called the Blood of Christ. And in front of me, what sweep, what drama!

I overlook San Juan pueblo and the trees along the river with summer foliage showing as a dark green band in the midst of desert. I overlook the vilage of Alcalde, its cluster of adobe houses barely visible. My gaze stops momentarily at the Black Mesa. I look above the mesa and behold the sky spreading immensely to the northwest, a blue cover over the valley of the Chama, over the village of Abiquiu, the Ghost Ranch, Navajo Canyon, Cebolla, Tierra Amarilla, the land of massive red earth fifty-five airline miles away, and beyond, the mountains of the Continental Divide.

Nearer at hand is the gap in the western rim where the Chama flows in to join the Rio Grande. Through that gap what peoples have passed! It is the only exit from this part of the Rio Grande valley to the lands of the west and northwest. In two thousand years what migrations it has witnessed, what treks! And who are those ancient refugees—or pilgrims? People going out, people coming in, they had to pass through the Chama-gap.

South of the gap is the Pajarito plateau, lightly holding on its huge palm the ancient Puye cliff dwellings [and] the modern mechanically mushroomed town of Los Alamos, dedicated to atomic energy research and, man's larger world being what it is, concerned with the manufacturing of atom bombs. Should just one—one such bomb—accidentally go off, it would cause more havoc everywhere around than two thousand years of nature's storms and man's unmechanized anger. Behind and towering above the plateau is a great mound-like blue mountain whose name I have never been sure of. Perhaps it is Palvadera (or Valle del Caballo). At any rate it is part of the jagged mass of the Jemez range.

I see an ominous black storm form above the Jemez, blot out the peaks, engulf the slopes, then move on with its terrifying charge of lightning, thunder, and heavy rain up the valley of the Chama, chasing the ghosts of people who have gone that way. Now a second storm shows up north beyond Velarde. And still a third, far to the south. In that southern storm the lightning splits horizontally through the blue-black clouds and the clouds stream down to earth in solid bands of water. From it no sounds come. It is too far away. Three storms occurring simultaneously and all within view, and not a drop on me or within miles of me. Between the storms the sky appears in vast blue stretches, the sun floods down, the world is brilliant and serene. This world can have its storms and yet outshine them. It can contain them and remain a world. And the storms, I must tell you, are terrific where they hit. But one atom bomb storm would burst it asunder.

I sit in my parked car with the top down, having a grandstand seat for this mighty spectacle. I am, for the time being, an immune spectator. I am in sunshine. I am in the valley of the shadow of God. And am not satisfied.

I like to see the shadows of hills. But I can see the hills too. I would not like the shadows if I could not see the hills. Yet it is true: the shadows witness that the hills exist. They are promises cast on our earth by the sun as it slants against the reality. I cannot see God; His shadow does not satisfy me. God's world is not enough when you yearn for Him. I yearn. I yearn to see, to be a participant, not a mere spectator, I yearn to merge with the Life whose physical aspect is the only aspect visible to my eyes. The outer magnificence reminds me of an inner splendour. And so I yearn. And I think.

Say that God is as this vast world. Here it is. Here He is. My relation to Him is as my relation to it, is it not? I am not really part of Him, not consciously at any rate. I am an outsider, an exile. An exile from large-ness and from abundance and from glory. I am a warm-blooded creature but do not flame. I seek warm things and want warm life; but do not care as I was meant to care, nor love as I was meant to love. I am a conscious being but do not unite, not with myself, not with [creatures?] [creation?]. I am a spectator. No, not even that. I can behold the Rio Grande world. I can contemplate it. I cannot see God. I am not a seer. I am, as I say, Him-blind. The sun slopes in the west, and I am in the valley of the shadow of God—and in the shadow of the bomb.

[1947?]

Santa Fe Sequence

Santa Fe is cupped in hills. Red hills dotted with dark green clumps of piñons and cedars encircle it, protect it, cradle it. The city rests in a hollow of Southwestern earth that would seem to have been made for it by nature millions of years ago, that patiently waited until men found it and established their dwellings. Now it is outgrowing the cup, spreading out and up onto the rim, into the hills.

Santa Fe cupped in hills. This was my first impression of it, and it will be my last; but it [is] not quite accurate. There are no hills to the southwest, no rim. In the direction of Albuquerque the land is relatively flat, the cup is open. But you will see why I have my picture of it if you come down from the north and pause on the hill near the Cross of the Martyrs. There below lies Santa Fe, hills to the north, and to the east, and to the south and to the immediate west. You see the dome of the State Capitol rising above surrounding trees. You see trees and trees, green, green, and as much of the houses and buildings as the trees will let you see: governmental buildings, churches, stores, dwellings. In winter when the green has vanished and the trees are bare, the houses stand out and their color is so like the color of the earth that they almost blend. In winter too you will see piñon smoke rising from the chimneys, and if your imagination is good you can get a whiff of the pungent aroma even up on this hill. Except for a few brick and stone buildings, you might think you were overlooking a very large pueblo. But no, in this city are things and ways the Indians did not and do not know of, nor the Spaniards of an earlier day. This city you are overlooking, this Santa Fe, is the mother-city of the modern Rio Grande world. And it is under the shadow of the bomb. All cities, all cities everywhere are; Santa Fe knows it is.

[1947?]

California

Caromb

They should have arrived in the morning, the cool bright-haze morning of clear and misty things, the forward-gleaming morning. Two young people in love should have arrived when the sun warmed the earth and the pine trees were like torches. They would have seen vast shoulders of earth covered with primeval verdure sloping to the sea. They would have seen the sea itself, bright blue like the sky with a roaring fringe of white where the rocks made foam. The cottages would [have] seemed like tanned young faces with eyes opening. They would have sensed great land and something vast and spiriting. They would have loved Caromb as a place to be in love.

But they arrived when the pine trees gathered shadow and the black wing stirred all forms to hunch and creep; when the mountains loomed ominously like huge death-stones moving to close one in; when the sea was bleak and chill and lonely; when dogs barked; when houses began to creak and strain; when seals on the far rocks rolled sounds across the empty waters; when the wind moaned and the sea pounded. It was ghost-hour in Caromb. It was the hour of the black wing. It was close to night and the time of covered consciousness. * * *

The road was bordered by pine trees now, and occasional clearings, sometimes white fences and white ranch houses. All the farms were called ranches. This was ranch country. It was a harsh word, ranch; harsher than farm.

They were on the road to the peninsula, a road over the earth, the deep earth, blocks of elements, events, and dry fire. The body of earth speeds, and the body of man is carried along.

Be with us always, earth,
Let us not fall below,
But hold our wingless feet
As they rest upon you.

The road to the peninsula. On and on it went, further and further
from the highway; and as grey twilight came a chill entered him [John].
The landscape seemed weird. He began feeling they were headed towards a remote, other-world, entirely cut-off spot, a place of frightful
happenings. There was a brooding here, a peering tragic something, as
though all of this ground had suffered a catastrophe, perhaps a sinking
under water, a deluge of its life—and now, though again emerged, it
could think of nothing but its tragedy. Voices seemed as if shouting at
him, "Who goes there? Why are you entering this over-shadowed land?
You had best keep out." * * *

[John and Marian rent a house in Caromb.]

The drive home was short through the earth at sunset. They took the
outer drive winding along the shore between the beach and the wave-
worn rocks. Far to the west the sun was sinking behind a band of slatey
clouds. The sea was turning slate-like. The breakers, livid-white,
pounded on the sand. "It is very much the sea to-night," said John, "but I
would like to see a ship. It is too empty. There should be boats, fishing
craft, sailboats, along here, but I suppose it is too exposed. This really is
the vast wide ocean—oh, bleak, bleak, and vast and empty, oh, thou
ocean."

As if moored to it, a large dark cloud overhung the mountain south of
the valley, casting the mound beneath in sombre shadow. Up the valley
there was light, a strange soft twilight haze which illumined the hills as
they folded down. "Look at that," said John, "ominous, lyrical, and magnificent. I have never seen such oppressive beauty." * * *

He felt the high slopes folding down on him, bearing down, hemming
him, pushing, rolling like huge shoulders upon and against him. From
this view the frame of the mountains did indeed look like the protruding
ribs and bones of giants too large for their graves.

Somehow the vegetation made it worse. He would rather have been in
a bare jagged canyon or among the stark sand-hills of the desert.

It was still. Nothing stirred. The leaves were still. Only the purr of the
car and the noise of its tires on the gravelled road. It was empty. Suddenly
with a start he realized it was empty, fertile but empty. There were no
cattle grazing on the slopes, no horses in the yards, no sheep in the pens,

no men in the fields. Not one single man, one human figure, had they seen. Yet everything was orderly and cultivated. It gave him an eerie feeling, as if invisible hands had worked a fertile valley for food they would never use.

The road began winding. The valley narrowed. It narrowed and narrowed. Increasingly he felt oppressed and hemmed in. The twisted hills loomed above and about them. Rocks thrust out. All earth seemed to be leaning down and closing itself.

At length they came to a sight which made even Marian want to turn back. They were approaching a group of trees more strange than any they had ever seen. The trunks were as large as great oaks. They were colored a ghastly grey. And ghastly grey were the limbs and the queer foliage which bore them downward. The trees seemed dead, yet they were alive, a live forest of them. To John they seemed like gaunt arms stuck up from the earth with the hands fallen at the wrist—as though some body underground had thrust up a hundred arms in a vain attempt to grasp the air and disentomb itself, and, failing—there the livid bones stood with fingers trailing.

They turned back quickly. As they neared the mouth of the valley John felt space again and was glad he was emerging at Caromb. The trip had done at least this for him. But they had run under clouds again. The air was chill. Marian thought she saw a man in a field. It was only a scarecrow, and there were no crows, no men, not a single living soul. Somewhere off in the distance a dog barked and as they skirted the sea they seemed to hear a different kind of bark, perhaps seals. They wondered if there were seals far out on the rocks of Point Goros. * * *

[John goes for a walk with Alice, another character in the novel.]

From the start he felt he should walk cautiously, as if he were entering a land inhabited by unknown peering creatures. The path was bordered by high brush. He saw trees, and they were curious. Soon they were passing through a sort of forest. The trees, mostly pines, were the strangest he had ever seen, weird, stunted, wind-blown, with amazing wild shapes and of scaly grey hues. Some leaned forward. Some shot back— products of the unceasing sea winds like gales. Some looked like flying witches. Some hunched and crept. Some were jagged and broken, grotesque. Some were gruesome, as if alive but fatally mutilated. Some were intact, squat, dark, powerful. All seemed in frenzied movement. Yet nothing moved. It was as though the legions of the air, under a potent curse, had been changed into trees with consciousness, and rooted in this inferno where they could strain and reach and rip and tear but never leave their rocky anchorages.

Down a slope the rocks and the sea could be seen.

From far rocks came the barks of seals. * * *

[John and Marian are now in their house in Caromb.]

They awoke in the morning, the cool bright-haze morning of clear and misty things, the forward-gleaming morning. Their mood was serene, tender, singing. They arose and opened the French windows. Sunshine washed and warmed the earth. The pine trees were like torches. They saw the valley curving in and the hills folding down, far far away. They saw vast shoulders of earth, the giant mountains, covered with primeval verdure sloping to the sea. The sea, bright blue like the sky, lifted wave after wave, on-coming, to break on the beach. Across the bay near a cove was a fringe of white where the rocks made foam. Behind the rocks was an arm of land and beyond the wind-blown arm, towering above it, were the stark high ranges browing the coast to the region south. They sensed great land and something vast and spiriting. With consciousness blended and translucent they experienced morning Caromb. * * *

[John and Marian drive into the mountains.]

Mounting, mounting, they wound up. Once they glanced back and saw, lower than themselves, a long misty cloud hanging over the valley, and beneath it, far far down, the tiny cultivated plots of the valley's floor. The air was rarefying. The altitude affected their ears. * * *

They went through a pass and all at once were startled to see a vast scene, a huge creation of sweeping valleys and canyons, plateaus, and majestic mountain ranges. It was like the other side of the world, totally unlike the region of Caromb. There was nothing sombre. All was bright. The dominant color seemed to be rose-purple, and the wash of the sun.

"Will you see that!" John exclaimed. Marian was seeing it with all her eyes. "It is unbelievable," he said. "It is like the earth just after creation, prehuman, preanimal, preorganic. Only the vast bare skeleton, but what grandeur!"

As they rolled on they saw but one sign of human habitation. A ranch house, appearing no larger than a bird, perched on a high grass-covered knoll—there it rested, diminutive and remote, sealed in silence, motionless, engulfed by space, lost in magnitude.

"And look, Marian," he said, "it has a white fence about it!"

At one place they stopped the car and got out. It was bright, warm, immensely open, and all was silent, a vast impalpable silent world of pure still force. From far off, perhaps from far down, there came to them the tinkle of a cowbell. Before them was a large curved mound richly grassed and with wild flowers. Beyond and below it they could discern the green floor of a valley. Perhaps this was the pasture-land from which the sound of the bell had come. As they looked up and off the plateaus stood and the vast ranges, stark and grand.

John smiled and sighed. Truly they were out of Caromb, but . . . "No man or men could ever inhabit this," he said. He spoke in hardly more than a whisper. "They could not conquer it. They could not exploit it. They could not pollute it. Not the slightest mark could they make. A large city would be as easily engulfed as the ranch house. Their own voices would terrorize them. The acoustics are extraordinary. If I raised my voice and shouted I do believe it would carry, a thousand times better than over water, to that most distant peak." He made as if to do it. He checked himself, he was checked by the silent imminence.

"No, this is a home for gods. I've often heard the phrase but never before have I seen the actual place. For gods, for winged beings who could take food from the air, who could dwell in the air as well as on earth—and I can see a great populace of them, dazzling and magnificent, flying from stark peak to stark peak, gliding down to the green valleys, lingering on the plateaus, rising from the valleys to the stark peaks, arriving and departing for stars, for the great bodies of the inhabited universe. Truly this is the port of the gods. Or perhaps it is their theatre where they gather to see plays depicting the history of the cosmos." * * *

[1932]

America's Proposed Riviera:
A Chicagoan's Impressions of Los Angeles

It is a distinct thing, this Los Angeles region, like nothing else you have ever seen—physically, I mean, as a place, as a locale, produced by Nature and man for the eyes to see. Nature fashioned it like no other place, not like New England, the South, the Middle East, not even like California a hundred miles north. Drive north less than a day, approach San Francisco, and you will be in an entirely different country and climate, something more like what one has known, perhaps, in Maine, Connecticut, Illinois, or Wisconsin. Los Angeles is different—and, so far as the works of man are concerned, deliberately so. Granting, as some say, that we

Americans have in us a strong streak of exhibitionism, boosting and exhibiting our cities even more than ourselves, Los Angeles was bound to become a show-place.

Nature lifted mountains, scooped out basins, raised hills, split ravines, opened canyons, dug arroyos, smoothed out valleys. It is as if here she had the intention of fashioning every form she knew. And then she invited men from everywhere to come and settle, first, in the basins, and next on the hills. And they came from everywhere, as they did to Chicago, and within an incredibily short time filled this vast area with cities and towns and villages so numerous that it is a feat even to memorize their names: Los Angeles itself, Pasadena, South Pasadena, Altadena, Eagle Rock, Glendale, Hollywood, Beverly Hills, Westwood Village, Bel Air, California Riviera, Santa Monica, Ocean Park, Venice, Redondo, San Pedro, Long Beach, Culver City, and many more. Yes, Nature and man both made variety, an amazing variety—an exact opposite of the monotony and sameness and uniformity of the Middle West.

To my sight, the dominant color of the region is reddish purple. Again different from the grey or brown tone of the prairies. This reddish purple wash is over everything, the mountains, the valleys, the basins, the hills. See mountains in the background, always mountains in the background, the highest ones with snow. See thick clusters of houses in the basins. See white houses, a brilliant galaxy of them, scattered over all the hills and even up the mountain slopes. See patches of vivid green occasionally breaking in between the acres of reddish purple earth. See orange and lemon groves, large flower nurseries, palm trees. Know that westward is the coast, the palisades of Santa Monica, the long wide beaches, the blue ocean. See a blue sky and a bright sun. See the land sweeping down and curving up, up and down, around, and winding, like a scenic railway—and the long slopes of encircling mountains. And you will see the Los Angeles region somewhat at I saw it. And you may also see reason why it is the proposed Riviera of America. * * *

A fair number of the people who came to this region, who are still coming, are, as everyone knows, from the Middle West and New England. They were and are in revolt against, or, in any case, in reaction against, the cold stingy climates of their former homes. Out here, then, there can be no cold, no climatic harshness. They won't have it so. They exalt the fine warm bright days. If the weather betrays them they try to conjure the betrayal out of existence. They try to appropriate the climate, possess it, and make it obey them. This is why they feel so personal about it. Southern California naturally favors them. But if, now and again, it does not they band against it and work mental magic. They simply will not have this weather like the weather of their old homes.

Out here, too, the land must look tropic. In the beginning there were no palms. But palms are very tropical looking. So palms were imported. People who have seen the tree grow where it is indigenous make fun of these Los Angeles growths. But what matter? To those who now dwell in this region, but who once lived in Kansas or Iowa—back home the gnarled oak before the door meant hard work and close saving—now, the two palm trees in the front yard symbolize leisure and enough to spend. It is the symbol which counts. It is of not much importance that the palm itself is but a transplanted thing. In fact, so much the better. The people themselves are transplanted, and therefore they may well feel a tender kinship with the tree.

Yes, back home they had to work. It was hard unpleasant work. So here in southern California there must be leisure and play. This is why the Riviera idea has sprung up and taken hold. This is why the real estate firms know it is a selling idea. Truly there could and there my be a delightful thrilling Riviera here. But there are several serious obstacles. One is that too often what we mean by leisure is lazing, loafing, doing nothing, sleeping and drifting and occasionally puttering about it. Neither delight nor thrill can come of leisure of this kind. Thus, for example, one of the unkind but partly true observations made of the people of this region is that they are mainly old people who have come to the Coast to die. A second obstacle is that, also too often, what we mean by play is merely amusement of the Coney Island type. And there is, in truth, much of Coney Island, in the Los Angeles region. Thus there is danger that it may become, not America's Riviera, but, on the one hand, America's cemetery, and, on the other, America's main cheap amusement resort.

Nor is there to be any hard drab dismal reality here. The reaction against reality has given rise to an amazing variety of things romantic in their way, and artificial. It is not without reason that Hollywood, the movie capital of the world, is located in this region.

Here too there must be health, spelt with a large H. Back home there was sickness, disease. People have come to this country to escape illness of all kinds, to have conditions which are good for their bodies. There must be Health. And so, they are concerned with their bodies, concerned enough to make up for all past lack of concern. The degree to which they take life physically is equaled only by the degree to which they take to the by now famous Los Angeles cults. One feels that if good intentions produce good fruits, one should soon see springing up on this part of the coast a race of athletes and saints. Los Angeles has the Olympic Games this year. * * *

As regards what man has produced, what man has done to and with this geographical setting—it is as if southern California set out to be everything the rest of the country is not, the exact opposite of all the other states and sections—and half succeeded, half failed in the attempt. * * *

One of the most impressive buildings in Los Angeles is a new structure, a huge affair, a fifteen million dollar county hospital. What is it? Does it express, to the extent of its cost, the desire for health? Does it express the prevalence of disease? Is it a tribute to the one or to other or to both? In any case, here it stands, a symbol of the city. Approach Chicago and you will see the steel mills of Gary, the oil district of Whiting—or you may see the Merchandize Mart. Approach Los Angeles and you will see this new white enormous hospital. * * *

In Los Angeles there is everything under the sun—a vast medley which, in its way, is as I have suggested, distinct, different, unique, a distinctness which somehow has arisen from an accumulation of imitations—and this is strange enough. Take, for example, the matter of what we may call architectural styles. I have never anywhere seen so many different shapes and colorings. Perhaps here too there is an expression of a reaction, a reaction against the standardization of houses so frequently seen in the Middle West. Here, it is hardly an exaggeration to say that no two places are alike. Individualism, surely, and perhaps a sort of romantic [communication?].

In Hollywood there are two great movie theatres, one Chinese, the other Egyptian. There is a pyramid. There is a Greek Theatre. Save in the case of the Five and Ten Cents Store one looks in vain for anything American. Woolworth's stores and markets. Most of the other structures show the influences of somewhere else. Perhaps again a protest, a rebellion against America's provincialism. Certainly a desire for the exotic, the romantic, the artificial. This is Hollywood, where the wish to be conspicuously "otherwise" reaches its apex.

In dwelling house styles one sees the influences of the Spanish, the French, the English, the colonial, the southern. These influences are dominant. Even in a wealthy residential district like Oak Knolls, a not large and quite restricted area, I saw as many different designs as one would see if he travelled the length and breadth of America. As I drove about my impression increased that most everything I viewed bore a sign which read, "Made elsewhere." Most things had come about as a result of an idea of something. Few things had sprung up because they had to spring up, just here, and pursue an inevitable natural growth. Yes, artificial. Even some of the fruits and the flowers would die unless they were artificially irrigated. By the way, this artificial irrigation—it explains why some California fruit is tasteless, why some California flowers are odorless. Yet, certain of these forms have been planted, and they do grow.

grow. This is the amazing part of it—this *growth* of imitations, of artificial, of transplanted things. Something will come of it. Something surely will. For have no doubt, the Los Angeles region is growing. In this it is something like Chicago. It is a huge stomach, a huge mouth and digestive tract. Just at present there is much that does not belong in it, at least, not in the present forms. But this foreign, unusable stuff may be eliminated. The rest may be worked over and absorbed and transformed into genuine Los Angeles substance. If and when this happens it will be the most extraordinary thing produced in America.

But to return, for a moment, to the houses. Of all the styles the Spanish or the mission style seemed to me to be best suited to the locale. But about these mission houses, as about others, I noted again and again a certain feature. The exterior would be white. This was as it should have been. In the sunshine it would appear bright and brilliant. A happy place to live in, one would feel—as long as he looked at its exterior. But let him go inside. There he would find darkness, dark boards, dark paint, dark wallpaper—and by dark in this case I mean drab and dismal. And so many of the rooms have low ceilings that the darkness seems to bear down on one, oppressing and depressing him. Just the opposite is true of Chicago houses. Their exteriors often are ungainly or forbidding; their interiors usually are warm, rich, attractive, liveable.

Why, I asked myself, why these dismal interiors in sunny California? My question itself suggested one answer, namely, that sunny California was too sunny, too bright, too brilliant too continually. People needed places of refuge from it, dark places in which they could escape and rest from the glare. Another answer came. Many of the people who built these bright exteriors dark interiors were from Kansas, Iowa, Illinois. So then, though outwardly they were influenced by California's brightness to the extent that outwardly they conformed to it; yet, inwardly, they remained as dark Kansas and Iowa had made them, and these dismal interiors were expressions of their past lives willing out—inevitable expressions of the darkness and hunger which had gripped and stamped them during most of the years of their life.

At a dinner party in Hollywood I was asked where I was living. My answer caused a shock. "What," my questioner exclaimed, "Pasadena!" And he lifted his brows as if to add, "Of all places! Good heavens, man, what are you doing there? You should be in Hollywood." Why he felt I should be in Hollywood was obvious enough. Hollywood is, in its way, the artistic center of the Los Angeles region, and writers, artists, and dancers tend to gravitate there. As one person put it, "If some writer or artist you have known has disappeared and you wonder where he is, look and you will find him in Hollywood. They all turn up there." What a magnet, what a center of influence for good or bad it is! The closer one gets the more one feels its power of attraction. I think it was Keyserling who said that Chicago might spread and spread until it had included and absorbed all of America. Yes, truly. But I feel that Hollywood and the movie world are already doing just this.

Why my questioner felt as he did about Pasadena puzzled me. I liked Pasadena. And after seeing Hollywood I liked it even more. Later on I asked about the matter and learned that Pasadena, among some, had the reputation of being *the* locale for genteel elderly folk. True, it was the seat of the California Institute of Technology which drew a man like Einstein. If one was a scientist, yes, certainly, he would be in his element in the Caltech life. But for a writer, an artist . . . No, Pasadena was an old folk's home, even an old folk's paradise, a garden for greying good people who were quite retired from the interesting stream of life. In short, of this entire region it especially was a cemetery for those who had come to California to die. It was no place for a young person with or without talent.

This reputation may have been true of the Pasadena of some years back. I do not know. But I am sure it is only partly true, if at all, of the Pasadena of today. The Pasadena I saw was one of the finest, one of the brightest small cities in America. Since business is the dominant form of our life, one can obtain a fairly accurate sense of a town by seeing and experiencing its main business district.

Colorado Street, Pasadena's main street, might almost be called a gay promenade. It is wide and open to the famous southern Californian blue skies and sunshine. One sees mountains in the background. Its stores and buildings are modern, well-kept, white. Some of its shops are smart, serving a fashionable clientele. All of the shopkeepers, the salesmen and trades people are courteous, friendly, and pleasant to deal with. Its atmosphere is a happy combination of the small town and the cosmopolitan. Anyone who likes good things, whether he be an American or a European, would feel pleasantly at home strolling along this main street.

The tone of it might be compared with that of Michigan Avenue north of the bridge. I may mention, by the way, that one of the parallels I saw between the Los Angeles district and Chicago was this: that in Los Angeles also the smart shops are moving away from the crowded business zone. Just as in Chicago, north Michigan Avenue is becoming *the* place, so in Los Angeles west Wilshire Boulevard is becoming *the* place. So similar are the happenings that one might call Wilshire Boulevard the Boul Mich of the Pacific Coast.

In feeling, Pasadena reminded me somewhat of Winnetka. Like Winnetka it gives the impression of being well-kept, well-run. It is, of course, considerably larger than Winnetka. In Winnetka there is nothing like Colorado Street, nor like the Caltech. And too, Pasadena is far more of a tourist place, a health place, a climate place. But, like Winnetka, it is a locale of well-conditioned people, conservative but not reactionary, of people interested in the arts and sciences, education, and the more advanced happenings of the day. Its conservatism was particularly appreciated by me after I had seen "the life" of Hollywood. And it is of interest to note that of all the towns grouped about Los Angeles, Pasadena, like Winnetka in relation to its group, is said to have the best in the matter of education and schools.

There is, of course, nothing like Hollywood in the Middle West, or anywhere else, for that matter. Hollywood, as everyone knows, is quite unique—yet in its case too, to some extent, the uniqueness somehow arises from an accumulation of reproductions of things found elsewhere. There are bits of Greenwich Village, Broadway, Coney Island, and many more besides, all gathered about the magnet of the movie world. And this movie world—it is our modern dream-maker. It standardizes dreams and sends them out so that by paying anywhere from five cents to two dollars we can have, any time we want, a waking dream which lasts two hours. It is our factory of romance.

I had been told that at a certain hour of the afternoon one could see strolling along Hollywood's main street the prominent figures of film-land—and also, hosts of imitators of these prominent figures. I was prepared, then, for a parade of celebrities and manikins along a promenade which would set them off. Yes, the parade took place; but the setting, namely, Hollywood Boulevard, disappointed me. It was rather cheap and garish and unkept. For brightness and fineness of quality it was not to be compared with Pasadena's Colorado Street. If the movie world produced the former, whereas greying elderly people produced the latter, I felt that the old people had much the better of it as regards taste and style.

On Hollywood Boulevard, however, there is one notable thing—Sid Grauman's famed Chinese Theatre. I went there one evening to see Greta Garbo in *Mata Hari*. The picture was not very good. Garbo did not stand out. In a sense, she did not create her character. The opinion is increasing that she never or seldom does create a character. Her popularity as a screen actress is on the wane. But as a person, as a living figure, just the opposite is true. She is an idol, and she is becoming more so. Everyone who spoke about her raved, women especially. She is a woman's actress. Men are not so enthusiastic.

As for the theatre itself—we have nothing like it in Chicago. The Balaban and Katz places, the Oriental, will lead one in the general direction, but the Chinese Theatre out-does these. It is more expensive, more lavish, and, in a way, it is in better taste. In fact, if one accepts it for what it is, there is something impressive and thrilling about it.

It is a huge affair, without balcony or gallery, done in a style which one might describe as a movie theatre architect's idea of what the American public believes to be Chinese. Huge Chinese motives of structure and design are repeated in every possible place, on the pillars, on the walls, on the ceiling, and, in smaller patterns they are reproduced on the rugs and carpets and on the backs of the red leather seats. About them there is something, yes, obvious and vulgar, but also fantastic. Together with the exotic color effects they do indeed place one in a strange, somewhat oppressive, but glamorous world—a world of unconcealed, even exaggerated artificiality—a setting quite in keeping with moving pictures.

As I sat there looking about my appreciation of it increased. I began feeling that here in truth was the right sort of theatre for the movies. Formerly I had preferred the small cinema theatres done with modernistic simplicity, nothing ornate, nothing lavish or Babylonian, but all, however stylized, rather severe and geometric. Now I felt the cinema theatres were more in keeping with photographs—which are or can be art products, whereas this Chinese Theatre was just the place for *moving pictures* of the Hollywood brand—which are artifices. This theatre is, then, a sort of symbol of what is undesirable, desirable, and distinct in Hollywood. More than this, it is a symbol of one feature which is common to the entire Los Angeles region. It is a show-place—and one need be in the locality no more than a day to know that, as I suggested in the beginning, the whole area is on show and to be seen. The days, the weather, the climate, are on show. "See this," you will be told, "see this glorious bright warm day. This is typical of southern California." At first you are very glad to see it. Perhaps it was for this that you have come to the Coast. But when your attention is called to the weather, to the climate, day after day, week after week, you wish they would leave the days and the weather alone. You become very conscious that you are a visitor. You come to dislike being a visitor, a sight-seer. You begin feeling you are or should be or shouldn't be a climate-hound. You begin realizing that the people of the region are "climate-conscious" with a vengeance; and that, though they may have lived in the place for many years they themselves are still sight-seers, they still retain the psychology of visitors.

The geography is on show, the mountains the hills, the arroyos, the canyons. Each person will tell you of the interesting places. He will more or less insist that you see them—and often, with a generosity which one does not often encounter, if you have no car he will offer either to loan you his or to drive you about. Yes, you will find friendly, generous, hospitable people there.

And of course the houses are on show, particularly the palaces of movie stars and of millionaires from the Middle West and the East. One would expect this. Rather unexpected is the degree to which lesser places, small homes, stores, and restaurants also so to speak feel they are on show and will be seen. To catch the eye, for example, they have a way of making the shape of a building bear out its name. To call a place "The Coffee Pot" is not enough. The sign, even a glaring neon sign, is not enough. The building itself will be shaped like a coffee pot. A building which houses a restaurant specializing in lobsters will be shaped like a huge lobster and painted a boiled lobster red. A hot dog stand will have a hot dog shape. And so on. Certainly one does see and remember them.

By the above I do not mean that all of the region impressed me as a curious playground. It did not. Nor do I mean that all the region is on show, and that it does not deserve being seen. On the contrary, one should see it. It is worth being seen—though here as elsewhere one cannot help but question now and again as to whether man should have the power to add to or subtract from or in any way change his physical environment, so often do his products harm or disharmonize with the natural setting, so often do they harm or disharmonize with himself.

But everyone, I think, would be impressed and perhaps thrilled by the scene along Sunset Boulevard westward out of Hollywood through Beverly Hills to Santa Monica. Below you, to the south, spreads Los Angeles. As you drive along you look down upon it, and over it, and on clear days one can see, over the city roofs and steeples, some distance off, a range of hills sloping to the sea. You look up and see hill upon hill; and on most of the hill-tops and dotted all over the landscape are white houses with red tiled roofs, a galaxy of them, gleaming in the sun light. It is like a fairyland, a magical place. One might well believe that both gods and angels had looked with favor upon this region. * * *

[1932?]

VII

Epilogue

Editor's Note

In the early 1920s, Toomer came to know Alfred Stieglitz and Georgia O'Keeffe through mutual literary friends like Waldo Frank, Gorham Munson, and Hart Crane. Toomer was thirty years younger than Stieglitz, and admired him as something of a father figure. He enjoyed visiting Stieglitz and O'Keeffe at their country house, The Hill, in Lake George, New York. At The Hill Toomer appreciated the peace, the beauty of the land, and the sense of meaningful place created by his hosts and the countryside around the house. It was a good place to write, think, and talk. "The Hill," Toomer's tribute to Stieglitz, was included in *America and Alfred Stieglitz: A Collective Portrait,* edited by Waldo Frank, Lewis Mumford, Dorothy Norman, Paul Rosenfeld, and Harold Rugg, in 1934. "A Double Portrait" was probably written after Stieglitz died in 1946, perhaps shortly after Stieglitz's death when Toomer would have been especially moved to write about his friend.

"Music," a handwritten draft dated March 2, 1937, is from a group of pieces Toomer called "Psychologic Papers." The final entry in *A Jean Toomer Reader* is an untitled poem, handwritten, dated February 24, 1939.

Music

Music is an almost instantaneous evocator of inner-experiences not being had, not being thought of as possible, until the music begins.

Add music, and you can instantly transport yourself, *through inner-experience,* into a different world.

What outward changes in the form of your environment could possibly do this for you?

This illustrates the direct effectiveness of inner-instruments.

Music, however, though able to transport you into a different world, cannot keep you in that different world—no, not even if you yourself are a musician. Once it is over for the time being, you slide back into this world.

You cannot use it as a means of transferring your "I" from the ordinary consciousness (the outer-world), to the subconscious, (the inner-world), and definitely and permanently locating in the inner-world.

Music, in short, is not an instrument for the permanent transformation of a man—though it is a powerful agent, to be used in conjunction with a psychological technique. Nor can music, of and by itself, break down the false psyche and effect thorough catharsis.

But it is, perhaps, the most perfect example of the truth that, by certain agencies, we can move from the without to the within—and that, once within, from within we have a natural impulse to *give out.*

What man, full of song, wants to keep it to himself? There are no misers in music. There are no misers anywhere in the inner-world. Inner fullness must overflow, by the same law which governs the out-pourings of birds, reservoirs, and rivers. The singer is not content to sing only for himself; by the law of his being his deepest urge is to share his song with others.

[1937]

A Double Portrait

Where did Stieglitz live, where belong? Aside from your thoughts of his relation to New York and America, how did the man himself impress you? Did he give you the feeling that he belonged on the seventeenth floor of a skyscraper? In a city apartment? In the house on the hill at Lake

George? Can you think of any place in this world where he might have belonged? I cannot. It is true that he existed wherever he was without too great a protest. Much of the time he was or seemed as oblivious of his external surroundings as of the food that was put before him at meal time. True too, he must have felt a vital relationship established whenever and wherever he had work to do, creating, fighting for the advance of life against inertia and deadness. But the impression he gave me was that he was a traveller in these parts, an exile from another world, without home here. He was so unconcealed in his homelessness that he symbolized the state and acted as a magnet for many others, exiles like himself, but less sure of their status.

What can an exile do here? He can suppress his remembrance of a brighter life, close his vision, persuade himself that he is not an exile at all, and dig in. If he succeeds in this he becomes what we call adjusted. He can search for the way that will lead to where he belongs, make haste to go home. He can try to create in this world the atmosphere he longs for, bringing into this sphere something of the beauty and the meaning that he remembers more and more. He can endeavor to open this closed world to the light from above, to the light from within. He can point himself and point men to reality, and also to the ideals of worth, dignity and integrity which reflect the stuff we should be made of. The best of exiles realize who and what they are, press on to the goal that is called by many names, and, at the same time, make their contributions to the transformation of this world. The known Stieglitz was one of the creative people of our time. He did his part to enrich this world and our lives. I suspect that the unknown Stieglitz was heading, in his unhurried way, towards the realm that we too must long for, that might exist here and now were men to awaken.

The earth, just as it is, is sufficiently wonderful. If with even partially opened eyes we view its lands and waters and the things growing from the soil we have reason to feel that earth is enough. Heaven and earth, I surmise, are already married. It is our world, the world we have built apart from Nature, apart from our own true natures, apart from the radiant reality which some call God—it is this so-called human world that is, in large spots, in large blots, so drab, so ugly, so malicious, so unfit for life. It is this world and its wars and wastes, its despotisms, its organized enslavement of people, its propagated prejudices and hates, that ravage the earth and mutilate men. Anyone who fits into it dies as a man. Anyone who merely seeks to escape from it dies as a man. But to know that one does not and will never fit into it as it is, is a sign that the man still lives. And those who live work for change, growth, transformation. They create.

When he was not struggling against the blights of this world, Stieglitz lived apart from it; yet he had a marked ability to live with whatever in it was real to him, and valuable—certain people, certain paintings, certain photographs, books, horses, hands, faces, clouds—things that like himself were in but not of this murky sphere. Stieglitz could live with. He could extend himself into things, enter and come to know them so well that he could make them live for others, leading you inside them, making your relation to them a living experience.

No one who knew him would think of him as an ascetic. He had a vivid life through at least two of the senses, sight and touch. But in him there was a streak of natural asceticism. To most ordinary pleasures Stieglitz was indifferent; they did not exist for him. He did not smoke or drink. He took food in an absent-minded fashion, not unlike a child who would much rather be doing something else and eats only because it is an inescapable routine. Your typical ascetic has made himself that way as a means of furthering a conscious aim. He has had to fight against the temptations of the flesh, and often must continue the fight throughout his life. Stieglitz took no stand one way or the other. He enjoyed those aspects of bodily life that appealed to him. The others were as if nonexistent. His kind of asceticism was part and parcel of the life he lived elsewhere than in this foreign realm. It was part of his homelessness.

Best known for his work with and for photography, art, and artists, Stieglitz should also be recognized for his work with people. Others have done more to free people by political action. No one of our time did more to free them through the release of their creative powers. His was an inside work. It was a contribution to the large and essential work of internal change.

The temptation to be untrue to oneself is more dangerous than any lure of the flesh. The vice of mental and spiritual falsity is more corrosive than any bodily vice. I think it has always been so, and is particularly so today. Stieglitz represented integrity. To more than one person of my acquaintance his life demonstrated that integrity is possible. He had the power to arouse in others a feeling of the value of a man being true to himself. There are quite a number of people, not artists and writers only but people in all walks of life, who can say, "He helped me to be true to myself."

Stieglitz lived in himself. He lived in and from a center of being that was outside of the ordinary person and, for this very reason, somewhat free of the separatistic ego, in some measure related to the world above the self. The relationship was a potent one, capable of drawing others into it, as into an atmosphere, so that they too felt a larger world become real to them. It was a sense of the whole world, not merely of our separated part—the living world of earth and Nature, human beings in love and in conflict, joy, sorrow, and something of the universe.

He was in contact with an inner core of life and feeling, understanding, values. When silent, he lived in this center, sometimes in calm reflection, often in a brooding gloom. When he spoke, he spoke from it. He perceived with its eyes, and these were the eyes that directed his camera. His life at its best, his actions and influence all issued from that core, and were impressive if for no other reason than that so many of us seem to have no center at all. Stieglitz appealed to and often evoked what is buried in all too many people of our day. His was the magnetism that a quickened life exerts upon those who seek a life above this death, a force greater than this inertia, who want to live creatively and come to grips with the realities that lie behind the surface of things. In his measure he was an awakener.

He represented a way of living and creating. Though it was the unusual way of an unusual man, it gathered into its current all sorts of people through the years, giving to each of them something that he or she might take away and make his own. Even those who found cause to become disillusioned about him acknowledge that their lives were the richer for having known him, and that he speeded them on their ways. His was a natural way, uncalculated, perhaps unsought, the only way that he could live and be himself.

The mind is a trail-blazer. So is the heart. The mind tends to systematize the way it discovers. The heart makes its way differently. It sings, but never organizes. It opens out, leaving its record upon the malleable stuff of life.

Most of us must make effort. If we are to accomplish anything at all, our natural flow must be reinforced by power of will. There are a few who seem to live and accomplish effortlessly. Their natural flow is adequate. Such a one was Stieglitz. I am sure he had a will, I am sure he used it on occasion, and not always wisely, and of course he had had to struggle; but his creativity seemed to stem from an inner spring that had no dry seasons. During the twenty-odd years I knew him, his flow seemed never to diminish or, for that matter, to increase. It was a self-sustaining phenomenon. Through disappointments and sorrow, through bodily illness, there it was. Even towards the end when in some respects he was a feeble old man, waiting for death, weary of the mess that men make of life, their tangles, their betrayals, their seemingly irresolvable problems, it continued.

This natural creativity, his grasp of outside things as if they were within him, his contact with his own being and, through this, with the wide world of being and living—these, I take it, were among the elements of his mysticism. Stieglitz has been called a mystic, and he was one, a natural

one. His was a being-centered life. He abhorred "system," "organization," and effort to "make things happen." He opposed repressive ratio-
nalism. He prized the spontaneous, the identification of oneself with a
larger life, the capacity to be carried along by an effortless current of life
from deep levels, the ability to live now, experiencing the present as
though right here and right now all life were concentrated.

This is a rare type of man in any age. I sometimes think that in our age
it is a type almost extinct; yet this cannot be so. Should man finally lose his
mystical element he would become altogether mechanized, and if he
became so mechanized he would become altogether destructive. Should
all true inwardness pass away, so would all true outwardness, for the one
depends upon the other. We would become vessels of frustration and
hate, warring with each other because of what we had done to one another. Or we would become mere objects, stone-like, capable of striking
against each other but no more. This has not happened yet. That it has
not is certainly not due to the trend of the times. Rather it is due to the
fact that some people, of whom Stieglitz was one, successfully oppose the
trend and establish themselves in the human spirit, with power to kindle
others.

[1946?]

Letters and Excerpts of Letters to
Georgia O'Keeffe and Alfred Stieglitz

Sunday
13 Jan 24

Dear O'Keeffe,

Yours was no simple invitation to call; you opened the way and initiated a spiritual form. There were four of us, but the clear mobility of that
evening did not come from the lowest common denominator (as it almost
always does, whatever the group); it issued from the highest. This is
achieved only in rituals when religions are young.

Have you come to the story "Bona and Paul" in *Cane?* Impure and
imperfect as it is, I feel that you and Stieglitz will catch its essential design
as no others can. Most people cannot see this story because of the inhibi-
tory baggage they bring with them. When I say "white", they see a certain
white man, when I say "black", they see a certain Negro. Just as they miss

Stieglitz's intentions, achievements! because they see "clouds". So that at the end, when Paul resolves these contrasts to a unity, my intelligent commentors wonder what its [sic] all about. Someday perhaps, with a greater purity and a more perfect art, I'll do the thing. And meanwhile the gentlemen with intellect will haggle over the question as to whether or not I have expressed the "South".

Before so very long, I'd like another evening with you.

Jean

137 S St., N.W.,
Washington, D. C.,
Wednesday.
[Feb., 1924]

Dear Stieglitz,

Words, pure words, do not come from the motion that accompanies internal break-ups, inward re-buildings. I am broken glass, shifting, now here, now there, to a new design. And because I am in this city, physically soft and quiet, I am glass fragments blown by a low wind over asphalt pavements. * * *

Toomer

c/o Mrs Abbie Clark,
Tenant's Harbor,
Maine.
4 Aug 25

Dear Stieglitz,

I wish my hand could fashion what my eyes see. This is a country for the brush and camera. Some of these houses have been weather-beaten until they're quite marvelous. And what a perfect little harbor! But the old fishing days are over. No more ships are being built here. As the auto has replaced the horse on land, so the motor is replacing the sail on sea. And our urban communities, our superficial city folk, are spreading out everywhere.

I'm having a fair time. I've [sic] out fishing cod and haddock with one of the old fellows. I've heard a number of real sea tales. I've experienced the humanity of this section. And I've written a bit. How much longer I'll stay, I do not know. I'm quartered at a summer boarding house, quite good, but if the city moves in here, I'll move elsewhere. At present, I'm the only one. But four or five are expected within a day or two. I didnt [sic] leave New York to meet it here.

my [sic] best to O'Keeffe, and you.

Jean

439 West 23
20 Sept 25

Dear Stieglitz,

* * * For the first time, I'm really reading Herman Melville. Moby-Dick in particular contains such energy and revelation that I'm preparing an interpretive essay. Melville surely was an American, and a true brother-in-search for the source and essence of all clouds. The other day I saw a cloud that could have been the White Whale that Melville challenged for its wonders. There is a real parallel between the sea and whales, and the sky and clouds, between you and Melville. But you are more positive in spirit, and he had less mastery of art.

Your letter was so fine-toned that I want to come up and give my own note to the song.

my [sic] best to Georgia and you [sic]

Jean

439 W 23
Saturday
[Oct., 1925]

Dear Stieglitz,

* * * A human being needs *right conditions.* If he has to create *them,* he has a hell of a time creating anything else. * * *

Toomer

care of American Express Co.,
Calcutta.
October 21st, 1939.

Dear Stieglitz,

* * * If I have not yet reached Heaven at least my feet are more firmly planted on the Earth. As every jumper knows, one must have good purchase on the ground in order really to spring up.

Best greetings from us in India to you and O'Keeffe and all in America.

Toomer

Tired, I have come to the door

Tired, I have come to the door
    of the deep rest;
Exhausted, I have come to the gate
    of the deep force;
I have come. I wait.

[February 24, 1939]

Textual Notes

PART II

[page 41] Cut last paragraph of p. 15 to top of 19 of original ts. Contains psychological and philosophical discussion of ordinary awareness and "Being-Consciousness" and the possibility of brotherhood through the unity of consciousness. These thoughts tend to break up the narrative because, as Toomer notes, "These realizations came to me, as may be guessed, not at the time of the events on which they were founded, but later" (p.18).

[page 42] Cut pp. 21 to top of 22 of original ts. Narrative interrupted with somewhat repetitive discussion of detachment from the body.

[page 44] Cut three paragraphs of p. 26 of original ts. An elaboration on the unconsciousness of human beings, these paragraphs break up the narrative and are redundant in light of the complete text.

[page 56] Cut pp. 50 to first paragraph of 53 of original ts. Disrupts the narrative with discussion of how now, as he writes this autobiography, Toomer is mostly back in the premystical state of being bound to the body.

[page 61] Cut Chapter X, "Three Notes," pp. 64–71 of original ts, an essay discussing, with hindsight, the insights the mystical experience gave Toomer. Most of the points in this chapter are clearly implied and demonstrated in the preceding and following pages of the narrative.

[page 71] Cut pp. 89, after break, to 92 of original ts, on the "sleepy state" of the average person, fully discussed and implied earlier in the narrative.

PART III

[page 82, "Germ Carriers,"] "Germ Carriers" is an excerpt from p. 11 of Toomer's second draft of "Preface #3" for "Book X."

[page 86, "The Negro Emergent,"] This is a somewhat rough ts draft with two slightly different versions each of pp. 4, 9, and 10. I have used the pages forming the more coherent whole.

[page 92] Cut last half of paragraph, bottom of p. 9 of original ts, a short but rambling digression on discovery.

[page 95, "Not Typically America"] This ts has a few written insertions not in Toomer's handwriting. I have not included these in this rendition.

[page 95] Cut opening paragraph on p. 1 of original ts ("Preface #3"), a parenthetical statement about Toomer's poem "Blue Meridian."

[page 101] Cut from top of p. 10 to end, p. 13 of original ts ("Preface #3"). Here Toomer mostly discusses the purpose and philosophy of the proposed "Book X" for which this preface was written.

[page 101, "Fighting the Vice"] This excerpt begins on p. 8 of original ts ("This May Be Said/The Inside Story").

[implications?]: unclear handwritten word over "statements."

[page 103] At this point on p. 12 of original ts ("This May Be Said") Toomer wrote, "I wrote him [Johnson] the following letter." Apparently Toomer planned to place his letter of refusal to Johnson here. (See the letter to Johnson in the next chapter.) The letter does not appear in this ts. After the place for the missing letter, I have cut the next three paragraphs describing a book Toomer says he is writing on his views of race in America.

[page 104] Cut from middle of p. 13 to end, p. 15 of original ts ("This May Be Said"). A discussion of the publicity Toomer had recently received for his "mixed marriage" with Margery Latimer.

[page 107, "The Americans"] Cut second paragraph of p. 1 of original ts. A discussion of the proposed book to which this essay is an introduction.

PART VI

[page 219, "New York"] At this point on p. 2 of original ts of "Break," Toomer placed a poem, "The Lost Dancer," which has now been published in Darwin T. Turner, ed., *The Wayward and the Seeking: A Collection of Writings by Jean Toomer* (1980); and Robert B. Jones and Margery Toomer Latimer, eds. *The Collected Poems of Jean Toomer* (1988).

[page 221] Cut last two pp. of "Break" from bottom of p. 5 in original ts, a philosophic-religious musing.

[page 221, "The Brilliant Brotherhood"] This excerpt begins on p. 135 of original ts and continues to p. 137, the end of Ch. XX.

[page 223, "Doylestown"] This excerpt begins at the bottom of p. 11 of original ts.

[page 225] Cut at middle of p. 15 of original ts. Here Phil Gosh begins a philosophical speculation about "tree consciousness" as related to human consciousness. The next excerpt begins at top of p. 34 of original ts.
Cut at middle of p. 34 of original ts to top of p. 36.

[page 226] Cut at middle of p. 36 of original ts to the break on p. 60.
Cut at bottom of p. 60 of original ts to letter to Ramsey on pp. 61 and 62.

[page 233, "The South"] Cut in the middle of p. 1 of original ts of "The South in Literature." The remainder of "The South" is from "Notes for a Novel."

[page 234] Cut in the middle of p. 4 of original ts of "Notes for a Novel," where Toomer writes briefly of a proposed novel. The excerpt ends with Toomer's note at bottom of p. 4, to end of ts on p. 5.

[page 239, "To the Land of the People"] Cut at top of p. 3 of original ts of Ch. VII, "Incredible Journey." Final paragraph of this selection is from p. 27 of original ts of "The Angel Begori."

[page 240, "The Dust of Abiquiu"] Toomer did not number the pages of his notebook; the pagination is the editor's.

[page 243] Cut at bottom of p. 5 of original ms. The following two sentences are from the bottom of p. 9.
Cut end of p. 9 of original ms. The next excerpt begins at top of p. 18 of original ms.
Cut final paragraph of p. 18 of original ms to top of p. 19.
Cut at top of p. 20 of original ms. Selection continues from bottom of p. 5.

[page 244] Cut at middle of p. 7 of original ms to top of p. 9.

[page 245] Cut at bottom of p. 9 of original ms. The next paragraph is from top of p. 8 of original ms.
Cut at middle of p. 8 of original ms to top of p. 10.

[page 247] Cut middle of p. 14 of original ms. Selection continues with final paragraph of same page.
Cut at end of p. 14 of original ms to second paragraph of p. 16.
Cut at middle of p. 16 of original ms to final paragraph of same page.
Cut from end of p. 16 of original ms to top of p. 21. Continue to bottom of p. 23.

[page 259, "Caromb"] Cut after first two paragraphs of p. 1 of original ts to top of p. 3.

[page 260] Cut from bottom of p. 3 of original ts to bottom of p. 23.
Cut at middle of p. 24 of original ts to top of p. 51.

[page 261] Cut at middle of p. 52 of original ts to top of p. 202.

[page 262] Cut middle of p. 202 of original ts to top of p. 216.
Cut at middle of p. 216 of original ts. The next excerpt is from first paragraph of p. 136.
Cut second paragraph of p. 136 of original ts. Continue selection with third paragraph of same page.

[page 263] Selection ends at bottom of p. 137 of original ts.

[page 264, "America's Proposed Riviera: A Chicagoan's Impressions of Los Angeles"] Cut from middle of p. 2 of original ts to top of p. 3.

[page 265] Cut at top of p. 5 of original ts. The next paragraph in the selection is from bottom of p. 2.

[page 266] Cut from top of p. 3 of original ts to top of p. 5.
Cut from middle of p. 5 of original ts to top of p. 6.

[page 271] Cut final two pp. (15 and 16) of original ts.

Selected Bibliography

PRIMARY WORKS

Cane NY: Boni & Liveright, 1923. (Rpt., NY: Liveright, 1975.) (Edition, *Cane: An Authoritative Text, Backgrounds, Criticism,* ed Darwin T. Turner, NY and London: Norton, 1988.)

The Collected Poems of Jean Toomer, ed Robert B. Jones and Margery Toomer Latimer; intro by Jones. Chapel Hill and London: University of North Carolina Press, 1988.

Essentials: Definitions and Aphorisms. Chicago: Lakeside, 1931. (Rpt., ed Rudolph P. Byrd. Athens and London: University of Georgia Press, 1991.)

The Wayward and the Seeking: A Collection of Writings by Jean Toomer. ed with intro by Darwin T. Turner. Washington: Howard University Press, 1980.

SECONDARY AND OTHER WORKS

Baker, Houston. "Journey Toward Black Art: Jean Toomer's *Cane.*" *Singers of Daybreak* (Washington: Howard University Press, 1974), 53–80, 107–108.

Bone, Robert. "Jean Toomer." *The Negro Novel in America* (New Haven: Yale University Press, 1965), 80–89.

Bone, Robert. "Jean Toomer." *Down Home* (NY: Putnam, 1975), 204–238, 301–303.

Bontemps, Arna. "The Negro Renaissance: Jean Toomer and the Harlem Writers of the 1920's." *Anger and Beyond,* ed Herbert Hill (NY: Harper & Row, 1966), 20–36.

Byrd, Rudolph P. *Jean Toomer's Years with Gurdjieff: Portrait of an Artist, 1923–1936.* Athens and London: University of Georgia Press, 1990.

Durham, Frank, ed. *The Merrill Studies in Cane.* Columbus, Ohio: Merrill, 1971.

Fullinwider, S. P. "The Renaissance in Literature." *The Mind and Mood of Black America* (Homewood, Ill.: Dorsey, 1969), 123–171.

Hutchinson, George B. "Jean Toomer and the 'New Negroes' of Washington." *American Literature*, 63 (Dec 1991), 683–92.

Kerman, Cynthia Earl and Richard Eldridge. *The Lives of Jean Toomer*. Baton Rouge: Louisiana State University Press, 1987.

Lewis, David Levering. "Stars." *When Harlem Was in Vogue* (NY: Knopf, 1981), 50–88.

McKay, Nellie Y. *Jean Toomer, Artist: A Study of His Life and Work, 1894–1936.* Chapel Hill: University of North Carolina Press, 1984.

Munro, C. Lynn. "Jean Toomer: A Bibliography of Secondary Sources." *Black American Literature Forum*, 21 (Fall 1987), 275–287.

O'Daniel, Therman B., ed. *Jean Toomer: A Critical Evaluation*. Washington: Howard University Press, 1988.

Perry, Margaret. *The Harlem Renaissance: An Annotated Bibliography and Commentary* (NY: Garland, 1982), 138–158.

Reilly, John M. "The Search for Black Redemption: Jean Toomer's *Cane*." *Studies in the Novel*, 2 (Fall 1970) 312–324.

Reilly, John M. "Jean Toomer: An Annotated Checklist of Criticism." *Resources for American Literary Study*, 4 (Spring 1974), 27–56.

Rosenfeld, Paul. "Jean Toomer." *Men Seen* (NY: MacVeagh/Dial, 1925), 227–233.

Rusch, Frederik L. "The Blue Man: Jean Toomer's Solution to His Problems of Identity." *Obsidian*, 6 (Spring-Summer 1980), 38–54.

Rusch, Frederik L. "A Tale of the Country Round: Jean Toomer's Legend, 'Monrovia.'" *MELUS*, 7 (Summer 1980), 37–46.

Rusch, Frederik L. "Jean Toomer's Early Identification: The Two Black Plays." *MELUS*, 13 (Spring-Summer 1986), 115–124.

Scruggs, Charles W. "The Mark of Cain and the Redemption of Art: A Study in Theme and Structure of Jean Toomer's *Cane*." *American Literature*, 44 (May 1972), 276–291.

Scruggs, Charles W. "Jean Toomer: Fugitive." *American Literature*, 47 (Mar 1975), 84–96.

Thompson, Larry E. "Jean Toomer: As Modern Man." *The Harlem Renaissance Remembered*, ed Arna Bontemps (NY: Dodd, Mead, 1972), 51–62, 279.

Turner, Darwin T. "The Failure of a Playwright." *CLA Journal*, 10 (June 1967), 308–318.

Turner, Darwin T. "Jean Toomer: Exile." *In a Minor Chord* (Carbondale: Southern Illinois University Press, 1971), 1–59, 121–132, 140–143.

Wagner, Jean. "Jean Toomer." *Black Poets of the United States from Paul Laurence Dunbar to Langston Hughes*, trans Kenneth Douglas (Urbana: University of Illinois Press, 1973), 259–281, 531–532, 541–542.